FROM OPINIONS TO IMAGES:
ESSAYS TOWARDS A SOCIOLOGY OF AFFECTS

ULUS S. BAKER

EDITED BY
ARAS ÖZGÜN AND
ANDREAS TRESKE

Theory on Demand #37
From Opinions to Images:
Essays Towards a Sociology of Affects

Ulus S. Baker
Edited by Aras Özgün and Andreas Treske

Cover design: Katja van Stiphout
Design and EPUB development: Eleni Maragkou

Published by the Institute of Network Cultures, Amsterdam, 2020

ISBN print-on-demand: 978-94-92302-66-3
ISBN EPUB: 978-94-92302-67-0

Contact
Institute of Network Cultures
Phone: +31 (0)20 595 1865
Email: info@networkcultures.org
Web: http://www.networkcultures.org

This publication is available through various print on demand services. EPUB and PDF editions are freely downloadable from our website: http://www.networkcultures.org/publications.

institute of
network cultures

Cover illustration: Diagram of the signifier from Deleuze, Gilles and Félix Guattari, *A Thousand Plateaus: Capitalism and Schizophrenia*. Minneapolis: University of Minnesota Press. 1987.

CONTENTS

We have lived at least one century within the idea of opinion which determined some of the major themes in social sciences... In short, social sciences were designed in terms of opinion; asking people what they think about themselves, their lives, their stories, their issues, their problems. And I believe that social sciences have been transformed into a kind of doxology, but I'm tending rather to oppose this status of sociological research. My problem here is that; sociology is epistemologically—or logically—tending rather to become a general opinion about opinions; of what people are supposed to think about themselves and others. And this a clear distinction from the early emergence of social sciences and social research in general... And, through this, in social sciences, we have lost the ability to create (what we may call) the life of affects—an affective life...

— Ulus Baker, from *What is Opinion?* video lecture[1]

---

1   See: Ulus Baker, What is Opinion? Video prod. Aras Özgün, 2001.
     http://www.vimeo.com/465275260.

PASSING THROUGH THE WRITINGS OF ULUS BAKER

Ulus Baker (1960 - 2007) was a Turkish-Cypriot sociologist, philosopher, and public intel-lectual. He was born in Ankara, Turkey in 1960, to Sedat Baker, a prominent Cypriot psychiatrist, and Pembe Marmara, a well-known Cypriot poet. He studied Sociology at Middle East Technical University in Ankara, where he taught as a lecturer until 2004. Ulus wrote prolifically in influential Turkish journals such as *Birikim*, *Toplum ve Bilim*, and *Virgul* among others; made some of the first Turkish translations of various works of Gilles Deleuze, Antonio Negri, and other contemporary political philosophers; actively contrib-uted to *körotonomedya* collective (an Ankara based collective of young radical artists and intellectuals which had been influential with their online publications between 1996-2008); and frequently gave public lectures and seminars in alternative scholarly spaces as well as teaching as a lecturer at Middle East Technical University and Istanbul Bilgi University. Baker's prolific and accessible work, the novelty of issues he introduced to Turkish speak-ing intellectual circles enthusiastically, and his humble social manners and appearance, earned him a widely shared positive reputation in early age. Baker died in 2007 in Istanbul, where he mostly lived in the final years of his life.

The following texts in this edition are edited from essays and notes Ulus Baker wrote between 1995 and 2002. They have been with us for many years. We have observed and sometimes participated in their development, witnessed their lengthy writing process, shared notes and fragments in a continuing discussion with Ulus Baker, but also with many of our friends, his students, colleagues, and professors. After he died in 2007, many of his friends started to collect and share his plethora of unpublished writings (which proved once again what a productive mind he had, considering the amount of his published work despite his early death). Parts of the following text have been published in Turkish already in various publications[1] or online for many years, mainly in *körotonomedya* archives,[2] or were shared as lecture notes in discussion groups. Some of the texts have been parts of his doctoral thesis at the Sociology Department of Middle East Technical University. We included in this edition an interview one of us gave (in the inherent virtual presence of the other) after Baker's death: *On Cinema and Ulus Baker*.

Much of Baker's writing branches out in many directions departing from his criticism of sociological research turning into an analysis of peoples' opinions. Main lines of discussion that emerge from this question are: a historical exploration of the notion of 'opinion' as a specific form of apprehension between knowledge and point of view and a deeper look into 'social types' as an analytical device deployed by early sociologists—which form the first part of this edition; followed by the association of the form of 'comprehension', the 'social types' postulate with Spinoza's notion of 'affections' (as a dynamic, non-linguistic form of the relation between entities)—which forms the second part of the book; and,

---

1   See for example: Ulus Baker, *Kanaatlerden Imajlara: Duygular Sosyolojisinde Dogru*, Istanbul: Iletisim Yayınları, 2010.
2   See; Köronotomedya, http://www.korotonomedya.net/kor/index.php?index.

finally, the possibilities of reintroducing this device for understanding our contemporary world through cinema and documentary filmmaking, by reinstating images in general as 'affective thought processes'.

These essays are not structured linearly within and among themselves. Baker's writing loosely proliferates into many directions, as if circling certain problems rather than tightly developing successive arguments and expositions. Readers will notice frequent parentheses and inserts (references, comments, thought fragments, assertions, proclamations, side notes) in between sentences and paragraphs. These inserts connect to other essays; the fragment of thought they signify becomes a link to another discussion in another essay. Some of the essays end with a feeling of incompleteness remaining as passing notes on the subject, thought frag- ments within themselves. Yet these ideas resonate with larger problematics Baker tackles, sometimes become further explored in other essays, or otherwise, create fissures and layers in the loose texture of ideas Baker intends to weave. This thought process would be familiar to people who had the chance to attend to Baker's public lectures, seminars, and talks: Tangen- tial threads connect, and the rotating flow of ideas starts to form an outward expanding spiral, reflecting a non-linear thought process that aims to assemble a multidimensional construct with materials gathered from various disciplines of the social sciences and humanities. The terms Baker uses without explaining, or the comments he drops without referencing, together with the breadth of the discussions he pursues may create the impression of an esoteric nar- rative at first sight, particularly to readers who are rather used to following such discussions in academic forms and formats. Creating a 'narrative' is certainly what Baker is after, yet, despite such dropped-in comments, mentions and terms, it is also clear that Baker intends this narrative to be accessible to any curious mind, rather than being esoteric, rather than aiming to be understandable only by those who are already equipped with graduate-level of familiarity with philosophy, sociology, film studies, media studies, psychoanalysis, history, political thought, literature, etc. In most of the essays, Baker explains pivotal complex ideas and debates with incredible clarity, in a highly comprehensible manner. Therefore the writing style of his narrative rather reflects his thought-process, a flow of ideas, which he doesn't mind sharing with his reader. We tried to keep this form of writing intact in our editorial work on the texts.

Readers will also notice reappearing and revolving themes and discussions throughout the essays. Ulus revisits certain questions, themes, and arguments again and again in his writing. Yet, the careful readers will also notice that these are not repetitions; every time he revisits a motif, he recomposes it by adding something new or recombines it by positing it next to a new theme or rephrases it with a new intensity. Another peculiarity of Ulus' writing is his use of terminology; he prefers to summon original French, German, Russian, Greek, and Latin concepts and terms at times or integrates these into the flow of text without the customary reference to their English equivalents. We perceived these as signifying the heterogeneity of his thinking and writing and preserved them with minimal interventions (such as providing explanations and translations where we deemed necessary) in the editing process.

Readers will further notice that, despite the theoretical richness and philosophical depth of Ulus' writing, his discussions are decisively not meta-theoretical, but anchored in and oriented towards everyday relations and social processes. After all, his main concerns are to overcome a gradually developed deficiency of mainstream sociology in understanding today's society, to explain the form and substance of everyday social relations, and redeem images as *thought processes* directed towards this end. *Passing through* (as he likes to say) Spinoza, Deleuze, Foucault, Simmel, Freud, Husserl, Mills, Vertov, and a whole history of sociology, philosophy, cinema, and media theory is a necessary engagement in this sense, but not the main goal.

We mentioned above that these texts have been with us for many years. What we mean by that is not only a collegial familiarity with them, but a deeper level of participation in Ulus' practical and contemplative life. We encountered Ulus in the early 90s, at specific moments of our lives, in the specific political and cultural context of Ankara, and our close friendship continued until his untimely death. This friendship has been transformative for all of us, included many other bodies and nodes, spanned across many psychogeographical, social, intellectual, and creative contexts, most of which culminated in the *körotonomedya collective* of which we were a part. We believe the interview from 2007 after Ulus' death, with which we conclude this edition, sheds more light on Ulus' standing as a public intellectual in these transformative times, his personal life and our friendship.

•

We are very grateful to the Institute of Network Cultures and Geert Lovink, who made this project possible. We would like to thank the Turkish publishing house Iletisim Yayinlari for their collaboration, and especially Tanil Bora for his support. Kemal Yardimci's assistance in recovering and formatting certain references in the editing process has been indispensable. We would also like to thank, on behalf of him, Ulus's many friends and colleagues at körotonomedya collective, and, Berrin Balay and Middle East Technical University's Audio-Visual Research Center (METU-GISAM) for supporting him in the process of writing these texts. We thank our partners Lale Gülden Treske and Deniz Atik Özgün for bearing with us in the course of the lengthy editing process.

•

And thus, passing through his words, he is with us.

Andreas Treske & Aras Ozgun

Urla, 2020

1. A SOCIOLOGY OF AFFECTS

When questioned about the founders of structural anthropology, Claude Lévi-Strauss, who actually introduced the term itself, answered they were Caduveo villagers. Again, Félix Guattari was serious when he proposed that the *analysands*—the analyzed people in the psychoanalytic treatment—should be paid, and no less than the analyst, since they are investing or *putting to work* their unconscious productions. The *first structuralists* were really Caduveo villagers, and psychoanalysis, as we will see in a later part of this book, could never be established without the quite clever participation of an intelligent hysteric girl, Anna O., from the very beginnings of Freud's studies. We don't hesitate to take these affirmations as our point of departure in these essays, which will be a research into the possibility of what we call *sociology of affects*, instead of the mainstream *sociology of opinions*.

My investigation will begin with a critique of what we may call sociology of opinions, nowadays far distant from its founder, Gabriel Tarde's vision. Academically set values of social sciences (and of sociology in particular) have created a massive doxology out of opinions (which are always in a dynamic flux) by collecting, filtering, interpreting and archiving them.[1] There is still a profound epistemological problem: Sociology actually tends to become an opinion of opinions, which is an opinion among others, and that would be interpreted by any 19th century human scientist pretending to establish the *objectivity* of science as quite an insulated basis. Marx was telling us that one should never ask a culture, an age, or a people what they think about themselves in order to understand what they are. Our primary concern hence will be to question what lies in this methodological trajectory and metamorphosis since the 19th century, when the human sciences were first established. This transformation is characterized by the gradual disappearance of a typically affective entity, which had been often present in the works of early sociologists: the social types.

The term was clearly formulated by Georg Simmel, who was capable of illuminating a number of social types in his extraordinary work on the conditions and landscapes of modern life: the Poor, the Jew, the Stranger, the Worker.[2] No sociologist of this early epoch could have done without the process of passing through the creation of social (or socio-psychological) types—the Protestant for Max Weber, the Lumpenproletariat for Marx, the Bourgeois for Sombart, the Consumer for Veblen... If there is something that defines such creation of social types, it is nothing but a capacity of early social scientists to make them analytical entities, which, at the same time, coincided with their quality of becoming-events. One could speak, for instance, about *social classes* only when they could be visualized with their traits, characteristics, foundations, and

1   Gilles Deleuze and Félix Guattari, 'L'anti-oedipe', *Capitalisme et schizophrénie. 1,* Paris: Les éditions de Minuit, 1972.

2   Georg Simmel, 'Die quantitative Bestimmtheit der Gruppe', *Soziologie. Untersuchungen über die Formen der Vergesellschaftung,* 1908, pp. 68-94.

everything else. Hence, as shown by Rosa Luxemburg, we can talk about class in two senses, the first as an abstract category for economic and political analysis, and the second, as corporeal groups, communities of people, both becoming objects and subjects of capitalist production relations.

Then, we should inquire into the conditions of the disappearance of social types in today's sociology, and ask whether this disparity is something endemic in today's globalized living conditions, or it is merely a failure of academicized social sciences to create social types—to our knowledge, the last prominent creator of social types was C. Wright Mills, with his *white collar*[3] and *power elite.*[4]

It is necessary for this inquiry to proceed through literature and cinema, since not only sociology, but the novel of the 19th century and the cinema of the 20th century were also creators of social types. We arrive to Dostoyevsky's *Idiot* through Balzac's types in 19th century literature, and cinema (even in its merely burlesque form) presents us with *The Tramp*[5] as the Migrant, who was nothing less than a social type.

My first argument for the possibility of a sociology of affects is that the creation of social types and landscapes is essential to any reconstructive effort in sociology. By this we do not mean that we should simply reconstruct the landscape of late 19th century Europe, since our landscapes and milieus are quite different now. We are only insisting upon the strong connections between affects, and the possibility to visualize them in concrete life situations. This is why we will have to go beyond simply illustrative visual sociology in order to reach what we may call documentary. The sociology of opinions generally distrusts the visual, forces it to obey the text and the commentary, and pretends to be the only analytical power that can study this immense world of images that coexists with modernity since the invention of photography.

Not only for methodological but also for pedagogic purposes, we intend to position a sociology of affects in parallel to documentary filmmaking; the former lacking images, and the latter, generally, some theoretical awareness. We consider this as pedagogically important since we can easily observe how every successive generation rather thinks more with images than with texts, and how powerful today's technological imageries are.

As we learn from Spinoza, images never cease to create and represent affects. We do not need Hegel to remind us how images and passions overwhelmed entire historical periods. A long history of iconography involves political acts such as *iconoclasm*, and no social event could proceed without inscribing images. As Nietzsche pointed, the typical reaction of people to any innovator, for example to a scientist, is asking them to show it in images.

---

3   Charles Wright Mills, *White collar: The American middle classes,* New York: Oxford University Press, 1951.
4   Charles Wright Mills, *The power elite,* New York: Oxford University Press, 1956.
5   Editors Note: Charlie Chaplin's fictional character featured in a series of Chaplin's films starting from *The Tramp* (1915).

Imagination, a faculty so long admitted with contempt, tends to become necessary for creation in modern times. This also means that the image of thinking itself has also been transformed: For the Greeks, up to medieval times, thinking was the reflection in our poor minds of the ideas that are immutably located somewhere in the heavens; in modern times, thinking is a human activity, at least since the *Cogito* of Descartes, and it operates as a power that enters into our collective circuits, transgressing the cerebral boundaries of the Subject, stimulating, inciting, pulsating other ideas, constituting social events.

We know that we neither should, nor could revive the old Greek opposition between *doxa* (opinion) and *episteme* (knowledge). Knowledge tends to become more and more pragmatic, and that is not without risks: The difficulty of discerning between knowledge and information properly is a characteristic of our times, and we can no longer revive such old distinctions unless they serve the stimulation of new ideas. It is for this reason, we suggest looking back into Spinoza's philosophy (which is a philosophy of the future, in our opinion, rather than a philosophy of the past) in order to reformulate a modern image of thinking. For Spinoza, thinking and knowing were nothing but affections of a body-mind continuum, which suggested that they were also of social and historical continua.

Thus, our inquiry in the following essays will summarily proceed as follows:

Sociology tends to become *a sociology of opinions*—an accumulation, filtering, and summarizing of opinions, which are the most unstable social eventualities. This imposes a fundamental epistemological problem—an opinion (not knowledge, nor even information) of opinions. Journalism and video-archives can do this much more easily and are already doing it better.

We are suggesting a *sociology of affects*, which we believe was already present in the insightful and *illuminative*[6] period of the birth of the human sciences, coupled with the creation of *social types*.[7] Either the modern conditions of life or an endemic incapacity of the way in which the social sciences are practiced in today's academic settings and conceptions—or perhaps both—render the characterization of *social types* as affective entities difficult today. Thus, although we can no longer adopt their typologies, we can still rely upon the works of the *founding fathers* (particularly Simmel and Tarde's) for gathering clues about how to interpose *social insights* into social phenomena.

This sociology of affects should be a twofold experience: an encounter with cinema, especially but not exclusively with documentary film, and with Spinoza's profound understanding of human affections.

The encounter with cinema presupposes an observation: Until recent past, sociology, semiology, and history of arts could pretend to *analyze* cinema as an ambiguous part

---

6   Walter Benjamin, 'The Work of Art in the Age of Mechanical Reproduction', trans. Harry Zohn, in Walter Benjamin, *Illuminations*, ed. Hannah Arendt, New York: Schocken, 1969 (1935), pp. 217-52.
7   Simmel, 'Die quantitative Bestimmtheit der Gruppe'.

of aesthetic culture. As Réda Bensmaïa points, now it is cinema that tends to become capable of analyzing everything, including sociology. In fact, this is not a new phenomenon or a turning point as Bensmaïa suggests.[8] Cinema has always been not a text, but a way of analyzing social phenomena, of making the invisible visible.[9]

The social sciences today are much habituated to the investigation and inspection of texts (readings, intertextuality, dialogism, structuralism, deconstruction, hermeneutics, psychoanalysis, etc.). It is impossible to oppose the usefulness of such powerful tools, we can only suggest using these mercifully. Yet, the shadow of opinion contaminates such well-intended probes, transforming them to an almost plethoric accumulation of a ceaseless continuum of interpretations. The common Derrida reader and interpreter now working in academia operates under the assumption of a positivism of texts and readings even when criticizing the positivistic method. And the *Verstehen*[10] approach too, in spite of many successes, never ceases to be an *opinion of* opinions—perhaps, if not an amalgamation, in their singularity this time.

We will suggest an archival mode of sociological presentation (including the visual, the audible, the text as signs), and to develop a montage-thought in the combined domains of sociology and documentary film (rather than only a collaboration or illustrative help), which we believe was inherent in cinema but not in the textual mode of representation. We believe this would lead to important pedagogical consequences. Perhaps the most important book of sociology ever written, *The Sociological Imagination* of C. Wright Mills,[11] should be rewritten in such a fashion, taking into consideration not only the opinions, but also the concrete life experiences visually represented as affects.

Last but not least, all that happens in the domain of life-experiences today—from the televisual (in which, tele stands for distant) representation of devastating wars to the rapid eruption of mass communication from the public realm over the private and even intimate spheres—show that we are now in a phase of transition in the age of images. Images are no longer restrained in the representational limits of graphics, painting, and iconography, and they are not merely technical-images in the way photography and cinema had been according to Vilém Flusser. What we see now before and around us, with digital video and electronic images on ambient screens, we would like to call as thought-images. This type of images had been perceived and discussed as being immaterial in the past, in reference to their temporality and intangibility, as opposed to the materiality of the images in the age of the printing press. They now somehow materialize as surrogates for what we called knowledge or information in the past.

8   Réda Bensmaïa, 'Le Cinéma comme opérateur d'analyse.' *Surfaces* 1, 1991, http://pum12.pum.umontreal.calrevues/surfaces/vol1 lbensmaia.html
9   Dziga Vertov, *Kino-Eye: The Writings of Dzigo Vertov,* trans. Kevin O'Brien, forw. Annette Michelson, Berkeley and Los Angeles: Univ of California Press, 1984.
10   Editors Note: Verstehen refers to understanding the meaning of action from the actor's point of view, and has been perceived as a concept and a method pivotal to the rejection of positivistic social science.
11   Charles Wright Mills, The sociological imagination, New York: Oxford University Press, 1959.

2. WHAT IS OPINION?

Pascal's Bet

When Blaise Pascal, mathematician, physicist, and devout Christian, asked 'Does God exist?' in the 17th century, he certainly was not trying to gather the opinions of the people around—whether they believed in God or not. Nor he was interested in knowing whether or not God really existed, since this was only a question of heart and not of knowledge. The God Pascal believed in was certainly the God of the Judeo-Christian religion, the One who commanded to Abraham to kill his son, the one who has been incarnated, transformed into Man through the body of Christ.

We are far from the conditions and concerns of Pascal's time today. Pascal was not yet interested with what people were thinking about themselves or of God's existence.[1] What people thought (generally in a foolish way) absolutely meant nothing for the excellent mathematician and the inventor of the calculus of probabilities. He was rather interested in the *thinking-existence* of man.[2] When one imposes such a question today, it is foremost a matter of learning, for gathering information about *opinions*—as in a TV panel or public debate in our society of spectacle, which is rather tending to become essentially a *society of opinions*.

Today, in our quasi-liberal age, social scientists do not mind inserting questions like 'Do you believe in God?' in their questionnaires, in their pretentious effort to understand what happens in the social life, in an entirely similar fashion with television debates, where the anchormen raises such questions, having seated the believers on their right and the non-believers on their left. Such scenes became possible through a historical process of laicization, overcoming precisely those crucial moments when Nietzsche screamed 'God is dead!', and Heidegger asked 'Are we still capable of a God?'. Eventually, we can now conduct a study of religion and religious life, no longer with reference to *truth*, but rather with reference to *opinions*.

---

1   In a democracy, no one cares about our views, whereas in a repressive (totalitarian?) society every statement we make is examined for political properness. Evoked by Slavoj Žižek as a burning issue, we—our opinions, products and ideas—are taken seriously only in *totalitarian* societies. Hence, as Žižek and Agamben have attempted to point out, democracy itself tends to become totalitarian.
    See: Slavoj Žižek, *For They Know Not What They Do: Enjoyment As A Political Factor*, London; New York: Verso, 1991.
    See also: Giorgio Agamben, *Homo Sacer: Sovereign Power and Bare Life*, trans. Daniel Heller-Roazen, Stanford: Stanford University Press, 1998.
2   'Man is but a reed, the most feeble thing in nature; but he is a thinking reed. The entire universe need not arm itself to crush him. A vapour, a drop of water suffices to kill him. But, if the universe were to crush him, man would still be more noble than that which killed him, because he knows that he dies and the advantage which the universe has over him; the universe knows nothing of this. All our dignity consists, then, in thought. By it we must elevate ourselves, and not by space and time which we cannot fill. Let us endeavour, then, to think well; this is the principle of morality.'
    Blaise Pascal, *Pensées*, New York: E. P. Dutton & Co., Inc., 1958, p. 97.

Yet, things were different for Pascal. For him there were at least two kinds of *truth*; truths of heart and truths of reason. What he intended to do was by no means opposing them to each other, but rather combining their respective ways of thinking. But how to combine them, since he was sure that through his heart, he believed in his God, beyond any reasonable doubt? Yet, Pascal was a mathematician who invented the mathematical rules of probability as a rational means for creating second orders of precision, and he would use it in order to convince both himself and his opponents (Atheists, Dominicans or Jesuits) not to the existence of God (which was impossible, since belief in God is a gift of God, not something to be reached through reasoning), but to the misery and failure of the one who doesn't *bet* for His existence. Thus, one has to use mathematical rules which are obviously gifts of God—which, however, also show our finitude in this infinite universe while ensuring that we are at least the *thinking reeds* even if we are only *reeds*. As Pascal applies his calculus of probabilities to his main question, 'Does God exist?', there appears only two possible answers: betting to His existence (the believers', ultimately Abraham's position), and betting to His non-existence (the atheists' position). To these, the posterity of existentialism (especially Soren Kierkegaard) would add a third choice, that of not betting at all—which, in fact, is a non-choice, and the skeptics' worse position. Hence, in accordance to the calculation of probabilities and chances, it appears to Pascal that if one bets for the existence of God and He exists, one will gain his salvation only by sacrificing one's finite and miserable existence (through devotion to God)[3]. If one bets for His existence and He doesn't exist, one will lose nothing more than his miserable life forever. Finally, if one bets for His non-existence and He exists, the loss will be the eternal salvation accompanied by a miserable, finite life, and yet if He doesn't exist, one will gain nothing more than this worldly life. Hence, everything shows that it is in ones interest to bet for the existence of God.[4]

Nadine Gordimer points to how opinion was detached from truths in late modern times, whereas the probability of correspondence between two notions was still possible in Pascal's age:

---

3   'Qu'on s'imagine un nombre d'hommes dans les chaînes, et tous condamnés à la mort, dont les uns étant chaque jour égorgés à la vue des autres, ceux qui restent voient leur propre condition dans celle de leurs semblables, et, se regardant les uns et les autres avec douleur et sans espérance, attendent à leur tour. C'est l'image de la condition des hommes' (Pascal, *Pensées*, pp. 199-434) which reads as follows: 'Describing the miserable *existence* of human beings in this world we have people condemned to death, and they are killed one by one, strangled before the eyes of the others, the remaining ones after each execution must have to see their *condition* in the fate of their *others*. And they are envisaging each other with pain and there is no hope. They are all waiting their turn.' Pascal's image of the human condition could evidently be compared with Plato's famous allegory of the cave in his *Republic*. But this is also relevant to Bergson's account for *religion* and *morality* –'La religion est une réaction défensive de la nature contre la représentation, par l'intelligence, de l'inévitabilité de la mort' (Henri Bergson, *Les deux sources de la morale et de la religion*, Paris: Oeuvres, PUF 1970, pp. 1086); here, 'Religion is a defence of Nature against the representation, provided by the intellect, of death'.
4   Pascal's Wager: It is rational to believe in God since: 'If God does not exist,' he argued, 'one will lose nothing by believing in him, while if he does exist, one will lose everything by not believing.' It makes sense to cover Pascal's bet... If we win, we win eternity. If we lose, we lose nothing.

In the beginning was the Word. The Word was with God, signified God's Word, the word that was Creation. But over the centuries of human culture the word has taken on other meanings, secular as well as religious. To have the word has come to be synonymous with ultimate authority, with prestige, with awesome, sometimes dangerous persuasion, to have Prime Time, a TV talk show, to have the gift of the gab as well as that of speaking in tongues. The word flies through space, it is bounced from satellites, now nearer than it has ever been to the heaven from which it was believed to have come. But its most significant transformation occurred for me and my kind long ago, when it was first scratched on a stone tablet or traced on papyrus, when it materialized from sound to spectacle, from being heard to being read as a series of signs, and then a script; and travelled through time from parchment to Gutenberg. For this is the genesis story of the writer. It is the story that wrote her or him into being.[5]

The *power of the word* was nothing but this detachment from its status as the agent of *conservation*—of ideas, concepts, sounds—towards a state where it would eventually tend to become *creation*—a creation of opinions, or literature. Gordimer is critical about the *capture* of language by TV talk shows, arguments, backed by *electoral campaigns* emitted through satellites, walking towards a new kind of God and existence, the way the word tends to become a measure, a calculus.[6]

Through all these calculations and *scales of argumentation*, as the semantician Ducrot would call it[7], we may observe the birth of a new way of philosophizing, which is that of the Existentialism, towards Sartre's understanding of the *necessity to choose*. In our modern world, it seems that this choice, whether it is about the *existence of God* or any other issue—including freedom—, is not marked by a necessity but only by an arbitrary involvement of subjects. For the feeling of solemnness and of necessity, we need philosophy rather than common sense and public opinion.[8]

---

5   Nadine Gordimer, *Writing and Being*, Nobel Lecture, 7 December 1991, https://www.nobelprize.org/prizes/literature/1991/gordimer/lecture/.

6   Gordimer outlines the *doxological* and performative nature of writing, as a problem of existence, and this existence is for others, which she sees as the *humankind*: 'The writer is of service to humankind only insofar as the writer uses the word even against his or her own loyalties, trusts the state of being, as it is revealed, to hold somewhere in its complexity filaments of the cord of truth, able to be bound together, here and there, in art: trusts the state of being to yield somewhere fragmentary phrases of truth, which is the final word of words, never changed by our stumbling efforts to spell it out and write it down, never changed by lies, by semantic sophistry, by the dirtying of the word for the purposes of racism, sexism, prejudice, domination, the glorification of destruction, the curses and the praise-songs.' (Gordimer, 1991, 3)

7   Ducrot Oswald, *Les échelles argumentatives*. Paris: Éd. de Minuit, 1980.

8   It is useful to recall Baudrillard's almost defeatist account for *hyperreality* in this context, in which *existence* remains below the universe (Robert M. Maniquis, 'Introduction: English Romanticism and the French Revolution', *Studies in Romanticism*, Cambridge: MIT Press, 1989, pp. 343-344.) Baudrillard 's Fatal Strategies is nothing but a Pascalian account of the *possible* and the *probable* in social consciousness—there is connection between *opinional* Pascal's wager and the *postmodern signs* and *hyperreality*.

Pascal's wager also shows us the extent of our distance from the beginnings of modernity, at least from a philosophical perspective. Betting today is part of a general regime in
which judgments and choices circulate universally, generally taking the form of images,
shows, debates, political confrontations of ideas, and everything passing through TV.
Opinions, even when they are about important matters—such as the existence of God,
can easily circulate and, while being restrained in many kinds of totalitarian regimes
which are not less based on the circulation of opinions and overt lies, *the* opinion is
what creates individuals and social groups by the single movement of their expression.
Our parliamentary democracies are nothing more than a *public opinion research*, once
contested by Friedrich Pollock, the Frankfurt School sociologist, since it is now almost
impossible to understand the difference of our *electoral systems* from a simple *research
into public opinion*.[9] One can also add to this situation the very problematic question
of opinion polls in political issues, since the so called *voting behavior* could easily be
infiltrated in our *statistically* defined and organized societies, and there are those who
hope, with the use of devices like the internet, that the political system could be controlled by the electorate through the continuous variations of opinions and campaigns.

The Concept of Opinion, Ancient and Modern

When the Ancient Greeks were talking about opinions, they tended to become philosophers, a new person, since every person was entitled to have opinions. Hence,
the Greek polis excluded those who suspend their opinions and judgments—and the
resulting crime, that is, *non-participation* in public affairs either by ways of neutrality
or escapism (the *apragmosyne*),[10] was punished by the heaviest sentence, the exile[11].
Foucault interpreted Ancient Greece as a *society of spectacle*—while not in the same
way with ours—yet, they were in fact societies of opinions in their own way and under
their own social conditions. Something essential for them seems to be the opposition
they sustained between *episteme* (wrongly translated as *knowledge*, since it had a
narrower meaning than its translation) and *doxa* (again, wrongly translated as *opinion*,
since it had a larger meaning than its translation). Commentators of Plato or Aristotle,
as well as the historians of Antiquity, have interpreted this opposition as the point of
departure for rational philosophizing, the ascendance from the sensible to the intelligible, from illusion to knowledge. Yet, the studies of Jean-Pierre Vernant and Marcel
Detienne show us that this opposition of *knowledge/opinion* was not quite simple, since
there were many *discourses* aimed at the life of the polis, and none could claim to be

---

9   Friedrich Pollock, 'Empirical research into public opinion', trans. Thomas Hall, in *Critical Sociology:
     Selected Readings*, ed. Paul Connerton, New York: Penguin, 225-236.
10   For a detailed observation of the apragmosyne as one's own affair, See: Lynn B. Carter, The Quiet
     Athenian, Oxford University Press, 1986.
11   We know that exile was the heaviest sentence, something more than death, since Socrates preferred
     death to the escape; unless a kind of cosmopolitanism (yet to come with Alexander, destroying the
     grounds of the *polis*, in order to establish the *imperium* in Roman sense) was conceived and accepted,
     the polis was assumed to behave as a *community* (the *koine*) and as a *limitation*, since Aristotle in his
     Politics was able to measure the exact and adequate number of citizens even for non-ideal city-states
     (See: Aristotle, *Aristotle's Politics*, Oxford :Clarendon Press, 1905).

more than an aspiration—these were the discourses of the Old Man from the Orient (the sage or wise man), the rhapsode or myth-teller (the Poet), the philosopher (who loves wisdom, without being exactly *wise*), and the sophist, who was exactly the *man of opinions*. It is sufficient to read the Socratic dialogues of Plato to acknowledge the existence of a continuous struggle among these *pretenders*.[12]

The confrontation of opinions was essential to the Greek polis, since it was believed that the truth would unmask itself only through such a confrontation. In other words, *truths* that involve the episteme could only arise from the doxa's that conceal them, as an essential procedure. It could be accurate to treat the classical Greece as a *society of opinions* with some important reservations in this respect. Certainly these societies were those of Logos, the *common word*, and of consensus that is restored on every public issue. But they also feared much from the abusive powers of the orators, to the degree that they felt they should *discipline* their abuse of language. They had even created a *science of speech* (as in the Rhetorics and Poetics of Aristotle) to be publicly deployed as a general project of *Paideia*, the life-long education of the citizen, starting from adolescence.

Hence, all shows that the opinion was not something to be simply eliminated in the Greek way of prudence. We know that their juridical system was contaminated by an obsession with rhetorics and well-speaking, rather than well-established laws. The Greek polis, which is a society against state in the terminology of Pierre Clastres, did everything to control the speech it once freed, to put it at a distance from the speakers, imposing equality amongst them.[13] This means that, while a *society against state*, the Greek city was not denuded of power relations, which had to be decoded from the struggles around opinions. Due to the *larger sense* of the doxa, the Greek city was a *political* entity.

It is interesting that the relationship of Greeks with their language appears to be one of the most controversial aspects of our problem today. Language was really a Logos for them; that is, something more than what is expressed or communicated in the speech of a person. Even more than a *house of being*—as later interpreted by Heidegger—, they believed that we dwelled in language only insofar as it was the Greek language, the Logos. The poet Pindarus was pointing to a *language of Gods*, who could *name*

---

12   Jean-Pierre Vernant and Marcel Detienne, *Les ruses de l'intelligence: La mètis des Grecs* (Flammarion: Paris), 1974 (= Cunning Intelligence in Greek Culture and Society, University of Chicago Press, 1991). Marcel Detienne, *The Creation of Mythology*, University of Chicago Press, 1986.

13   A more adequate word than equality in this context is isonomia, meaning equal distance from the point of arrival or departure, which is the same. Hence comes the Greek ideal of the medium—the placing of the power simply in the middle of pretenders, for example, when, a legendary king leaves authority to the people, which would be the definition of the isonomia. Anaximander has been the founder of the idea of the middle (meson), through which he reformulated the notion of the infinite as a dynamic entity: The apeiron means unbounded, that is, something capable of decentering everything, rendering any kind of centralization impossible. (See: Pierre Clastres, *La Société contre l'Etat: Recherches d'anthropologie politique*, Paris: Minuit, 1974)

the beings with their proper names.[14] In Plato's dialogues, a particular problem never ceases to emerge, and reaches the point of absurdity: What are the *correct* names of things? It is as if names had to belong to things, rather than human language. The result has been the almost perfect *logocentrism* of the Greek, since any other language was perceived as impossible to be understood—the *varvaroi*, the barbarians, are nothing more than those whose speech cannot be understood by Greeks. We should have to wait for the *opening* of the Greek polis, the emergence of trade and the sparking of new philosophical sects, essentially the Stoics, who were strangers and bilinguals, for the radical transformation of such vision of language[15]. They were *cosmopolitans* right there, in their language and their understanding of it, while teaching non-interference into *political affairs*. It is important to note that, interestingly, this teaching is not in contradiction with the political involvement of the late Stoic philosophers—as we know that some of the latest were some of the greatest political orators of Rome, such as the Roman emperor Marcus Aurelius, and Cicero, or Seneca. There was no contradiction in their political involvement, since we observe an major transformation of all that significantly relates to political affairs: language being freed from the boundaries of *intelligibility* and tending to become pure speech and expression, the dissolution of the polis as a closed community of language (to give way to the imperial order of multitudes and cosmopolitanism), and more importantly, language now focusing on and designating *actions* rather than *names* (as in Pindarus, or in Epicurus, contemporary and rival to each other), and appearing as an instrument of *command* rather than something which we are born into (the Logos), as pure *rhetorics*.[16]

At the moment the Western civilization came to join the Judaic world, language suddenly left the level of expressing opinions to gain a higher, infinitely supreme dimension of designating actions, verbs. Everything was now understood as the Command or decree of God, and no other possible word could circulate, with the exception of human speech which was nothing but a faint echo of the Logos. This language was absolute, physically dense (the Verb becoming Flesh) and its grammar was nothing but the way which every philosophical-theological démarche should follow. Language was the cosmic order which defines correspondences, possibilities and haecceities, and a new science of interpretations (hermeneutics) was born at every level of intellectual

---

14 For some commentators, and not without philologically justified reason, this *language of Gods* was no more than the ancient Phrygian, tending to disappear in Western Anatolia in the times of Pindarus. We can also endorse the ongoing speculation about the Oriental origin of most of Greek gods. But nevertheless, gods spoke in Greek language, at least in the concrete language of Homer and Hesiod.

15 Stoicians were the ones who invented the first *philosophy of language*, since their emergence coincided with an epoch when language could be assumed something like trade, which had been denied by the Greek philosophy as *non-philosophical* activity up to then. Now, within language, somethings could be exchanged just like the commodities in trade, and Stoicians called this as *semeion*, the sign, corresponding to the money-sign of the commerce (Kristeva, Bréhier, Deleuze & Guattari...).

16 While the Stoic notion of Logos is directly derived from the Heraclitean one, I believe that it received a completely new sense in their use, and referred to belonging to language, and only language as *speech acts*, rather than to the profound order of the *phusis*. It is necessary to note how the word Logos was used for everything in Ancient Greece—reason, measure, justice, language, speech, everything... (See: Cornelius Castoriadis, *Les Carrefours de labrynthe*, Paris: Seuil, 1972).

activity.[17] Human opinions were no longer the words in which truths were hidden and waiting to be extracted by dialectics, but only illusions, compared to the supreme order of the divine Command. Having an opinion had been redefined as obedience to the *dogma*—to a *doxographical order*.

This is why 17th century philosophers, and Pascal in particular, were the masters of an essential revolution: They just begun with questioning the nature of the Command, the voice of Scriptures, in order to free the language to became *expressive*, rather than a mere representation of the divine command. This was the task, we will see, of Spinoza in his *Tractatus Theologicus Politicus*. The new conception of opinion, developed by Spinoza, was nothing but a *necessary illusion* which nevertheless was a necessary point of departure for attaining rational and intuitive thinking, the *adequate ideas* and the knowledge of *essences*, including our own. It is typical of Spinoza to use the word *opinion* as synonymous with *imagination* (imaginatio). It points to our faculty to think with *images*, which are both ideas and affections of external things in some parts of our body (senses), whose causes largely escape us since these ideas and affections can endure after their causes disappear. The devalorization of *mere opinion* continued, but with a new definition: Opinions are nothing but truths about ourselves, concerning our bodily affections in the world, which are not comprising the knowledge of relations and of the causes. Spinoza never believed in what we today call *falsity*, since there are never false ideas but only opinions that are mutilated by our life-conditions, and partial illusions related with our incapacity to think. Hence, Spinozism has never been an absolute rejection of the *opinion* (imaginatio) but rather a search into capacities inherent to it, for reaching to higher levels of thought.[18]

In our modern times, we assume that opinions are not parts of any knowledge, but rather ambiguous collections of ideas, feelings, knowledges, information and emotions. When Karl Mannheim, the founder of a *sociology of language*—rather than the *sociology of knowledge* (*Erkenntnissoziologie*), as it has been generally assumed—renewed the question of opinions, his inquiry was formulated in the context of modernity: the press, the culture of images, news, political pamphlets in circulation, state bureaucracies operating through reports, campaigns, cases, and public opinion polls. Yet he asked a fundamental question beyond all these fluctuating and chaotic flows: What compels us to believe in a column in a newspaper, a speech of the leader of a political party, a *conservative* or *revolutionary*, *progressive* or *reactionary* text or discourse? With this question, we are already in the heart of a sociology of opinions, which will gradually lose the radical nature of this fundamental question. It is possible to use

---

17   See: Michel Foucault, *Discipline and Punish: the Birth of the Prison*, New York: Random House 1977. *See also:* Gilles Deleuze and Félix Guattari, *A Thousand Plateaus: Capitalism and Schizophrenia*, trans. Brian Massumi, London: Continuum, (1972) 2004.
18   No one could deny the importance of this Spinozist conception of necessary illusion when we see it at work in Althusser's and Pierre Macherey's theories of ideology. Yet we believe that their Spinozism could not be complete unless we reach a genuine understanding of the world of images and opinions, and correspondingly, take them serious.

Occam's razor[19], with the hopes to benefit from the constant fluctuation of opinions, and claim that what is progressive or reactionary are not texts in themselves, but the people who uttered or written them. Surely, we don't believe to the existence of *texts-in-themselves*, just like that there are no *images-in-themselves*, without *intentions* or *subjects* who wrote, uttered and represented them. However, in modernity, opinions and their expression have gained a different amplitude which did not exist in pre-modern societies: They no longer belong to the domain of *knowledge* (and unlike the Greek understanding, they do not disclose *truth*). As Foucault once mentioned, when a journal asked a question to its readers in the 18th century, this was a *real question*—meaning, a question whose answer was still unknown. For example; the famous *Answer to the Question of What is Enlightenment* was written by Kant for *Berliner Monatschrift* (a monthly magazine). When such questions, including the one pertaining to the existence of God, are asked today in newspapers, blogs, reviews or TV discussion panels, they do not require *answers*, at least no more than *sociological opinion polls*. The journalists or researchers asking these questions are no longer interested in the true answer even if they don't exactly know the truth either. Or, the answers would merely be *confirmations*, if not *justifications* of actual problems that are set into the agenda by the media. An important philosopher of *communications*, Jürgen Habermas, would remind that what is at stake in today's mass media is not, and can never be, the *truth-values* or even *truth-claims* but only opinion-claims and arguments, produced in different circumstances than those of scientific wisdom or everyday aspirations. Communication has never been *systematically distorted*, since distortion is already its essence, vectoring towards the notion of *disinformation*.

Again, it is difficult to grasp why there is such a term as *public opinion* today, since, we already learn from the Greeks that *opinion* is always something *public*, it belongs to the speeches in the agoras, and it does not exist before it has been publicly spoken and expressed. And, following the effective dissolution of the City-State, the *koinoneia*, the Roman *res publicum* has never been separable from the public discourse, which is nothing other than individual claims to truth in tribunals, forums and assemblies. Yet in modern times, we have the concept of the *public opinion*, as if there could be something called an *opinion* that is not—or not yet—*public*.

A second, rather *modern* reappraisal of the opposition between *knowledge* and *opinion* comes from Popper and his followers, for whom science is not simply knowledge. Knowledge is, and should always be *doxa*, and not *episteme*, since the latter is not justifiable in its very Platonic origin. Thus, Popper is never interested in epistemological issues (yet, not without being critical about *epistemic* traditions in his work *Open Society and its Enemies*[20]), which opens the way for an understanding of *knowledge* as a kind of the despotism of the intelligible. Evidently, Popper's approach belongs to a kind of

---

19   Editors Note: Occam's razor is the problem-solving principle that entities should not be
      multiplied without necessity, in other words, 'the simplest explanation is most likely the right
      one'.
20   Karl Popper, *The Open Society and Its Enemies*, Routledge, 1945.

doxology, which already pretends to constitute a *logic of scientific wisdom* by relying upon the empirical principles of a *scientism*. There is no doubt that his *scientism* and his logical presuppositions (the 'falsification' theory) that led him to denounce an entire philosophical tradition from Plato to Marx, had evidently passed from Hegel's idealism.

In the *logical* context, however, the word *doxa* or *opinion* seems to refer to a set of Ancient Greek ideas and notions in the vicinity of *episteme* (knowledge). Seemingly both terms refer to ideas that can objectively be true or false, but with a clear and important difference: There is no such thing as *false knowledge* since falsity denies the very existence of knowledge. This self-contradictory character of *false knowledge* is in a way preserved in the work of Spinoza, who already seems to denounce the paradigm of *certitude* developed by his pseudo-predecessor Descartes. We will expose Spinoza's vision of *knowledge* and *opinion* in the next essays, while it seems to be sufficient to state that there is a radical rupture inaugurated by Spinoza in the context of the opinions, as *necessary illusions*, for now.

The classical understanding therefore imposes determination of opinion as a statement that can be either true or false. But this refers us back to Pascal's theorems of probability. We can now discern that, when Blaise Pascal urged us with his question concerning the existence of God almost four hundred years ago, he was not interested in finding an answer. He knew that the faith in God was a gift of the God Himself. Nor was he interested in the opinions of others, upon which, as we generally do today, polls, TV panels and shows can be based. He was not trying to define a sphere of *clear and distinct* knowledge of God and of His existence, since no definition of God could be available to the finite intellect of man as an ultimately finite being. Neither was he believing in the worth of any proof of God's existence—such as the Anselmian *ontological* proof, or any other metaphysical proofs.

Neither interested in the *opinions* of the people about the existence of God, nor in the intelligibility of this existence (the logic of proofs), Pascal could be treated almost as a nihilist, or an ultimate skeptic, while his piety obviously prevented him from all dangers of this sort. His God, who revealed himself through Bible, and the entirety of Christian civilization has necessarily existed. By imposing this question, Pascal seems to interrogate something beyond the *existence* of God, since an Atheist or Skeptic could never be convinced in the existence of God without having the grace coming directly from Him. His question effectively was not about the existence of God, but about man, whose conditions of existence condemned him to finitude and infinite misery. His famous wager (if you bet on the existence of God and God really exists you will gain your eternal salvation; if he doesn't exist, you will lose only your finite existence, nothing more; if you bet on the non-existence of God and He really exists, you will lose your salvation, and finally, if He doesn't exist, you are nothing but a miserable being who have passed his life without believing in anything) actually means that Pascal compares the positions of those who dare to bet in the existence of God and those who don't, rather than really inquiring upon the existence of God Himself.

Opinion as a Problem of Social Sciences

One can consider the entire domain of sociology as dominated by questions of opinion that transform the discipline into a vast doxology,[21] *serving* to create filtered agglomerates of opinions, judgments, answers to prevailing questions which have already lost their weight, and altogether transformed into sets of information. News media and mainstream documentary films proceed in a similar fashion in general—they ask people their opinions in order to learn about their life, environment and public issues. Friedrich Pollock in his classical article 'Empirical Research into Public Opinion'[22] observes the presuppositions of the mainstream sociology as practiced in American w*elfare society*: Whenever a question floats around in public, everyone appears to be eager to respond to it, yet, such answering attempt is quite illusory, since the question itself effectively create a fundamental bias—one is often led to *choose* an answer from the already provided ones that had been placed into agenda before the question is imposed. Moreover, we have to remember Bergson's famous *questioning of questions*: From the very depths of our language we associate the criteria of truth and falsity only with the answers, and not with the questions or problems themselves. When we face a question, we already presume that there must be a *true* answer to it. It is essential, therefore, to redefine the task of philosophy by the truth-value of the questions and problems themselves. Bergson's questioning of questions seems to depart from Kantian way of considering *true questions* and *false questions*. We can also remember Marx now, who asserted that every historical epoch only poses those problems it is able to solve. Opinions, in this sense, appear to be the outcome or function of the act of questioning, setting problems, issues, agendas, interrogations and pursuits.

The problem of opinions raise a major epistemological problem in the practice of social sciences from a formal point of view: What would be the epistemological character of social sciences if not a certain form of axiology, once they adopt methods that would force them to become *opinion of opinions*, a mere opinion among many others? Today we are far from the origins of social sciences in the 19th century, when a certain *ontology* was still relevant—in Comte, in Spencer, up to Durkheim. If mainstream sociology today tends to become a doxology, then, even the most anti-positivistic tendencies, such as critical schools, deconstruction, and post-colonial studies derived from the continental philosophies (French philosophy and German critical school) also belong to the same horizon. Hermeneutics or *understanding*, as well as *textuality* eventually share the same and common doxological character with what they attempt to criticize. What does *understanding* mean, if not pointing to a fundamental belief that people understand themselves better than anyone else? This problem was imposed twice in philosophy of social sciences: first by Nietzsche, when he warns us about the *decadence* of the sociology, notably of Spencer's, necessarily sharing the characteristics of a *decadent society*, and secondly by Heidegger, who has engaged in the criticism of the notion of *hermeneutic circle* in Husserlian phenomenology.

---

21   Gilles Deleuze and Félix Guattari, *What is Philosophy?,* trans. G. Burchell and H. Tomlinson, London and New York: Verso, 1994, p. 155.
22   Pollock, 'Empirical research into public opinion'.

Whatever the *decadence* of such 19th century *scientism* had been, the epistemological ambiguity that had been present in the foundation of social sciences has never failed to give its fruits: From Marx's critique of political economy to Weber's ceaseless creation of *ideal types* as figures for *understanding*, a new epistemic subject was born, which could not have been reduced to a mere doxology that occupies so much of social scientific practices today. The *founders* of social (or human) sciences created and invented what Georg Simmel had called *social* or *psychological types*. In Marx, not only the Proletariat but also the Intellectual, the Lumpenproletariat, and the Petty Bourgeoisie were typical, incarnating their social positions in a class society. This means that they could both be considered as classes and concrete social subjects at the same time, all together constituting social bodies that possess a variety of characters. This was the way in which Weber considered *the Protestant* or the *Puritan*, Veblen considered the *Leisure Class*, and Sombart discussed the psychology of the Bourgeois. At the extreme, French sociologists even considered the fundamentally amorphous *masses* or *crowds* as socio-psychological types, as exemplified in the works of Gustave Le Bon. Le Play designed perhaps the largest empirical inquiry into the life of the *working people* in Europe.[23] At any rate, the extreme case was Georg Simmel who not only coined the word, but also worked through the creation of a series of *socio-psychological types*: the *Migrant*, the *Poor*, the *Stranger*, the *Jew*...

It is clear that *realist* and *naturalist* literature was able to create *socio-psychological types* long before the social sciences: From Balzac on, we have the Bovarysme of the realist novel, and *Nana* is no one but a social type in Zola. We have the Idiot of Dostoyevsky, and the Russian novel never failed to operate through the creation of types—the *public employees* of Gogol, the *Nihilist* of Turgenev... Realist novel was bringing forth something quite different from the Romantic *individual* which resembled an *ideal*, an expressive individuality that culminated in the superhistorical Great Man of Hegel. A socio-psychological type is always different from what we may call as the *individual*, that prominent ideal and abstraction of bourgeoisie. Everyone acknowledged the existence of *classes* in the 19th century; it is remarkable how Marx emphasizes the fact that the concept of social class was forged particularly by French bourgeois historians like Thierry and Guizot rather than being his creation. A social type, whether in *historiography*, *literature* or *sociology*, cannot be reduced to a *class* or to the general and abstract notion of an *individual*. It stands in almost *halfway* towards these entities: They are evidently *individuals*, and *members of a class*, if not outcasts at all from a certain point of view, but what matters is that they belong to a kind of *singularity*. They are not *individuals*, or *categories*, but rather *constructs* of societies themselves—possessing concrete lives, traits, affects and ideas. According to Simmel, the task of sociology is to transform those *traits* through which a social type is recognized, to a *social form*, or rather, to a unique formula. Hence the formula of the *Stranger* would not be *the wanderer who comes today and goes tomorrow*, but rather *the person who comes today and stays tomorrow*. Similarly, there is no *Poor* before being defined as *poor* by society in a given, concrete social context, and its existence transformed into a problem to be solved by charity organizations, churches, humanitarian campaigns.

---

23   See: Pierre Guillaume Frédéric le Play, Frederic Le Play on Family, Work, and Social Change, ed. Catherine Bodard Silver, University of Chicago Press, 1982.

It is quite important to distinguish *socio-psychological types* from *conceptual personae* invoked by Deleuze and Guattari. Since the Platonic dialogues, we always have had conceptual personas; Socrates himself, the *Sophist*, the *Idiot* (not Dostoyevsky's but Descartes'), *Zarathustra*, the *Priest*, the *Other*... Conceptual personas are needed in constituting subjects responsible for ideas, which is not necessary for socio-psychological types, who don't need to be expressive of philosophical notions.[24]

Another important question is whether psychoanalysis also worked through socio-psychological types. In its Freudian version, the fundamental distinction between the psychotic and neurotic seem to forge an insightful typification. But who is typified here as the *patient*, a socially and psychologically *affected* individual, answering to therapy or not, as the sole Freudian criterion for such a distinction? From a Simmelian viewpoint, a *Patient* could be seen as a *socio-psychological type* only insofar as the subject of a socio-historical institutionalization such as the *clinic*, and this is what Foucault did in his history of madness—narrating the story of the *mad* becoming *patient*.

Hence, a socio-psychological type can never be surveyed without a corresponding landscape, milieu, and environment. This environment is social, since the nature is not a creator of types—it can only be generated by society. Consequently, it is difficult to define the traditional and rural conditions of life with reference to social types: The *Peasant* is a social type only with reference to the urban, modern life, against which s/he tends to become perceptible, as an outsider, as a potential or actual immigrant. We should keep in mind Spinoza's argument that 'But nature forms individuals, not peoples; the latter are only distinguishable by the difference of their language, their customs, and their laws'[25]. Socio-psychological types are certainly events that are introduced by modernity.

Now, our main concern will be the gradual demise of *social types* through the evolution and academization of social sciences. The birth of the *sociology of opinions* in the hands of Gabriel Tarde at the end of the 19th century was determined by the affective and contagious nature of opinions, and their productivity in creating new, constitutive social forms, forces and institutions.[26] In other words, social types in their communicative individuality are essentially *affected* and *affective*. They generate certain affections in themselves and others. They are traversed by what we like to call *sociology of affects* rather than of *opinions*—which are also a certain type of affects among others.

Thus, we should epistemologically criticize and falsify a series of assumptions through which human sciences have traditionally or actually condemned as if these were *Platonic* ideas: that of *personality*, that of *society*, that of *individual*. The first notion has

24   Deleuze and Guattari, *What is philosophy?*
25   Baruch Spinoza, *Tractatus Theologico-Politicus, Part IV*, trans. R. H. M. Elwes, Project Gutenberg Ebook, 2014 (1997), p. 160, http://www.gutenberg.org/ebooks/992.
26   Gabriel Tarde, *On Communication and Social Influence: Selected Papers*, Chicago: University of Chicago Press, 1969.

long been the fundamental assumption of a psychology claiming to investigate the *depths* of human essence. And when Tarde's major opponent Durkheim was trying to create a methodological framework to delineate the domain of sociology, he passed individuality to the realm of psychology, keeping the sui generis status of the *social* as a fact (*fait social*). In other words, Durkheim has tried to formulate an ontological, if not real distinction out of a methodological distinction: A social fact is defined as what not only goes beyond the individual, but also begins from just there, where the individuality ceases to exist and the sanction begins. Social facts defy anything that can be individually and subjectively identified—such as division of labour, the notions of the sacred and profane, etc., and distill an objective, ontological entity called society out of them.

Beyond all the merits that can be attributed to Durkheim and his followers in shaping sociology as a modern discipline, such methodological perversion seems to be the point of departure for the demise of social types. In the debate between Durkheim and Tarde the former had been the winner, leaving to us to rediscover the merits of the latter, especially in regards to our main issue here, replacing the sociology of opinions with a sociology of affects. It is evident that social types are affective, but how should we evaluate their disappearance from the domain of human or social sciences? Whether such disappearance is a natural outcome of the social conditions that developed throughout the 20th century remains an open question, but not only social sciences but also literature and cinema today seem to have ceased to operate through creating social or psychological types. Social types, as events that modernity introduced, have seemed to lost their classical characteristics and moods, and almost entirely disappeared only to reappear once again in Charles Wright Mills' works, as *white collar* and *power elite*. Rather concerned with *opinions* and *masses* (with the theses of so-called *mass society*) modern social sciences tend to work with *general* or *generic* concepts, which are quite distant from the perceptual character of the descriptions of social and psychological types. *Identity* and its *crisis*, *plurality* and *pluralisms*, *relativity* and *perspectivism* are some of these key notions today, which do not lead to inquiries beyond what still remain as the major epistemological problem of contemporary social sciences today; being an *opinion of opinions*.

I am merely attempting here, to remind the importance of social types in the history of social sciences, basically with reference to works of Simmel and Tarde with their *insightful* originality. This is a criticism of mainstream sociology as well as its epistemological presumptions. In this attempt, we will keep a critical distance from the categories of what we would like to call *juridico-legal* ways of thinking, which have become fashionable today, especially in Europe, following the influential works of German thinkers like Karl Otto Apel and Jürgen Habermas.

No longer interested in the opinions of the people Pascal was retired to the *Cœur*, leaving his *mathematical-scientific* research behind, to join the mystic experience of surrendering himself to God and of *Theodycée* as a pious Christian. He accounts his experiences induced by meditation as blissful. His was no longer a contemplation of the world, which could no longer give anything other than pain and suffering, and remain as a stupid basis to shape the making of the new science and art, yet, but rather of the internal life, of the interior of this feeble and powerless subject before his God, the infinite and omnipotent.

God has no image, even when He says that he created man according to His own image. For a long time this was interpreted in religious hermeneutics as purely a metaphor. And if God, not having an image, cannot be grasped through imagination, He cannot be grasped by our cognition either: We have no concept of God, nor do we know anything about Him, nor about the judgment he will impose upon us, nor about destiny and its enigmas. We are only charged to believe. We must choose Him and His order, the divine Command. Pascal is clear about it: A Command is something to be obeyed, not something to investigate. His attitude, however, is quite different from that of ordinary believers, who obey the Commandments for earthly reasons or conditions (such as fear of death and of the Final Judgment), or due to a lack of liberty imposed by the traditions regulating their lives, which make the operation of *opinions* impossible and control the community's life patterns all at once. All these can constitute almost a second nature of man that determines his choice. A tradition well formulated by Tertullianus[27] not only makes obedience a strict minimum for the believer, but also attributes unconditionality to the idea of choice. In this context, a statement such as 'I believe since it is absurd' would be somehow self-evident and refer to a pseudo-rational premise—if it were not absurd but rational, the notion of belief would not make sense in its context. Really, people only believe in what they don't know and understand, rather than what they do.

The novelty of Pascal is that he suggests the idea of *choice* in an entirely new form. He offers a limited number of alternatives, but one has first to *choose choosing* before making a concrete choice. This is the primary point of interest in Pascal's *wager*. And this is the non-philosophical (or rather, theosophical) way he tries to pass beyond *mere opinion*.

I should repeat that the Greeks have contrasted the *doxa* (opinion) and the *episteme* (loosely translated as knowledge) once again now. Their model was that of dialectics in its pre-Kantian sense, an *old* form of dialectics, in which everything happens in the context of a gathering and confabulation, and everyone involved tends to become a pretender—as in the model of Symposium. As Marcel Detienne argues, the Greeks were quite interested in the powers of speech, its persuasive and rhetorical force.[28] The Greek polis has always been a society of speech, an oral society. But they also feared from this power and always strived to control the speech by developing measures for restraining its abuses and institutionalizing it. Jean-Pierre Vernant shows how, in Ancient Greece, many different *speeches* were confronting each other in the heart of the city: There was the *muthos* of Poet, the *sophia* of the Oriental Old Wiseman, the *episteme* of the Philosopher, and the *doxa* of the Sophist.[29] This did not mean that every one of them shared the same basic terminology and rules of conduct with each other, as if being in a constant state of *ideal conversation*.[30]

27   See: Wikipedia on Tertullian, https://en.wikipedia.org/wiki/Tertullian.
28   Marcel Detienne, *The Creation of Mythology*, Chicago: University of Chicago Press, 1986.
      See also. Marcel Detienne, *The Masters of Truth in Archaic Greece*, New York: Zone Books, 1999.
29   Jean-Pierre Vernant and Pierre Vidal-Naquet, *Myth and tragedy in ancient Greece*, trans. Janet Lloyd, New York: Zone Books, 1988.
30   Editors Note: Baker refers to the Habermasian notion of ideal conversation/communication here.

Institutionalization of the Sociology of Opinions

My aim here is not to lament for the loss of *social types* as devices of understanding used by early sociologists. But it is difficult not to notice how badly the conceptual and methodological arsenals of sociology have since been impoverished: In the past, when Marx used the notions of *proletarian* or *capitalist*, these were not only designating social classes or organic units in an analytical fashion, but also affective social types, with emotional responses, sensibilities, traditions, and various cultural traits. The sociologists of the time always worked through creating social types: the Protestant or Puritan in Max Weber, the *bourgeois* in Werner Sombart, the *leisure class* in Thorstein Veblen. But in the early times of human sciences no one was more creative than Georg Simmel in the production of these affective social types: the Stranger, the *blasé*, the Jew… Even the psychoanalysis of Freud had to refer to social types –the *neurotic*, the *hysteric* are social types insofar as laymen can understand what they mean without knowing one word in psychology.

As I mentioned earlier, one of the most important reasons of the elimination of social types lies back in Durkheim's methodological efforts to distinguish the domain of sociology from other human sciences—psychology, ethnology and history. His definition of *social fact* is meant to designate what is something beyond the individual, beyond the subjective or emotional motives. Society appears here as a sui generis objectivity, as a fact in itself. Nothing could be more harmful for the sociologist's creativity in social types than Durkheim's attempt. In the early periods of its academization, with Robert E. Park and his Chicago School, the social types were imported from Europe (under the influence of Simmel). But the eclectic nature of their methods (a kind of ruthless positivism transforming the Chicago City into a laboratory) invited the Durkheimian concepts. Such a migration of ideas can only be conceived in parallel to real migration of people from Europe to the New World, not only of sociologists or sociological theories, but also of social types—the case of *The Hobo* of Nels Anderson is characteristic in this context. But the Durkheimian danger has prevailed, to undermine the capacity of the institutionalized sociology to create notions flexible enough to constitute and survey the new social types.

The Grand Theories conceptualized by Robert K. Merton,[31] and exemplified by the case of Talcott Parsons seem to have completely eliminated the social type. This is the accomplishment of the Durkheimian vices: The detachment of norms and values from the concrete life of the individuals, putting the frame of analysis at the maximal level of nations or society at large. Thus, sociology appears as an attempt to derive individualities out of the integration of values and the persistence of norms, people seeming to flow and variate in an ocean that is society in a historical context. This is where sociology coincides with the notion of opinion: The *sociology of opinions* today is the questioning of social groups about what they think of themselves, their life and public issues. The constant reference of the early sociologists to social types was opening

---

31   Robert King Merton, *Social Theory and Social Structure*, New York: Free Press, 1968.

sociology into the realm of history, to construct genealogies of these types or classes. Asking for opinions evidently can reveal something of the individuals surveyed. But one can scarcely believe that this can reconstitute the ontic social situation by itself, since, as Pollock observes, the polls are biased in such a way that no mathematical-statistical instruments could redeem.[32] It is always as if one poses a question and the respondent now believes that he has to have an idea or opinion about the issue. Yet, in the fragmented modern life, with an extremely high level of division of labor, no one would be able to form and represent a global opinion —which would be contrary to the very idea of opinion anyways. We are trapped by the language, as Henri Bergson reveals: One is always inclined to locate the values of truth and falsity in the answer when solicited a question, even in the case of the most absurd, stupid questions. Bergsonian philosophy was, in this respect, an attempt to create a philosophical art of creating and posing *true* questions. In the domain of opinions, however, this is impossible, since the emphasis here is on the opposition of the free-floating opinions.

However, modern societies are —nonetheless objectively—defined by a large accumulation of opinions, which are made the primary subject matter of social and human sciences today. One should note that the idea of opinion, so long despised by classical philosophies—a mere *doxa*, opposed by the *episteme*, meaning knowledge since the Ancient Greece—gained importance and relevance in the development of modernity, and, alongside the development of modern representative democracies, opinion tended to become the yardstick of the *public*, as the modern concept of *public opinion* was forged towards the end of the 19th century. Whether the term *public* is a mere useless addition to the word *opinion* or not is not at all evident, since every opinion is somehow public: It is impossible to have opinion without expressing it. This is the case even as earlier as Plato's philosophy: The opinion is the appearance, as just it appears in the public debates, while it is always individually expressed. The knowledge can be something *hidden*, on the sky, in the world of *ideas*, but opinion is something always *public* (koinon) while possibly comprising the truth of knowledge. Yet it is not difficult to oppose the modern meaning of opinion to the ancient ones. For a long time, opinion was being treated by the thinkers and philosophers as the ultimate source, or even being of the error and falsity. This is determined by the very nature of the concept, the *doxa* as pure figment, or something expressed in one's speech. Still today, an opinion—in a TV show, a conference or a panel—is nothing but something which has to be opposed, but the modern form of opinion is not challenged by the knowledge, but just by another opinion. This distinction is to be treated as only relative: When the ancient philosopher opposed his *knowledge* against the opinions cultivated by the eminent *doxologists* of the time (the Sophists opposed by Socrates), he was doing so in order to extract truth out of opinions (of himself and of others in a public debate). This means that since the Ancient Greece, opinions opposed opinions, and this was exactly the political representation of the free citizens in public issues. This domain of human public experience survived partially through some modern ideas, especially in the classical period in terms

---

32   Friedrich Pollock, *Empirical Research into Public Opinion* in Critical Sociology, ed. P. Connerton, Penguin, 1976.

of the empirical concept of *common sense*, but this is precisely something different from our understanding of today's idea of opinion. At present, no one can be blamed for his opinion, as it is still opposed to others. Opinion has lost its value as a point of departure in attaining the truth. The truth, on the other hand, seems to be reduced to a formless agglomerate of opinions, in the public, to be extracted and formulated by specific devices of research, i.e. the *research into public opinion*.

Ultimately, an opinion is what transforms an individual into a master and subject of his thought, as a member of a group. The term *member* should be emphasized here, since there are never individual opinions, even when a single person expresses it. Opinion is a performative way of becoming a subject, a member of a group, even if the group consists in a single real individual. One of the best paradigmatic models of how opinion operates is given by Deleuze and Guattari: If there had been an Ancient Greek round table at stake (the Symposium) and cheese is served one of the invited persons would say 'This cheese is spoiled and disgusting!' and other people on the table would oppose him by claiming that 'This is the best of the Rochefort cheese, you are the one who is corrupted!'. So, every judgment in the realm of opinions is accompanied by another judgment, this time attributed to the one who expressed the first one. Gilles-Gaston Granger calls this a *generic subject*.

The social sciences' tendency towards becoming a series of opinions about opinions starts with the process of academization during early 20s, through the works of Chicago School sociologists. This process is marked by the domination of the two American journals in particular –the American Journal of Sociology, and the Public Opinion Quarterly (published by the University of Chicago since 1937, which we believe is the first *interdisciplinary* engagement in the history of social sciences, already in an era when Durkheim attempt- ed to clarify the boundaries defining the different zones of social sciences—especially between psychology and sociology). Whether public or private, opinion is constituted as the principal subject matter of sociology. And today, social sciences tend to become more and more inclined to rely upon the notions of subjectivity based on opinion. Contrary to the classical manner of considering the realm of the social as an objective entity, as in the 19th century (positivism and Marxism), social scientists today seem to develop conceptual devices, or a self-referentiality, which tends to constitute a kind of *positivism of the text*, or a kind of discursive-interpretative strategy of *reading*.

The Notion of the Point of View

At the heart of Marxist theory of ideology, one can find the criticism and transposition of Feuerbach's moralist statement towards a political context: 'Man thinks differently in a palace and in a hut', Feuerbach wrote, and added '[If] because of hunger, of misery, you have no stuff in your body, you likewise have no stuff for morality in your head, in your mind, or heart'.[33] Engels' criticism was particularly directed to the way Feuerbachian morality

---

33   Ludwig Feuerbach, as quoted in: Frederick Engels, 'Feuerbach', trans. Progress
     Publishers, *Ludwig Feuerbach and the End of Classical German Philosophy,* 1946 (1886),

was 'cut exactly to the pattern of modern capitalist society' despite his intentions. Yet, despite his moralist take on it, Feuerbach's recognition itself, that 'man thinks differently in a palace and in a hut', can as well be interpreted as not only one of the possible sources of a Marxist theory of *ideology*, but also its pivotal formula. We don't intend to engage in the discussion of the development of such a theoretical perspective here—We think it is futile to repeat the Marxist debates on *ideology* that occupied the philosophical circles two decades ago (Althusser, his followers and opponents), and we certainly do not intend to declare a new *end of ideology* at all. We just want to note that the formula Marx derived from Feuerbach's statement should be taken in its concrete and literal sense, as an inquiry on *thought* itself, about *thinking*, rather than ideology. The *material* character attributed by Althusser to ideology largely depended upon the institutionalization of ideological positions in general, through specific devices he called the *ideological state apparatuses*. This would inevitably lead to an understanding that everything in this world could belong to the domain of ideology—not only family, mass communications, trade-unions, justice, NGO's, schools, universities and political parties, but also the entire spectrum of daily life experiences. Yet, we still think that Marx's focus was on the act of thinking —if we can consider *thinking* is an *act*, from a Spinozist perspective, as 'man thinks', rather than ideology. In order to locate Marx's understanding of *ideology*, one has to reverse the formula: If a peasant in his hut comes to think like in a palace, than we can say that he had been caught by an *ideology*, that his *thought* is not justified in itself by the factual conditions of his position. This means that thinking is not a *universal* activity but a conditioned, devoted, and engaged position in the world. To think is to have a point of view, but not an indifferent, haphazardly chosen one. Marx could have pointed that a peasant in his hut is differently affected than an aristocrat in a palace, if he adopted a Spinozist terminology. Thought, if reduced to *consciousness* alone, as in the case of Existentialist philosophies (Sartre, Jaspers and Mounier), tends to be formulated rather as a matter of *choice*, assuming the freedom of the will as its primary condition. We don't notice such determination in Marx, who was aware that the peasant is not free to choose his point of view even if he thinks *differently*. And this *difference* is never generic but always specific in the social domain: There is no such thing as *to think differently* in itself; one always thinks differently from another, and these differences encompass the entire social world. One can think like a peasant as a member of a class, or as a child of the traditions, mores, habits, or appropriated morality. This is not necessarily what is meant by Marx, since we reduce *thinking* to *opinion* in this case, conditioned in a world of social transformations, fluctuations and unconscious choices. To be a member of a class can be an attribution, creating the peasant as a *social type* among many others, yet one can fail to acquire the point of view determined by the peasant life as it is. One should assume that there are as many points of view as there are individuals. Again we have the Spinozist formula to interpret such a determination of the plurality of points of view: Nature doesn't create nations, classes, or castes; it only creates individuals. This does not mean that nations, classes, families and other social groups are fictive, or that they don't exist, it rather means that one has to be an active participant to be a member of any or more of these human groupings, that these groupings are to be historically and genetically constituted.

---

http://www.marxists.org/archive/marx/works/1886/ludwig-feuerbach/ch03.htm.

One question that raises itself up here is how to conceive such a notion of the point of view. Strictly speaking, the notion of point of view has nothing to do with *opinions* and the ordinary notion of relativism. Marx never conceded that the *class point of view* was a specific opinion among others, as it was represented by a *pioneering* cast of socialist intellectuals; the class perspective leads to a kind of *truth*, as it has been repeated by Lenin, which has to be interpreted as the *constructive power* of the socialist life. The only difference between this *constructivist* understanding of truth and the older, traditional, or *scientistic* truth regimes (such as religion) is that, the former is not pre-established and disguised by the long traditions, dogmas and rules. The constructivist understanding of truth neither presents itself necessarily as a final destination. We have to reconsider the fact that Marx's cluster of thought never encountered the Nietzschean one: Nietzsche had profoundly understood that *truth* could be the *deepest lie*, and the futility of the notion of digging out the truth. In Marx, the same sense is attributed to *truth* only insofar as it is conceived in the context of a *historical process*, which is implicit in Nietzschean viewpoint. The truth in this sense can create the affect of *being-at-home* (which had been a Hegelian category that came to be formulated as the fact of Western philosophy: 'We are together in the house of the Greeks')—an understanding that suggests us to stop and relax after attaining a truth.

Having a point of view is the foundation of the modern philosophy since Descartes. It is also the implicit philosophical basis of modern institutions—revolutions, democracy, society of opinion, freedom of thought and human rights. Since the Renaissance, it has also been the driving force in arts, literature and especially in sciences. In this part of our investigation, we will try to expand the determinations of such *modern* idea of point of view together with its political, social and aesthetic determinations.

Today, we are appealed by our contemporaries from the West and the East, to recognize and repent for the *great sin* of a great French philosopher of the 17th century, René Descartes. Cartesian worldview is severely criticized by philosophers, sociologists, scholars of every kind as the construct that is responsible of the *subjectivity* of the conscious being, the mind-body dualism (and through that, of all kinds of dualisms) and of the *cerebral* focus of Western metaphysical thought. Some of these criticisms are obviously well established without being pretentious about the *overcoming of metaphysics*. Yet all seem to profess that it was Descartes who founded the modern thought, upon which the Enlightenment, the Kantian *critique*, and all forms of modern philosophies evolved. Here, we intend to focus on a point of reversal that occurred in Descartes' thought, to the *coup de force* implied in his invention of the Cogito.

Aristotelian Scholasticism and the revival of Platonism during the Renaissance have developed in the domain of an Ancient image of thought. To think was to *appropriate* an Idea through speculation, or to capture the *hidden* forms behind its *appearances*, as if these ideas or forms were located in the Heavens. Residing among the appearances, one had possessed only opinions, and thinking was conceived as an activity that was consist of speculating, defining, and categorizing species and genera. It is evident that the Socratic moment of *turning thought back onto itself* was only a comparable gesture, which in fact fortified the regime of truth by expanding it into human, political and moral affairs. Ionians, while limiting themselves to the discussion of selectively chosen moral premises in their philosophy, developed the rational project of inquiring into the Nature of everything.

The Platonic-Aristotelian mode of thought (and its continuation in Medieval theology and Scholasticism) somehow operates as a device or method of thinking that is deprived of every affect, emotion, illusion and even tradition. Until then, there had been no distinction between Descartes' meditative practice, and that of an Ancient philosopher or a Scholastic. They have been the kind of philosophers who over-valued the method (the logical or analytical) with respect to the content (ascertained as knowledge or *scientia*). All broke apart when Descartes raised his formulation of the Cogito ('I think, therefore I am') at the level of the 'definition of man'. The Aristotelian *classical* definition of man, as animal rationale, had been relying upon a classical mode of definition—one had to traverse the universe of *animals*, and then find out the *man* particularly in it, distinguishing this sub-group by a *differentia specifica* (specific difference), which in this case has been 'to be rational'. All had been a movement from genera to species in the general deductive context, in accordance to the Aristotelian formal logic of syllogism. What is it then, that makes Descartes' cogito—I think, therefore I am—sound like a definition? This is not only a new definition of man, but an entirely new definition of the definition itself, at least implicitly present in *Meditations on First Philosophy*.[34] We need to consider the complete formula of the Cogito to get a better sense of it: I doubt, therefore I think, so I am, therefore I am a thinking thing. Against his *theologist* or *materialist* critiques,[35] Descartes seems to be in anger, especially in his letter to Arnauld: 'I know that there can be my body who thinks in me; what matters is that I can *doubt* about this; that some kind of power in me can lead me to doubt about such a reality',[36]—this is exactly what Descartes calls as *thinking* (*penser*). One can even say that he has been the inventor of *thinking*, while for the Ancients, with the exception of the Stoics, thinking was generally the *internal thought*, the *dianoia* through which one necessarily encounters the idea by replicating its models, as Plato's *Meno* implies. There was an external relationship between the *idea* and the *internal thought*, and neither the latter was reducible to the former, nor the former to the latter. Thinking meant to be impregnated by an idea, which belonged to the Divine order that was out there, in the heavens, whereas the world of appearances in which we ordinarily live was only a distorted image of the world of eternal forms or ideas. It is clear that Descartes had been at the threshold of moving from the understanding of *thinking* as a replication or simulation of ideas towards a modern image of thought at this moment. In his *Principes de la philosophie*, he answers the question 'What is thinking?' by expanding thinking towards a new domain: 'Thinking is

---

34   René Descartes, *René Descartes: Meditations on First Philosophy in Focus,* Edited by Stanley
      Tweyman. Routledge. 34–40. London and New York. 1993.
35   See: George L. Klein, 'Randall's Interpretation of the Philosophies of Descartes, Spinoza, and
      Leibniz', John Peter Anton (ed.) *Naturalism and Historical Understanding*, New York: SUNY Press,
      1967, p. 85.
36   René Descartes, *Selected Correspondences of Descartes*, pp. 207–208.
      http://www.earlymoderntexts.com/assets/pdfs/descartes1619.pdf.

not only understanding, willing, imagining, but also feeling [sentir]'.[37] This means that an *affective* dimension is introduced in the classical notion of thinking. But what is much more important is that Descartes now develops a new image of thinking, thinking as a human activity: 'But once I kept myself secure from the fact that, at the moment when I wished to think that everything is false, it was necessary that me, who was thinking it, be something...'[38] Descartes clearly rejects to contend himself in affirming that man is a reasonable animal in the classical manner, since this time, one has to traverse the notion of the animal, and answer the question of 'what is reasonable', with a series of infinitely recursive questions.[39] His deduction is not that of a derivation, but a clear involution when he passes from *doubting* to *thinking*, and from *thinking* to *being*; that if I doubt, this involves that I think, and that I think equally involves that I am.

This relationship of *involution* is another image of *thinking*. When a Scholastic ventured into defining man, the concepts he used were not intrinsically related to each other; the notion of man could be thought without necessarily referring to the notions of animal, and of reason. Moreover, each of these notions could be found in different individual minds, or in the same individual mind differently, at different times. This is the case of the Cogito in Saint Augustine, where the identity of the *Ego Cogito* is raised up to the dimension of time, to his Odyssey from Paganism to Catholicism.[40] Descartes is replacing this image with a new one, in which, on the one hand the identity is reduced to the simple certainty 'I = I' and on the other, thinking is elevated up to the actuality of an act. It is as if *thinking* begins to have a *speed*, which is infinite in the formulation of the Cogito, but necessary for passing from one thought to another, from one affect to another. This is nothing but the invention of *subjectivity*.

This is a singular moment in the history of thought: It leads to many assumptions and implications—which are not only *philosophical*, but also moral, social and political. For the first time, thinking has acquired a new modality, as an image of a particular human activity or, in a step further, an action carried out by human being. As an activity, it has a speed and a trajectory, a *démarche* in the Althusserian sense, and thereby, there can be obstacles and barriers installed on its path. As the philosophical invention of subjectivity cannot be separated from the creation of the *modern subject*—in the *juridico-legal* sense of the word, man as a thinking being can affirm his *existence* only when such obstacles are removed or eliminated. Without the passage from the Ancient image of thinking to the Cartesian one, one cannot *claim* the *right* to think and express her/his thoughts. It is clear that the expression of ideas, and thinking in general had

---

37   René Descartes, 'Oeuvres', *Les principes de la philosophie Vol. 2*. Paris: Librairie Albin Michel, 1932, p. 95.

38   René Descartes, *Discours de la méthode: Part 4*, Paris: Fayard/Mille et une nuits, 2000.

39   René Descartes, *Discourse On Method, and Meditations on First Philosophy*, Indianapolis: Hackett Pub. Co., 1993 (1596-1650).

40   Philip Schaff, *St. Augustine's City of God and Christian Doctrine*, CCEL, 1890, http://www.ccel.org/ccel/schaff/npnf102. See: http://www.ccel.org/ccel/augustine/enchiridion.html for Enchiridion.

been persecuted and censored by the authorities in the past as well—by the State, the Church and the like. It is true that some people have always been persecuted and massacred for their ideas. But the modern claim to *freedom of thought* and its various manifestations—freedom of conscience, human rights, freedom of expression—would not be possible if modern societies have not been implanted with this new image of thinking as an action. The Cartesian coup de force, which is executed in the language of philosophy, unrolls a corresponding series of social transformations, expanding in the clusters of time and geography that we call the West, through which new *freedoms* are invented, and a new *society*, which we call the *society of opinion*, is formed.

The *point of view* can now be instituted outside the Cartesian understanding of sub-jectivity, but always in the domain opened up by Descartes' *coup de force*. His follower and major *rationalist* opponent, Baruch Spinoza still appraises reason and thinking as an act of the mind; the best political regime is the one that persecutes such act of thinking less (democracy). But what is characteristic in Spinoza is the way in which he incorporates the principle of the Cogito in the second book of his Ethics as an almost indifferent proposition: 'Man thinks'. This is certainly not in the *tone* of Descartes, who had been very eager to conclude his postulations as soon as possible (Leibniz accuses him with concluding his thoughts too quickly). In the *tone* of Spinoza, from the fact that 'man thinks' one can discern different point of view than the Cogito of Descartes. Thinking is nothing but *to have ideas*; as Spinoza abstains from defining *thought* in his work, while venturing into defining everything in due order *more geometrico*. Descartes cries: 'I think', 'I am a thing that thinks', whereas Spinoza coldly observes the fact that man thinks, without accentuating the act of thinking. Thinking, that is, having ideas, is nothing but an affection of human body in its encounters with external world. There is no point in stating that 'I am a thinking thing', since thinking is only a mode of affections and at the same time a general notion, whose isolation as a privileged act as such could destroy its affect. By *thinking* Spinoza refers to every affect that passes through us, all of which are anchored in the singularities of this world. It is impossible to conceive and generalize thinking as a discrete act; it is a perpetual activity that embodies the human mind.

Another moment comes with Kant, who too criticizes Descartes for arriving to conclu-sions too quickly, as Leibniz has done before him. One needs the Cogito as a receptacle in which the acts of analysis and especially synthesis are performed by the faculty of knowledge, but there is no room for saying that 'I am a thinking thing', simply because the notion of *thing* is not yet *explained*. According to Kant, the passage from 'I think' to 'I am' is justified, but from 'I am' to 'I am a thinking thing' is not a legitimate one. Kant calls this Cartesian attitude *material idealism*; by declaring the spatiality of the objects in our absence as either doubtful or indemonstrable, Descartes thereby admits 'the undoubted certainty of only one empirical assertion (*assertio*), to wit, 'I am'.[41] What Kant means is that Descartes, while recognizing the human thought as a non-spatial thing,

---

41   Immanuel Kant, *Critique of Pure Reason*, trans. F. Max Müller, New York: The Macmillan Company, 1922 (1781), p. 778.

reduces everything to a possible doubt we may have about our corporeal existence, yet everything is still to be determined and explained:

> The 'I think' is, as has been already stated, an empirical proposition, and contains the proposition, 'I exist'. But I cannot say, 'Everything, which thinks, exists'; for in this case the property of thought would constitute all beings possessing it, necessary being. Hence my existence cannot be considered as an inference from the proposition, 'I think,' as Descartes maintained- because in this case the major premise, 'Everything, which thinks, exists,' must precede- but the two propositions are identical. The proposition, 'I think,' expresses an undetermined empirical intuition, that perception (proving consequently that sensation, which must belong to sensibility, lies at the foundation of this proposition); but it precedes experience, whose province it is to determine an object of perception by means of the categories in relation to time.[42]

This is not a purely philosophical criticism of a metaphysical theme, if we orient ourselves to the new path Kant now conveys the act of thinking: Only deduced from the experience, 'I think' is not sufficiently determined, remaining merely as an empirical, non-methodic intuition. One can understand how Kant also aims for a coup de force within the philosophical reflection: This coup de force would be on the same grounds we have tried to expose concerning Descartes above, and it would culminate in the foundational logic of the Enlightenment and, among its newly emerging institutions, the most important one, the *reason*—or what the philosophers of the time were calling as *reason*. And in Kant, reason is presented a legislative faculty, acquiring an almost juridico-legal definition: There is nothing but reason to judge everything; but to judge everything, first the reason has to judge itself. The highest achievement of Kantian philosophy, the idea of critique (as Kant calls his philosophy as *kritische*, critical) would be derived from this somehow strange argument.

Hence, the Cogito institutes itself at the level of social structures as a significant component of the process of modernity, in contrast to the purely *cognitivist* aims of Descartes, and partially those of Kant. We will now look into only a few dimensions of this process, particularly, the institution of the subject in modern juridico-legal forms, who becomes the container of not only his *thoughts* and *opinions*, but also of his affects.

Implications and Consequences of Cogito

A promise determined the kind of religious obedience practiced in the Judeo-Christian culture; this was based on the priority of the *moral-magical* bonds between divinity and his people over any other relationship, especially the relations of property. This means that in these civilizations, God rather 'promised' a land to his people. This was different in the relationship of Greeks to their gods, although we don't share Michel Foucault's

---

42   Kant, *Critique of Pure Reason*, p. 802.

view that this was exactly what made them an inherently *political* civilization.[43] We neither intend to seek the semiosis of a nonpolitical form, or theme of power with a reference to the *Oriental* empires and theocratic regimes. Foucault himself stresses that this theme, which he calls 'pastoral power', remained as merely a theme or idea through which power relationships are ideally conceived by these civilizations, perhaps until the emergence of modern structures of power. There are many reasons to believe that a conceptualization of power, insofar as it is generalized among the people, can be *inscribed* through historical processes into the functioning of political and social institutions. We can ask why Foucault did not seek the same relationships between *discourse* and *power* he sought in modern societies in these Oriental societies starting from the classical period.

Yet, the discourse of the Cogito did not remain purely philosophical in the classical period: We have already implied that it lies, as an assumption at least, at the roots of what is called as *freedom of expression*. As thinking tends to be conceived as an act, this also brings the surfacing of the notion of external—and only external—obstacles that appear to inhibit and persecute such act. This was naturally a *universal* problem for the philosophy of the classical period—some philosophers, such as Giordano Bruno, were persecuted, and some, like Baruch Spinoza, were not able to publish their most important books. Such oppression had been the conditions of the *double-philosophy* of Leibniz and probably Malebranche, who expressed their philosophies at two discernible levels, one for the *learned* and one for the *ordinary* people. We can detect such *double-philosophy* from the fact that certain problems that exist in the former register do not appear in the second, and some *aporias* in the second are passed without any reference in the former. We don't merely refer to an old and long tradition of *esoteric* doctrine here. Esotericism, in the depth of its mystic and religious character, belongs to a different order than 17th century rationalism. We can only consider a compromise with the authorities for avoiding drawing the outrage from the notables (the priests, the Church and the politicians) who needed the masses to remain *ignorant*.

The philosophical problems faced by the new Cogito were not evidently *juridical* at first, although its process of expression created a new atmosphere in the sphere of legal norms, which cannot be reduced to Foucault's analyses about the transformations in penitential structures in the Classical period. It is true that we can also examine the emergence of a new kind of power that is invested not only in the domain of law and justice, but in every aspect of social life, permeating through the entire life-experience of modernity. But there was also the development of a new form of *opinion*, in whose image one can perceive the embryonic development of the modern societies of opinion in a crystallized form. What would happen, when we transpose the Cogito into the domain of *opinion*, rendering all former distinctions between opinion and knowledge indiscernible?

First, opinion is already framed in a continuity with knowledge in Spinoza's philosophy; and reasoning through *common sense* had already been fully validated in the Anglo-Saxon empiricisms of Hume and Locke. This was a new mode of continuity between opinion

---

43   Michel Foucault, *The Order of Things: An archaeology of the human sciences*. Routledge, 1989.

to knowledge and other cognitive-affective faculties—imagination, sensibility, aesthesis... Secondly, the development of the societies of opinion had its early roots in the 17th and especially 18th centuries, with the development of quasi-private, non-academic philosophical circles (even a solitary figure like Spinoza had a circle of friends, expanding from his country, Holland to Germany, France, and England). The 18th century, especially in France, was marked as the century of Lumières, with the emergence of various 'clubs' of ideas, such as the early period of the Jacobine Club. These were places where communication and fermentation of ideas took place. It appears that the Cartesian Cogito was incorporated in these non-institutional milieus as their constitutive element: Their claim had been the right to think and to *realize* the content of their thoughts, whatever these may be. Thirdly, the early examples of independent press and publishers' houses emerged in constant interaction with the above-mentioned milieus, tending to become their material means of production and circulation of ideas.

Sophism and Jurisprudence

Today, the philosophy of law can be contrasted by a new logic, an *outsider* logic in a Foucauldian manner, which is that of jurisprudence. The opinion about law has always been distant from the philosophy of law, whose in depth philosophical models in modernity were provided by German philosophers like Kant and especially Hegel. In Hegel, Right (*Recht*) is treated as almost the Idea, and his philosophy of right comprises everything, from phenomenology of the spirit to the realization of the reason. As the philosophical reflection was a question of *ought*, rather than a reflection upon the actuality, the idealist philosophies of right (the *Rechtsphilosophie*) were inclined to define the principles of right in everything they touch upon, including the invention of the inalienable human rights and freedoms, the definition of the *logic* of procedures, and the philosophical conventions through which the codes of law are defined. Today's brand of *universalist* philosophies, like Habermas and Niklas Luhmann, have developed a new *Rechts-philosophie* that is not lacking these early resources, but applying them to the actual conditions in more refined forms.

Every philosopher had to deal with affairs of law and rights. Investigating about law has always been a productive source of wisdom and a fruitful field of reflection for philosophers, from Ancient Greece to the present times. Yet we can identify a distinct philosophical thread that aims to transgress the idealization of the law, if not directly attack it. This is the *jurisprudential* thread, beginning with the Sophists. As Platonists claimed, Sophists cultivate and operate with the opinion, rather than truth; they tend to *relativize* all, create *situations*, or in modern philosophical terminology, *language games*. They organize performances of '*as ifs*', simulations, and pseudo-conceptual arguments. But they truly overwhelmed the established opinions of the people, and even within the framework of the Socratic-Platonic thought, their work could not be considered as merely destructive, since destroying an opinion was generally considered by the same philosophers almost as an initiation to philosophy. According to Aristotle, for instance, to persuade in rhetoric was an act of undoing the opinion. What mattered was to learn the art of persuasion, and that was the case with the great orators, and Sophists—the lawyers of the time. In Ancient Greece, this had been a singularly different semiotic-per-formative model of speech and language, which was inscribed within the folds of the political city. We will show later, in the context of the *social types* of the Ancient world, that the most *modern* figures of Antiquity were the Sophists. For them, philosophy, or thinking in general, was a preparation for the art of persuasion, for developing the capacity to argue. The endless recursive patterns of philosophical counter-arguments in the Sophist dialogue of Plato show that even the philosopher could do nothing out-side *argumentation* or *working through opinions*. Against Sophists, even Socrates turns out to become a Sophist. This was a deep rupture in the trajectory of ideal dialectics.

Albeit being matters of opinion, negotiation and argumentation naturally possess *posi-tivity*, which is absent in *thinking*. What can be a genuine distinction, between *thinking* as a procedure of knowledge and *arguing* about or negotiating opinions, after all? One can simply argue that I only have an opinion, whereas he possesses the truth. Which only means that, he believes in the truth of his opinion. Opinion, on its logical founda-tions, seems to be a horizon for every *apparition* of a thought or an idea. Certainly, this horizon must not be the ultimate one, since the Greeks believed in the Heracleitean premise at the outset, that *truth conceals itself*. This is a manner for predicting the Nietzschean theme, which reads *truth is the deepest lie; one digs and finds not the deepest item*, so one calls it *truth*. It is not ultimate, but it is the limit that repeats itself at every stage of argumentation as the basis of a self-reference: Opposing opinion and true knowledge imposes a challenge—opinion is open to *error*, but knowledge should be communicated as an opinion first.

The Critique of Language

What could the *critique* of language mean? Is it possible for someone to criticize some-thing outside of the language, even in the practical terms of everyday life? Most ordi-narily, when we criticize someone, we generally criticize one's behavior, temperament, attitudes, deeds or actions, and this means that we are still at the level of language—assuming, following Derrida, that these criticizable elements are nothing but contexts, and therefore can be treated as texts. Or, do we mean by this, a criticism of linguistic theory—something many theorists have been successfully conducting? This is a rel-atively prudent claim and it can be exemplified in many instances in the course of the evolution of linguistics, pragmatics, and philosophies of language. And thus every criticism should necessarily be a critique of language, since all of them are linguistic, pragmatic or philosophical events at the very same time. It would be convenient to note in this regard, how Plato already invented philosophy as a critique of language, due to the fact that it was born into the language (the logos) and ought to be perpetuated by language itself—at least until the arrival of more advanced philosophies, like Hegel's, that surpassed the idealism-realism polarity. Without attempting to reduce philosophy into a linguistic manifestation, we may at least tentatively maintain the Hegelian context in which everything that happens in philosophy, art and culture, as well as science and technology, is language and nothing but language. So, the critique too should neces-sarily be employed through and upon language.

The idealistic motives in such an idea of the *critique of language* can already be seen in the early idea of the Logos, as the pre-philosophical material of the Ancient Greek thinking. The notion that Logos governs the universe and Being (that it is what is common to all) among other foundational concepts are already the fundamental affirmations of Heraclitus, a *pre-philosopher* (or, if we borrow the official language of the historians of philosophy, a *pre-Socratic philosopher*, as he could not be a *philosopher at his time*, simply because the word *philosophia* and the corresponding institution was invented not even by Socrates but only later by Plato). And the first important critique of language is brought forth by Plato, as one of the core arguments of his ultimate *political* work, alongside the critique of opinions. Plato's is not a critique of language, but rather a criticism of certain ways in which language is politically or poetically used. If language was common to all—which is evident—it should serve to the Common, to the *koinonia*, in its use. The political significance of such a critique is already manifested in Plato's famous criticism of poets and artists, in respect to the *common* of the ideal city. Among the many ways of reading the well-known passages of the Republic, there is at least one which can render it as an attempt to criticize language as such, while such a criticism necessarily occurs only through language. There is still another evidence, that the Saussurean foundation of language (as distinguished from speech) is already present in Plato's dialogues. The only contrary clue is that there is a single word in Ancient Greece to mean both language and speech, *Logos*. As Castoriadis explains, the word *Logos* is not merely Speech-Language, but also Reason-Cause, Principle-Measure, etc. Therefore, it means *everything*—and thus, it is quite open to treachery and anachronisms of a Heideggerian search for *origins*.[44] Yet, it is clear that Logos can mean everything in itself, in the very primordial possibility of defining language. We simply think that Greek understanding of the *universality* of the Logos was, in an ordinary sense, that language can call, name and attribute everything. In other words, Logos coexists with *Cosmos* as its necessary *cultural* and *intellectual* component. We are opposing Castoriadis only at this point: That Logos means as many things as possible also signifies that Logos is entitled to *call* everything in Cosmos for the Greek philosophy in general. So, when Pindarus was talking about a *language of Gods*, he was probably referring to an old Anatolian language whose rules still prevailed in dialects of the time (perhaps the Phrygian), and which was capable to *call things with their 'true names'*. There is no doubt that even the act of criticism (in the sense of critical thinking) in its oldest sense is assumed as a *logocentric* phenomenon.

Therefore, Logos *reigns* over all only insofar as it can *name* all. This earliest insight has been reaffirmed by Nietzsche in his *Philosophy in the Tragic Age of Greeks*[45]; language commanded since everything it named was possessed, or become a part of an *open whole*—which was truly called later by Heidegger as the primordial meaning of *aletheia*, the uncovering of the oblivious. Yet Nietzsche, as a more culture-oriented thinker than the purely philosophical Heidegger, formulates the limits of such *universe*, retaining the philological elements intact and almost as imaginative dimensions; affirmation was an act of faith, but still remained as an act of language, of telling the truth, a *veri-*

44   Cornelius Castoriadis, *Les Carrefours du labrinthe,* Paris: Seuil, 1999.
45   Friedrich Nietzsche, *Philosophy in the Tragic Age of the Greeks*, Gateway Editions, 1996

diction. One provides, in addition to one's speech, signs about its very truth: acts of confidence, of conviction, of belief. In any case, these are pre-linguistic phenomena: They are either gestures or presuppositions—deeds or acts warranting the truth of the arguments. Logos argues before its acts towards *naming*, and even *naming* itself is an argument: There is a sublime moment when one can no longer excavate the volume of the world and calls that level reached as the *truth*. Names are therefore always *true*. When someone names something, there is nothing left to argue.

Yet, language does not only *name* but also *suggests, proposes, judges, teaches, criti-cizes*—it is a purely pragmatic potentiality. Even naming is a speech act, as the famous theory of names developed by Saul Kripke demonstrates. Socrates was deranged by Sophists and rhetoricians since they were teaching for money, and by doing so, using Logos in some sort of *commercial activity*.[46] We should note that Socrates' criticism of Sophists was not merely due to them teaching for money, but due to the fact that they taught the *use of language* in exchange of money. They were almost *linguistic impostors, language abusers* for Socrates. They were continuously postponing the act of *naming*—their procedure was the indetermination in language, that of a continuous argumentation, of pleading, and of an agonizing Logos.

Communication Theory: The Story of a Model

There is an interdisciplinary *discipline* today, which calls itself *communication studies*. It is saturated by at least two tendencies; first the theories of communication, and second, by what we may call *philosophies* or *pragmatics* of communication. The former has its starting point in the tiny *cybernetic* engineering affair (the so-called Shannon & Weaver model of communications); the latter is broadly articulated in the domain of *critical* philosophies of Karl-Otto Apel and especially Jürgen Habermas. It is necessary for our project of imagining a sociology of opinions to critically engage with this model of communication; first with the model itself, and later, it's unquestioned acceptance as a fundamental philosophical concept.

The Shannon & Weaver model of *communications*, as we noted above, belongs to the domain of engineering, and finds its provocative tenure in its *scientific* nature and its availability in a technological perception of the world[47]. It tells us that any instance of communication involves the coupling of an encoder and a decoder—the sender of the message, and its receiver. By the same token, there is a *message* sent and received between them, whose content is not of any concern. The message is sent through a trajectory, which is open to interruption from the surrounding environment (that is its *anthropic* dimension). This means that the *path* through which the message is sent is a *medium* that connects, yet the *environment* in which that medium exists in obstructs the message at the same time. The environment is the ambient world outside. One last

---

46   See: Saul A. Kripke, 'Naming and necessity', in *Semantics of natural language* (1972): 253-355.
47   See: Claude E. Shannon, 'A mathematical theory of communication', *The Bell system technical journal* 27.3 (1948): 379-423.

element should be added, and it is called as *language*. Here language is nothing but a system of codification, a code, which is applied to the substance of the message. The content of the message is coded by a given language, known by both of the parties, so that one encodes it, and the other deciphers it.

Last but not least, there remains still an ambiguous element, which is presupposed in the entire exposition of the communication phenomenon; that is the *content* of the message. This *content* should be left *ambivalent* for evident scientific reasons: Modern science, in order to be *modern* and claim *universality*, should describe and define merely the *forms* or *structures*, rather than *contents*. This is what makes Shannon & Weaver's model *scientific*.[48] The model is not concerned with *content*, since it is designed to be applicable to any kind of *content*. For the engineer, or the cyberneticist, the content would be *information*. This information belongs to the material order, and constitutes the *content* as such, but thereby, the difficulty (the recursive pattern of indetermination) only shifts. Then, one may ask 'What is information?'—as we are today acquainted with notions such as *information society*, *information revolution*, whereas we seldom have an idea about what information is.

What had been the initial applications of this model, which has been generally called *transmission theory of communications*? We will take the example of Harold Lasswell's sociology of *mass communications*, which has shaped the mainstream theoretical approaches to the subject matter, while uncritically adopting this general model of communications, and almost transforming it into some form of concealed *ideology*.

Lasswell was one of the first sociologists who theorized about mass communications. He lived in an epoch when the power of mass media had started to be questioned—when printed press effectively shaped political affairs, radio was in its heydays, and television was rising on the horizon. His awareness of his task under these circumstances became crystalized in the question, 'Who communicates?' Evidently, in every act of communication, there is someone who initiates the act. Yet this is not sufficient; without an audience, a message would be nothing. Hence, Lasswel goes on to describe the parties of communication as concrete agencies, instead of *notions* or *words* involved in the abstract model of transmission. What Lasswell calls *control analysis* is the answer to the questions: 'Who communicates?' For instance, 'Who owns this newspaper?', 'What are their aims?', 'What are their political allegiances?', 'Do they attempt to set the editorial policy?', 'Does the fact that they are republican account for the newspaper's repeated attacks on the Royal Family?', 'Are they subject to any kind of legal constraints?', 'How

---

48   Claude E. Shannon, whose initial ideas appeared in the article 'The Mathematical Theory of
      Communication' in the *Bell System Technical Journal* (1948). In its broadest sense, information is
      interpreted to include the messages occurring in any of the standard communications media, such
      as telegraphy, radio, or television, and the signals involved in electronic computers, servomechanism
      systems, and other data-processing devices. The theory is even applied to signals flow in nervous
      systems of humans and other animals. The signals or messages do not have to be meaningful in any
      ordinary sense.

does the editor decide what to put in the paper?'[49] These series of concrete questions are nevertheless determined by an obvious claim to *objectivity*—an empirical analysis into *opinion* becomes infused in the empirical questioning of *intentions* and matters of *ownership*.

For Lasswell, the second layer of any communicational analysis should be the message itself: The sociological transposition now requires including the analysis of the *content* of the message, which is assumed by Lasswell as some sort of *representation*. This time, his inquiry is organized around the questions of 'How?' For instance, 'How are women represented in tabloids?', 'How are black people represented in the films or TV programs?' We have to note that the majority of *sociological* researches today are constrained within this domain of inquiry; the *content* analysis is often limited to mere calculation of number of occurrences, and content research remain to be a matter of counting the number of occurrences of a particular representation, generally by comparing the results with *official* statistics—which is assumed to be somehow an objective criterion.

Then, there is the *channel* that is supposed to carry the message. What can be the sociological transposition of such a *material-physical* medium—such as the *airwaves* that carry our speech to the others, or electric cables transmitting signals or bits? Here, Lasswell's approach turns out to be a *practical* question: What are the relative superiorities and adequacies of various types of media for the efficient transmission of a given message? What channels should be used, without falling into the pitfalls, such as trying to communicate with a deaf person by phone? Beyond that, the inquiry becomes concerned with the *attraction* of media for particular purposes—does it appeal to the audience? Is such or such medium effective for our message? It is clear that Lasswell, as one of the first researchers in the domain of mass media analysis, was in fact concerned with the *practical* purposes rather than *analysis* proper.

Accordingly, the *audience research* becomes the most important part of the analysis within such a practical approach, and today, media industry is continuing to use ratings and similar statistics, just like the advertisers, to promote their *commodity*, which is, for the time being, condensed into the *message*. Yet, we don't communicate in a vacuum, in an empty space—there is a *society* to whom we communicate our messages, and this same society can also become an obstacle for the propagation of our messages. In communicating, we are supposed to have some *interests* or purposes—we normally communicate for persuading others, or achieving our intent. Since Lasswell was not concerned with interpersonal communication, but with the effects of the mass media, he did not pay attention to the modes of communication which are far from being *persuasive*, as in the case of everyday interpersonal relationships. This is the larger context of the question of *effects*, passing from *practical* questions to *pragmatic* ones. How is the audience affected by the messages? Are these effects approximating the intended ones?

49   Harold D. Lasswell, 'The structure and function of communication in society', *The communication of ideas* 37.1 (1948): 136-139.

And pragmatics transposes everything to the domain of *practical* purposes: Lasswell, as many others involved in empirical researches in public opinion and mass communications, fails to recognize the complexity of pragmatism in the context of language. Pragmatics, founded by two great American philosophers, Charles Sanders Pierce and particularly J. L. Austin, seems to me as radically opposed to simplistic *practical* inquiry. Austin argues in his *How to Do Things with Words* that, 'having an opinion about something' is fundamentally a performative speech act with illocutionary power.[50]

Social Types Towards a Sociology of Affects

We mentioned that birth of sociology is inseparable from the capacity of describing, or even inventing *social types*. This term has first been used by Herbert Spencer, who has tried to describe, rather obscurely, the types of societies according to their degree of complexity in terms of their structures. This is not exactly what we mean here by *social types*, since in the evolutionary approach of Spencer, the theme of evolution is so predominant that it is no longer possible to conceive types of societies outside his conventional axis of development from the *less compound* to the *more compound*. Spencer, however, had a second criterion for classifying types of societies, which was, this time, according to their internal configuration. When he distinguishes between the militant and industrial societies, the evolutionary schematism still prevails, but now, it is possible to conceive the presence of *militant* attitudes in the developed industrial societies. Spencer was so determined to apply his evolutionary and progressive schemes to every context that, the blunder was inevitable when such criterion was imposed upon concrete cases. In Spencer's conception, the types of social structure depended on the relation of a society to other societies in its particular environment. There is irrefutable empirical-historical observation that societies of different types can coexist. Hence, he goes on to define situations in which peaceful relationships correspond to those internal structures that are *weak* or *liberal* in nature, while *militant* attitudes correspond to austere and authoritarian social structures. The internal structure of a society is now determined not as a function of the degree of evolution, but rather on the state of conflict and alliance among neighboring societies.

Spencer never tried to define an individualized *social type* in terms of his distinction between the *militant* and *industrial* societies. He became rather one of the founders of a long-lasting political convention, which led social thinkers and politicians to believe in the necessity of an exact correspondence between liberalism with light industries, and heavy industries with rather authoritarian regimes—an idea that prevails even in Max Weber and Ernst Troeltsch. Spencer's distinction will empirically collapse under the Weimar Germany, and especially in the context of the social type described by Ernst Jünger, *Der Arbeiter* (the worker). Spencer was unable to grasp the landscape offered by *militant* and *industrial* societies, since he lacked concrete definitions of *militant* or *industrial* behaviors that could attribute concrete *social types* their characteristics. The industrious *Protestant* of Weber had not been conceived yet, despite Marx and Engels' observations on certain historical relationships between Protestantism and capitalism, and sociologists did not knew how to

---

50   John Langshaw Austin, *How to do things with words*, Oxford: Oxford University Press, 1975.

create social types as amalgamation of characteristic social relations within the tangible social landscapes. Wandering around a logic of distinction between militant and industrial societies, however, Spencer encounters the germs of the idea of a crypto *social type*—the *soldier* and his *compulsory* behavior:

> The trait characterizing the militant structure throughout is that its units are coerced into their various combined actions. As the soldier's will is so suspended that he becomes in everything the agent of his officer's will, so is he will of the citizen in all transactions, private and public, overruled by that of the government. The operation by which the life of the militant society is maintained is compulsory cooperation . . . just as in the individual organism the outer organs are completely subject to the chief nervous center.[51]

The industrial society too defines a character, which can obviously be attributed to a *social type* that remains undefined in Spencer's system: This is a society of *voluntary cooperation* and individuals self-restrain, whereby we can identify a prehistory of Max Weber's themes:

> (The industrial society) is characterized throughout by the same individual freedom which every commercial transaction implies. The cooperation by which the multiform activities of the society are carried on becomes a voluntary cooperation. And while the developed sustaining system which give to a social organism the industrial type acquires for itself, like the developed sustaining system of an animal, a regulating apparatus of a diffused and uncentralized kind, it tends also to decentralize the primary regulating apparatus by making it derive from numerous classes of its disputed powers.[52]

We can recognize here the *raison d'être* of the emergence of sociology in the 19th century: A new class without an official title is born—and it is not only the birth of proletariat, but also a new life-world which escapes from any known method of apprehension. The problem of *industry*, particularly following the process later identified as Industrial Revolution in England, soon became central to anything that can be discerned as sociological discourse.

Spencer had also characterized his distinction with reference to concrete historical transformations towards the turn of the century. The militant character is once more introduced within the settings of industrial society, which ought to be defined by some sort of liberalism and democratic spirit, with decentralized State, and cooperation through division of labor:

> If we contrast the period from 1815 to 1850 with the period from 1850 to the present time, we cannot fail to see that all along with increased armaments, more frequent conflicts, and revived military sentiment, there has been a spread of

---

51   Herbert Spencer, 'social Types and Constitutions', in Herbert Spencer, *The Principles of Sociology, in Three Volumes,* vol. 1, New York: D. Appleton and Company, 1894, p. 564, available at: https://oll.libertyfund.org/titles/2642.
52   Ibid., p. 569.

compulsory regulations. . . . The freedom of individuals has been in many ways actually diminished . . . . And undeniably this is a return towards the coercive discipline which pervades the whole social life where the militant type is pre-eminent.[53]

While the *freedoms* conceived by Spencer are nothing but the liberties of the industrial capitalism, defined by bourgeois rights of economic freedom and liberalism, he certainly grasped an essential *fin-de-siècle* transformation in the heart of this modern society—a *peaceful* and *industrious* beginning, following the entire set of conflicts of the 19th century, now tends towards creating a *militant* structure, with declining freedoms, centralization of the authority, and possibly, towards a strict disciplinary society.

It is interesting how 19th century literature and philosophy was much more efficient in characterizing *social types* and their surroundings, with accurate descriptions and the capacity to individualize them. All seems to begin with Balzac, the great literary figure who inherited from the classical literature not only Racine and Corneille's *tragedies*, but also the farcical or *folksy* types of Beaumarchais or Molière. The beginnings of sociology was so permeated by the notion of a *positive science* that the great founders like Comte and Spencer aimed at *generalizations* or *laws*, rather than concrete, individualized descriptions. Literature, on the other hand, through creating the long prose writing, the novel, was now able to express landscapes and social types much more accurately than any sociological description. Thus, as Dostoyevsky and Turgenev in Russia introduced those vivid and exemplary social types such as the *Idiot*, the *Nihilist*, the *Father of Family* (and series of descriptive events alongside them), Dickens situated his quasi-tragic types in the heart of the modern industrial landscape of the city, and Emile Zola, with his *naturalism*, created the atmosphere with all the environmental details, and characteristic figures almost resembling *spiritual automates* in his zone of writing. Everything shows that *social types* are first the invention of literature, before becoming means of expression in social and human sciences.

In order to create a social type, one needs imagination and capacity to be affected, rather than systematic knowledge of the issues and events. This does not mean that there is nothing systematic in the presentation of social types: Max Weber, and especially Georg Simmel had systematized and formalized the philosophy of social types in such a *scientific* way that their analyses can be given back to the domain of arts and literature more vividly than before. In order to create social types, one should be able to coordinate imagination, understanding of affects, and factual knowledge as the coalescence of a complex set of relationships. Borrowing the term *actor* from the domain of arts has been a genial turn in social sciences lately; but there are also those social types who cannot act, whose actions are suspended, or worse, are *represented* by others. We can now engage in developing a series of themes to clarify the impact of the emergence of social types in human sciences.

1. A social type can be visualized and understood by everyone, as it must be part of one's life world, or more concretely, social environment. Literature and the visuality of cinema, can easily accomplish this task by introducing characters who represent

---

53   Spencer, 'Social Metamorphoses', p. 587.

social relations, conflicts, causes and events. This is hard in social sciences, since the *scientific vision* requires generalization, and the creation of a *cumulative index* of all the themes that appear in their discourse. If we believe in the old Hegelian saying that science concerns with the *general* and art's task is providing the *general* through the *particular*, the powers of imagination are necessary in the observation and creation of social types. Yet, an individual portrait does not necessarily have to be a social type in arts and literature. From the *L'Avare* of Molière to the *Père Grandet* of Balzac, we have an entire set of important social transformations, revolutions, and the Enlightenment. The development of the rural capitalism explains the emergence of Father Grandet as a pure social type; he necessarily becomes the representative of a set of rural social relationships in the Napoleonic era. His conservatism is oriented towards future, imagined by him as his own survival through the family values of posterity. It is possible to develop an understanding of a set of social phenomena out of his example, such as the logic of conservatism, the decay of provincial values and life worlds, and a criminal conscience approaching the threshold of psychological abnormality.

2. A social type has a kind of *this-ness*. One can see them out in the corner of the street, a *Poor*, a *Mendicant*, a *Stranger*, a *Homeless*... Its *indexical* value, however, should also be expressed in the context of a theoretical or particularly analytical reflection. The social type is determined in-between *vita activa* and *vita contemplativa*, between the streets and the books. It is a connection between the subject and the object, between the academic discipline and life, between imagination and knowledge. The *sociological imagination* of Charles Wright Mills had been the construction of this bridge: It is not a sociology for the sociologists, but for the ordinary people, the laymen, the passer-by... His concept of *power elite* is the expansion of the everyday *awareness* of the masses, in front of three sectors of elites, military, political and economic, whereby the sociological expression of something which cannot be directly observed neither by masses nor by social scientists—who are only another social type, the *academic white-collars*.[54] His identification of the presence and the nature of the *white-collar* as different from the blue-collar industrial worker makes Mills one of the last great inventor of social types. The larger proletarianization of the masses and the seizure of a greater variety of work by advanced industrial capitalism creates a new social type; the office bureaucracy of the private sector, who has nothing to do with revolutionary ideas, but whose very appearance is part of a revolution in everyday life.

3. A social type should be analytically significant, besides its everyday existence: For instance, the proletariat in Marx and Engels' works has a twofold role—it is at once a *real*, politically defined social class, and at the same time, a part of an abstract network of capitalist production relations, which makes it an analytic-theoretical device to explain capitalist social relations. Such double conception of the working class is expressed more succinctly in Rosa Luxembourg's works, who warned about different levels of abstraction involved in this Marxist definition of social classes. Albeit the apparent set of correspondences, there can be a series of differences and disjunc-

---

54   C. Wright Mills, *White Collar: The American Middle Classes,* Oxford University Press, 1951.

tions between these two concepts of the class, since one is determined according to the capitalist production relations, whereas the other by the principle of multiplicities, networks and new and traditional patterns of solidarity—or occasionally, by conflict, as in the case of the emergence of social-democratic schism and the birth of fascism. It is clear that the first is defined according to the principles of political economy, yet the second is defined as a *social type*.

4. A social type is *affective*. It presents something *real*, a psychological persona, regardless of the level of abstraction and generalization in its presentation. This is another aspect of a social type which makes its literary apprehension more efficient. But it has also lead to a quite creative zone of sociological and philosophical writing—notably Simmel's powerful insights, Walter Benjamin's impressions and *illuminations*. The French style on the other hand concentrates on a more systematic and Cartesian definition of social types: The *affective* crowds of Gustave Le Bon are no less *social types* than Simmel's *Poor* or *Stranger*. Fin de siècle popular debates on the problem of *intellectuals*—occasionally through the Dreyfus Affair—constitutes a frame of reference for such conception of social type. In any case, a social type is determined by its *affects*, to be described as a set or constellation of affective, emotional relationships. The intellectual in France was quite different than the Russian *intelligentsia* as a loosely defined social cast in Tsarist period. The vagueness of French intellectuals was due to their detachment from professional, artistic or academic activities. They were defined by their *engagement* as a public force, as the *enlightened* actors of socio-political intervention into social affairs. The intellectual represents *himself*, not a class nor a social movement, and this is what makes him a participant of a new social movement, that of *des intellectuels*. They are caught between theoretical and practical necessities, which lead to specifically European reflection that required the coining of a new term, *praxis* which, would become a central concept in German Marxism through Karl Korsch, Karl Mannheim, and György Lukács' works. While belonging to a decadent society, these intellectuals were affected by the *most powerful of affects*, the *engaged knowledge* (Nietzsche).

5. Sometimes the affects are so deeply institutionalized in a historical period that it becomes impossible to detect the social type in the background of its social environment or milieu. These milieus can be *general*, as the urban landscapes of the *flâneur* (Poe, Baudelaire) or particular, as in the esoteric ambiences of Proust. The Turkish national novel after the Republican era is imbued by well-institutionalized *social types;* the soldier-bureaucrat, or the Ittihat idealists, somehow portrayed in contradictory modes of appreciation, depending on the political opinions of the authors. The *institutional* character of some social types are evident in the case of Mannheim, associating them with dogmatic sets of behavior, ranging between *ideology* and *utopia, progressivism* and *conservatism*. Again, Weber's description of the *ideal type* of bureaucracy can never be conceived without the conventional presence of an institutionalized social type. The *impersonality* of bureaucratic relationships is not possible without the presence of a new kind of social actors; the public employees are implicit social types, obeying to the inherent principles of rationalization. Impersonalization and the disenchantment

of the world, these two Weberian themes are not possible without the presupposition of the corresponding social types who remain hidden while providing powers of a theoretical explanation.

6. For Simmel, a social type is always constituted by the society. The *poor*, for instance is not defined by his own presence, and there are no social groups or classes *by themselves*. The social types, even when they are not *institutionalized*, are always captured in a network of social relationships and investments of power (to adopt a concept of Michel Foucault):

> In Simmel's view, the fact that someone is poor does not mean that he belongs to the specific social category of the poor. . . . It is only from the moment that [the poor] are assisted . . . that they become part of a group characterized by poverty. This group does not remain united by interaction among its members, but by the collective attitude which society as a whole adopts toward it. Poverty cannot be defined in itself as a quantitative state, but only in terms of the social reaction resulting from a specific situation. . . Poverty is a unique sociological phenomenon: A number of individuals who, out of a purely individual fate, occupy a specific organic position within the whole; but this position is not determined by this fate and condition, but rather by the fact that others . . . attempt to correct this condition.[55]

The *visibility* of the social type that Simmel describes here has another aspect that gives the social type its value and significance. Poverty is a distinct social phenomenon that provides the poor its visibility, but such distinctiveness is present in every social type—the *blasé*, the *stranger*, the *Jew*... Thus, a social type assumes the possibility and the capacity to be transformed into an object by the society that produces it. They are created by *points of view*, rather than consensus, or a sudden emergence. A Simmelian social type is always something codified. This means that a social type is determined by somebody else's point of view, by common people. That is why, because of their artistic essence that depends on subjective viewpoints, literature and cinema appears to be much more capable of capturing social types and making them visible, than the merely descriptive language of sociology.

7 A social type is necessarily *modern*, even if we can identify them in a historical fashion. Ancient philosophy provide with us rather *conceptual types*, to borrow a term by Deleuze and Guattari: The *Sophist*, the *Outsider*, the *Myth-teller* are conceptual, rather than *affective* or institutionalized types in Platonic dialogues. A social type is defined by *traits* or characteristics, rather than its own individual *point of view*. The positions of conceptual personae, on the other hand, are defined in the context of the established norms of a given *point of view*, which enables the type to judge, to talk and to reflect, just as the reader should do. Classical philosophical writing could not proceed without *dialogues* through which arguments were affirmed by the parties. Deleuze and Guattari

55   Lewis A. Coser, 'The significance of Simmel's Work', *Masters of sociological thought: Ideas in historical and social context* (1977): 177-194, pp. 182-183.

had argued about the internal connection between Descartes' 17th century *Idiot*, and Dostoyevsky's 19th century *Idiot*. Yet they failed to consider the fact that the latter appeared as a *social type* while preserving the nature of a conceptual person. Whereas the *Idiot* (Simplicius) was used by Descartes as somebody who fails to understand or simply subscribe to a philosophical argument, a commonsensical man who tries converse with his contenders—such as philosophers, or in their diametrical opposition, the theologists. The *Idiot* of Dostoyevsky, on the other hand, exactly does the same thing, blessing the philosophical arguments that he *fails to understand*, never the less he is portrayed entirely as a flesh and bone spiritual automate, as a character living in a material historical period and a concrete time: As Deleuze and Guattari maintain, he is the *Idiot* who wants to undo what has been secured by Descartes' *Idiot* during his conversation with the philosopher. Certainly, the Dostoyevskian *Idiot* wants the *absurd;* faith rather than knowledge, superstition or occultism rather than religion, blind activism rather than theory, but he is also the representative of a type of real people, visiting Europe to learn natural sciences, Hegel, and socialism as *positive* sciences. This is the characteristic of a certain brand of third world intellectuals who return to their country with ideals of development while the so-called *Developmental Studies* in the advanced capitalist countries are in a complete state of collapse.

8. Apart from being a coalescence of affects, a social type should be an *image*. This is quite obvious since we have already discussed that a social type should first be *seen* by the society before being designed as a representation or an object of contemplation. The Egyptians made images as hieroglyphic entities, destined to become ornaments or elements of the grace of kings and gods. The Ancient Greeks were prone to depict *ideal* or *formal* personae as sculptures. Oriental and Islamic iconography, as well as the European one throughout the Middle Ages, proceeded with pictorial depiction of the *divine*, its order and ornamental expressions, opposed by a more creative popular imagery, expressed in iconographies of folk culture, peasants, and heterodox religious sects. The Classical and Romantic art in Europe never ceased to revive and reproduce the *divine* themes in various, surely secular contexts: not social types as such but persons, who are part of the representation by painting, of the lights, colors, and patterns of the art. Then, all begins to change with two inventions: the photography capturing the *traces* of the passing time; and a new convention of post-romantic painters who draw studies, instead of drafts destined to be the initial stage the work. These studies, like the photographs they had been influenced by, were instantaneous moments of things, drawn without carrying out all the details and every feature, captured in the flow of time. The instantaneousness of photography and Impressionism in painting were able to portray the entire landscape of modern life together, and the social types would be part of this landscape. Dégas' *dancer* figure is clearly not a *social type* by itself, but we can argue that it is a part of the early modern urban landscape and life-world in which social types are involved. The *image* character of the social type is revealed in these impressionist paintings, which depicted moments of life in train stations, streets, coffeehouses, the dance studios. An entire photographic iconography, if not documentation of the ordinary life, has been accumulated during the 19th century; portraits, ceremonials, moments of life, and post-cards—depicting not only European or American scenes,

but also the exotic countries towards the end of the century. The social functions of photography had been already evident in the 19th century: It amplified the power of the press, the sole medium of the public opinion effectively shaping the social reality and the information flow. Still photography was able to capture life as it is at a certain moment at any place.

9. The birth of the cinematographic image has been much more powerful in reproducing the visibility of social types in the ordinary life. As a powerful means of communication, cinema soon assumed the function of a *document-in-itself*, like photography. But more than photography, whose distance from real life is evident in its stillness, cinematography amplifies characteristic of its signifier as a *trace* by providing them with the *illusion of movement*. The first films, regardless of their *magical* appearance in theaters, were presenting the traces of ordinary events. And a panoply of social types has been ever present in cinema—not only through *stylized* burlesque types, such as the Chaplin's Tramp, but also within the representation of the ordinary street life.

Tarde seems to be the sociologist with the most profound grasp of the concept of *opinion*. He recognized that opinion is not something remote from the complex networks of social relationships that are both historical determinants of the *present* situation, and in the course of his engagement with the criticism of the Durkheimian conceptualization of the *division of sociology*, he became further aware that *politics* should essentially be integrated into the domain of sociological research. This, according to Tarde, was a deficiency in Durkheim and his antecedents, such as Fustel de Coulanges (the author of *La Cité Antique*) and Loria—they failed to understand that an essential subdivision of sociology must be political sociology and the study of politics and opinions. In his book *Economic Psychology*[56] Tarde is engaged in comparing the *divisions* of political economy with those of the political science for revealing the interconnectedness of two essential relations: wealth (*richesse*) and power. If the subject matter of the political economy is the wealth, the subject matter of the political science should clearly be the power. He introduces the analogy between the human organism and the political power: The political power is to a human society what the conscious will is to the human brain. Two centuries of the politics of opinion in the Western world (notably in Europe and Northern America) succeeded in creating an image of *politics* that characterize the modern world. This is an image of politics as separate from and opposed to the private domain of domestic, everyday and ordinary relationships. The mediation and representation, shaping the *modern* institutions (in which the political life is deployed) tend to become essential attributes of such distinction—or sometimes *opposition*—between the private and the public.

As the researches into public opinion gained importance in defining the domain of social sciences in the 20th century, there had been a growing interest in sociology towards the subject of *masses*, *crowds* and their *individualizations*. The sociology of the *founding fathers* (to borrow an almost untenable expression of certain scholars who have tried to

---

56   Gabriel Tarde, *Psychologie economique, 2 vols*. Paris: Alcan, 1902.

write *official* histories of sociology, notably L. Coser)[57] was in fact the art of extracting concrete *social types* out of the amorphous crowds and masses of people in modern urban (and partially rural) settings. The image of the *ascetic* protestant or the puritan became an expressive figure for Weber when he inquired into the birth of the *spirit* of capitalism. The *flâneur*, through Poe, Baudelaire and Walter Benjamin was nothing but a social type situated in between the social processes of the fragmented modern life. Werner Sombart, Karl Troeltsch and Thorstein Veblen had discerned clusters of social relationships through the elucidation of various traits of a psychological-social character, the *Bourgeois*. And in French sociology, from Le Bon to Gabriel Tarde, we can observe how far the crowds and masses themselves can be treated as *social types*. Even the *political economy* of Marx is not deprived of social types—for example, the image of the *lumpenproletariat* as a social category is differentiated from the proletarianized masses.

The creation of social types depended had been related with early sociologists focus on the importance of the *particulars,* which had been significant both for their theoretical purpose and for the ongoing social life as such. A social type is in fact a coalescence of social relationships, raised up to the context of sociological analysis, while remaining in the field of *visibility* in actual life. This means that a social type, when properly defined and formulated, lives a twofold life; it first serves to the *analytical* theorization of the social scientist, but it also *appears* in the public domain—in the streets, in coffee houses, in social, economic, political, cultural activities. A social type is the thread through which the layman can understand sociology, the path defined by Charles Wright Mills as *sociological imagination*, while it cannot be reduced to an attempt to vulgarization, nor to be given simply as an *example*.

This *second*, non-analytic aspect of social types is important, since it constitutes the affective dimension of sociology. The key concept in defining a social type is the presence of corresponding social formula to each—the *Poor* in Simmel is not defined by one's income or even the degree of poverty, or by one's opinion or acknowledgement of oneself as *poor*. The Poor *appears* only when a given community takes some people as an object, creates institutions to cope with the presence of such object, develops social practices and judgments about it in order to regulate it. This is the way in which one of the last genial creators of *historical* social types, Michel Foucault had been able to find the formula of the modern criminal subject –the *dangerous individual*.[58] This is also a way to distinguish between genuine social types and those pseudo-social types. Actually, the present sociology of opinions that treats societies as *phases of agglomerations of social interactions* continues to be dependent on *social types*. Yet, we will argue that these are in fact *pseudo*-social types, since they are defined as *identities,* by the consequence of belonging to recognized *social groups*, as members of sub-cultures. When a sociologist goes into a field-research among the members of trade unions, her/his *subjects* are not real social types, unless s/he discerns singularities from the iden-

57   Lewis A. Coser, 'Continuities in the Study of Social Conflict', *Social Forces* 46.4 (June, 1968): 589–590.
58   Michel Foucault, 'About the concept of the *dangerous individual* in 19th-century legal psychiatry', *International journal of law and psychiatry* 1.1 (1978): 1-18.

tities revealed in the research. For example, the *yuppie* is not a social type insofar as it appears as a social category of the professional economic life in the *post-modern* age; it can only become a social type when a particular set of social relationships can be attributed to the description of such a social category in a tangible fashion.

The notion of *identity*, one of the central concepts in actual practice of sociology, undermines the capacity of social sciences to create social types. Ethnic and religious groups, each supposedly absorbed by an identity (or rather within a supposed *identity crisis*) are not yet social types. The Muslim, or the Turk in Europe, the Puerto Rican or the Black in United States, the Inuit tribal communities, are not yet *social types* while we can still include them to the general category of *migrants*. Identity is a category of the opinion, of political labeling, rather than a heuristic concept in defining a social type. It presupposes the mild democratic or liberal conceptualization of modern Western societies (and academies) to render the opinion with the highest referential value. Similarly, party membership or affiliation, to be the partisan of a cult or to be a member of a generation (pop music subcultures, cinema cults etc.), are not in themselves criteria for creating social types. In order to create social types corresponding to these categories, social science should produce a *flesh-and-bone* individuation which can operate at the level of the *visible*, certainly not in television, but in the everyday life at large. This is, we believe, one of the major failures of social sciences today.

Social sciences are not the sole creators of *social types*. As we mentioned earlier, plenty of social types have been created in 19th century literature (from Balzac to Zola, from Austen to Chekhov), on the background of the developing capitalist and urban landscape, and how throughout the 20th century, the representations of *social types* abounded in the domain of cinema, especially in the early periods of its development. This is the key to our particular interest in the *documentary* work of the Soviet cinematographer Dziga Vertov, whose cinematography is a genuine sociological reflection embedded into visual poetics. As we also mentioned, the domain of arts tend to be more adept than social sciences for creating and reproducing social types, as we are as much able to *think* through them as philosophy and science. Such adeptness is obviously due to the fact that art is able to produce direct, non-textual and un-mediated presentations of life. Yet, this Hegelian (or Lukácsian) notion—that arts can grasp the *universal* by departing from the *particular*—should be approached carefully, since the characteristic of the novel may not be the *presentation of the individual who represents its epoch* but rather the apparitions of *social types* in everyday life. In this sense, there is a concrete connection between artistic representation and the everyday life, and correspondingly, every sociology (political, historical, cultural, economic etc.) should be a sociology of everyday life.

A major dimension of our interest is directed towards the *affective* character of social types: A social type is either familiar or unfamiliar, communicated or excluded, but there is always an assemblage of affects that characterizes its presence. We can even say that a social type is made visible only insofar as it can be presented as an assemblage of affects, internal and external. This perspective consists the philosophical part of our interest, proliferating from the early modern discussion of affects provided by the 17th century rationalist philosopher Benedict de Spinoza, who developed a wholesome and comprehensive treatment of *affects*, the role of emotions, passions, and sentiments in individuals, in the processes of socialization, and in social life. Spinoza's work is a gateway for conceptualizing a *sociology of affects,* towards replacing the *sociology of opinions*. Sociologists like Le Bon, Gabriel Tarde and Georg Simmel were able to understand the importance of *affects* in social life—even in the shaping of social forms and structures. Georg Simmel has been concerned with the affective patterns in the creation of social types, since his sociological descriptions tend to be fragmented *impressions* of everyday life, here and there, felt by the sociologist before being reported to a deeper insight and analysis. This is the logic of the *actuality* of sociology, its difference from history or the so-called political science. There is a general misunderstanding about why Simmel and his various followers, such as the Frankfurt School scholars and Walter Benjamin, escaped from systematization. In fact, they were not avoiding systematic treatment; it was just their way of capturing the modern reality, which was based on the fragmentation of social life. The Spinozist definition of affects, such as *Love, Hate, Pleasure, Pain, Desire, Hope, Fear* etc., has to be considered as the unique foundation of the constitutive role of affects in social relationships. His major *rationalism* is echoed in the *minor* ones of the early 20th century, seeking the motives lying behind social reality—such as the utopianism and messianism in G. Scholem and Ernst Bloch, or the philosophy of sentiments in Renouvier and Henri Bergson. An important dimension of describing a social type involves treating it as an *assemblage of affects*, rather than a composite of opinions. Our examples in this respect are still in the domains of cinema and literature, as affective types can be directly visualized in artistic presentation, but only a sociology that can analyze and render concrete affects (individual and social) can provide a basis for the reproduction of social types.

Last but not least, we suggest a methodological perspective here, for the possibility of a sociology of affects. Affects are *seen* better than they are expressed through writing or even description, and we cannot afford to exclude the entire domain of *documentary* cinematography from the disciplines of social sciences. We believe that the cinematic means of presentation are no less *thoughtful* than the actual practice of social research, and perhaps they are natural *media* for the so-called *oral history* than any other statistical or observational treatment. The *concept* can reveal itself in cinema and video, and this is not necessarily limited to the domain of the *documentary filmmaking*, which pretends to be the direct *image* of the real. One can even say that the *staged films*, when they are true examples of genuine cinematic authorship, can analyze and synthesize social relationships much more profoundly than sociological researches. A great filmmaker like Sergey M. Eisenstein has been known to intend the *filming* of *Das Kapital* of Marx, an ultimate project which would be destined to accomplish the marriage of philosophy, science, and art in the domain of holistic expressivity.

The doctrines of public sphere tend to split human life experience into two parts—the public and the private. Only a sociology of affects can create the image of a society in which such distinctions in political, economic and cultural life are relativized or exhausted. The best examples of this are provided by the Third World cinema today, introducing new *affective* types together with a modern *ontology* of the image itself. Part of our interest lies in such an ontology of the image, and its place in the sociological treatment of the *societies of opinion* in which we live. As affects are always generated by images—the concrete Spinozist *affection* of the bodies, individual and social alike—the importance of this ontology in political life and its sociological treatment has to be revealed. Socially, every new generation tends to become more engaged with the images, due to the continuous development of audio-visual technologies in education and entertainment, as the entirety of everyday experience; modern politics and social practices depend on images, their reproduction, and manipulation more intensely. And the societies of opinion are societies of the image, of the spectacle,[59] of control,[60] virtuality, monitoring, and *interception*.[61] Thus, the *politics of the image* becomes an essential field of reference in our exploration.

C. Wright Mills and a New Sociological Imagination

When C. Wright Mills wrote his *Sociological Imagination*, sociology has already been *academically established* in United States, which was a tendency that was about to invade European academies. This was towards the end of Sartre's domination in France, and his critics was gaining ground in their struggle against Existentialism—such as Lévi-Strauss with his *structural anthropology,* and Jacques Lacan with his *re-reading* of Freud. In Germany, however, the Frankfurt School was still dominating the serious intellectual life and theory with major works of Adorno, Pollock, and Horkheimer. Heidegger was still silent, not only since he was not permitted by the French authorities to teach after the war, but also there was nothing left for him to ask to himself, like the question of *'can we still have a God?'*. The intellectual climates of the world, in their resistance against the *new-imperialism* of United States and the Cold War, started evaluating the very notions of *opinion* and *imagination*. Sartre wrote his *L'imaginaire*, and his opponent Merleau-Ponty questioned the conditions of *visibility*, of the world making itself visible, in his two books *Phénoménologie de la perception* and *Visible et invisible*. The Anglo Saxon *analytic philosophy* was still questioning the notion of *opinion* in its relation to *belief*. And this was also the age of the birth of *television*—the essential apparatus of filtering, interpreting, exhibiting and expressing opinions as *images*.

The formulation of *mass society* had its evident roots in Ancient Greece, and notably in the apparent elitism of the Pre-Socratics—as revealed by Heraclitus, who denounced the *nomos* of his fellow citizens of Ephesus: They relied on their *divergent* opinions, rather than what is *common to all*, which is Logos or Reason. And neither Plato nor Aristotle had an intensive affection for democratic values, as they always denounced the *fluctuating opinions* of the mob. In this context, Machiavelli and Spinoza appear to be rather ambiguous figures, since they attributed positive values to masses (the *mul-*

---

59   Guy Debord, *Oeuvres Cinématographiques Complètes*, Paris: Champs Libre, 1978.
60   Gilles Deleuze, 'Postscript on the Societies of Control', *October* 59 (Winter, 1992): 37.
61   Paul Virilio, *Guerre et cinéma: I. Logistique de la perception*, Paris: Cahiers du cinéma, 1991.

titudo of Spinoza) while denying them a properly rational attitude. The Enlightenment was at the same time the age of *disciplining* of the masses, ultimately with Napoleonic state apparatuses, as if the dominant powers disliked mass behavior, and the newborn sociology was intending to understand *mass behavior* to predict its explosions, emotions, and desires (the *positivism* of Auguste Comte, the *sociology of crowds* developed by Gustave Le Bon, and the *utopian socialisms* of Fourier, Owen, and Saint-Simon).

However, the question of *masses* or *crowds* is also the question of the *individual*. It was not possible to analyze the mass or the different behaviors of the *crowds* without identifying the *individual*. This question haunted the birth of French sociology from Le Bon to Durkheim. Le Bon intended to show the *leveling* function of the *crowd-event* (since crowds generally seem to gather together in *events*, revolts, revolutions, opinions, denunciations of *public enemies*). He believed that in a crowd, a professor could be reduced to the intellectually primitive level of a lumpenproletarian. A new *individualism* was born out of the general *fear of the masses*.

This *mass experience* is reversed in the works of C. Wright Mills: The mass is no longer something that revolts, causes problems, and jeopardizes the established public order. The public order is the basis of the mass society; the incapacity of individuals in managing their lives independently results in their acting in *support* of the power relationships. Mills showed the *mass* attitude as something both peaceful and stable, and *dangerous* at the same time. The *sociological imagination* remains as an attempt to make sense of life for the *individual* in mass. What we have here is certainly *imagination*, but not something that could be reduced to mere *opinion*. Imagination as such appears at the moment when an individual is able to visualize (even if s/he cannot *understand* properly) the coincidence of his or her history with so-called *public* or *objective* problems. Hence, Mills was attempting to *democratize* sociology, taking it from the hands of the *Grand Theoreticians* of the Academy (such as Talcott Parsons and even the *medium-range* theories of Robert K. Merton). We believe that his early death prevented him from developing his instigation further and offer an institutional framework for his *sociological imagination*.

And the word *imagination* in Mills, we believe, directly corresponds to what Hegel meant when he urges for a *pedagogy of concepts*, or Jean-Luc Godard for a *pedagogy of images* in the age of television, both referring back to the all-encompassing *Paideia* of Greeks. Imagination now tends to signify a kind of *awareness*, which should not be expressed as a merely *philosophical text* by some philosopher, sociologist, or scientist. If Mills denounces the *mass society*, it is for finding out the *individual in the mass*, to address to him, in a society where he is reduced to a statistical number or to a bearer of *opinions*. One has to dissociate the term *pedagogy* from its academic, scholarly, and class-based contexts.

Hence, Mills first attempts to show that there is no possibility for a sociologist (who corresponds in his *academy* to the *white collar worker* in other places) to observe how *decisions are made* by the *power elite*. If he was capable to write a book on the *power elite*, this was not a study through *knowledge*, but through *imagination*, which is necessary for denouncing the established order. The three general *orders* of the power elite, however, were already present everywhere—the military, the political, and industrial... This *everywhere* presupposes an *agenda* where *truth* escapes us, the masses, to which the *academician* also belong. Mills' is not a *conspiracy theory* as we understand today, since he really believes that sociology is still possible and that it is almost a *laboratory science*. Truly, sociology can *positively* work as if societies themselves are *laboratories*, and there is nothing to be troubled about such *indignity*. Mills in fact reveals us that his *sociological imagination* should do laboratory work, not in the sense that one can construct a laboratory-observation of social affairs, but in the sense that we are already living in *laboratories* constructed by the political powers and their command structures.

Sociological Imagination and Sociological Images

Visual, sound, or audio-visual material used in social research projects can never be seen as mere *supplements*, like illustrations that come to aid scientific observation whatever its nature is—textual interpretation, empirical research, participant observation findings. This is because visual and auditive experiences are not less *thoughtful* than philosophical, social-scientific, or anthropological investments of human thinking. They are based on more sophisticated modern *thinking machines* than texts, such as cinema, video, and todays electronic interactive media forms, which seem to penetrate into living culture deeper than the merely textual means and *cerebrality* of academic thinking. There is a simple reason for this: Every new generation tends to become more audio-visually oriented, rather than remaining as *readers*. They no longer perceive *images* and *sounds* as *things* that need to be interpreted, or contextualized, and commented upon, or as *supplements* or *illustrations*.

Discussing *opinions* and *affects*, we have already mentioned that the notion of *social types* is in a continuous decay. This decay is a symptom of the main *event* of our times: We have universally developed quite *wrong* audio-visual apparatuses—the television and partially the internet. The latter still remains as an *open* question, since it is difficult to foresee what will become of it in the future. The decay of social types today intersects with the emergence of pseudo-social types: the yuppie, the hipster, the hacker, etc.

Television is a *time machine*: It governs and orders time, fragments it in accordance to the exigencies of work and leisure time, it re-ordinates and re-creates time. The fact that a larger part of the world population lacks internet access at the moment is not an objection to our point[62]: With the already planned technological integration of the internet with television, the situation will change in a close future. Projects like the *information superhighway*[63] in United States, and Bengemann Report in Europe motivate such integration today.

However, we mentioned that our societies of *opinion* are commensurable with what Deleuze describes as *societies of control*: You are *free*, at least for having an opinion, but you are

---

62   Editors Note: This essay was written in late 1990's, when internet access was still available to a global
     minority.
63   Editors Note: The term 'information superhighway' was coined in mid-90s, allegedly by Al Gore, in
     reference to the development high-speed internet connections across US.

still controlled. And this control is largely audio-visual (monitoring of life), in contrast to the *writing* and *discourse* of the Foucauldian *disciplinary societies*, which have been questioned at least in a *liberal fashion*. This *questioning* remains *liberal*, that is, remain at the level of denouncing *disciplinary* structures, claiming *rights* towards a future citizenship, and of free flows of information in the information superhighways. Everything seems to be arranged towards avoiding the mistakes of *disciplinary societies*: The Napoleonic universal systems of education, *medical care*, *science*, *employment*, and the Freudian system of *childcare* have deteriorated today, and it seems that no one knows how to substitute them.

The major question of Mills' *sociological imagination* already has an answer: The *mass society* has became laboratory, where *grand theories* are invited to make observations and even experiments—among the cornerstones of the development of *academic* sociology were, the serial studies by Robert and Helen Lynd[64] about the engineering of an *electoral campaign* in Middletown, and especially Gunnar Myrdal's *military research* on the American Soldier.[65]

It is evident that a social scientist cannot create a *social laboratory* by himself or herself—otherwise huge cabinets of doctors of sociology should be constructed, inviting families, tribes, social groups, even classes and some *pratico-inerte* material with existential problems. Yet this *laboratory* is already established: once by the *societies of discipline* made visible by Foucault, then the *mass society* of Mills. The latter is evidently a pseudo-society, a project that will never be accomplished, since we have already learned from Gabriel Tarde that masses have to be composed by individuals. Mills shows that a sociologist here is the assistant of a *power elite* (a non-social *type*), he or she belongs to the order of *white-collars*, and he or she is not among the *holders* of power (in Foucault's terminology) but their *supporter*.

Foucault seems to start with an excellent image: *Ceci n'est pas une pipe* of Magritte, which is a painting that simply shows us a pipe, and below the image of the pipe reads the sentence '*This is not a pipe*'. Foucault interprets this paradox that involves both the visible and the utterable (language) in a little book, which, in our view, hints at his entire

---

64 See: Robert Lynd and Helen Lynd, *Middletown: A Study in Modern American Culture*, New York: Harcourt, Brace, Jovanovich, 1929.
  See also. Robert Lynd and Helen Lynd, *Middletown in Transition*, New York: Harcourt, Brace, Jovanovich, 1935.
65 A ruthless kind of pragmatism, almost denying the existence of some immanent problems is invoked by Myrdal when he declares that: 'It has become recognized that the most promising field for research is the *no man's land* between the traditional disciplines. There is one concept which the economist or the sociologist can keep blurred, namely the concept of *economics* or *sociology*; for it can never be a premise for a rational inference. In reality, what exists are merely problems to be solved, theoretical or practical; and the rational way of attacking them is to use the methods which are most adequate for solving each particular problem.'
  Gunnar Myrdal, 'Conference of the British Sociological Association, 1953. II Opening Address: The Relation between Social Theory and Social Policy', *The British Journal of Sociology* 4.3 (1953): 210-42. Accessed June 27, 2020. doi: 10.2307/587539.

work of detaching the visible from the textual (discursive).[66] In his archaeologies of language, of social sciences, of madness, of crime (to which he was always able to find out corresponding *social types*: the *madman*, the *erotomane*, the *dangerous individual*, and so forth), and of *work*, Foucault seems to visualize the entire social experience in the model of a painting, with its historical *ruptures* and analytical consequences which still remain to be interpreted.

---

66   Michel Foucault, *This is Not a Pipe*, trans. James Harkness, Berkeley: University of California Press, 1983.

3. WHAT IS AN AFFECT?

Empathy

A sociology of affects is that of *sense* and *intuition*: This means that it already belongs to the order of the *practical knowledge* (phronesis) of Aristotle. Yet, we don't believe Aristotle could help us much in this moment, as today's *practices are* no more guided by *knowledge* but only by information and opinions. Neither could Freud. We have already been acquainted with the basic notions surrounding the concept: double identification of opinion with *imagination* (Spinoza) on the one hand, and with *affects* on the other. Yet affects have a broader meaning, since they are lived-experiences, rather than the representations of experiences. Opinion presupposes the *affect* in the sense that an opinion or judgment already reflects an affective situation, rather than its *knowledge* in the classical sense of the term.

We have two fundamental models for considering *affects*: The first is that of psychoanalysis, mainly as it is developed by Freud,[1] and the second, which will use as the foundation for the critique of the former, is Spinoza's doctrine of *affectus* (emotions) developed in the *Third Book of Ethics*.[2] The outcome of this exposition will be, we hope, a possibility in discussing the images of *social types* as *affective entities*, no longer as *types* that can be related only through recognition. A sociologist should be able *to be affected* by the social types he or she is assigned to contact.

Concepts like *empathy, identification, inter-subjectivity, Verstehen, understanding* are widely used in social sciences, psychology, cultural studies, and psychoanalysis as *methodological terms*, as if they are a part of the *method* but not of life itself. But this *methodology* still rests upon the presumptions of a sociology of opinions. Sociology, if it will correspond to Mills' *sociological imagination* has to use all these notions with precaution.

The word *empathy* is not a part of the Spinozist vocabulary, yet it can always be interpreted as the Cartesian and Spinozist form of *admiration*, which can be translated as *wonder*: a psychological state which does not refer to the experience of sentiment yet, but that is somehow different from *indifference* or *neutrality*. It is a kind of *attention*, or *initial perception*, which awakes in our psyche a kind of *interest* that is not satisfied through consumption, but through reciprocal apperception.

In social sciences, we are already acquainted with a series of methodological terms concerned with research techniques, and these are not less subtle and savage here than they are in mass media. *Participant observation* is one of these. The anthropologist or ethnographer thinks that her/his prize will be higher in getting information once s/he adheres to a social group and *participates* to it. Mills questions the foundation of such belief: *Participation* already changes the nature of the thing that is *observed*.

---

1   Sigmund Freud, 'Inhibitions, symptoms and anxiety', *The Psychoanalytic Quarterly* 5.1 (1936): 1-28.

2   Benedict de Spinoza, The Ethics PART IV: Of Human Bondage, or the Strength of the Emotions, The Project Gutenberg EBook, April 15, 2013 [EBook #971] Release Date: July, 1997 First Posted: July 5, 1997, http://www.gutenberg.org/cache/epub/971/pg971-images.html.

In any case, to the degree that it excludes *empathy*, *participant observation* brings the misuse of the term *participation*. For Plato, there were three kinds of *participation*, yet only one kind of observation—that of the eternal *ideas*. The first was simply the material, natural participation: This is a complementary form of participation; its *participants* compose the totality of the thing, constitute a whole, combining with each other to complete something. The second was somehow *demonic*, the form of participation in *possession*. Possession has always been a state that requires the *purge*; such as the Church's mobilization against witchcraft, as it happened in the Middle Ages, or the psychiatric or medical mobilization for *saving* the individual against the dangerous and contaminating *disease* to which s/he *participates*.

Then comes the third meaning of *participation*: One participates in an *idea* with all his being. This is quite difficult to understand today since we are quite remote from the Platonic world of ideas. This is not yet the Cartesian *Being=Thinking* equation; one can *participate* only to a *model* derived out of an *Idea*, which is nothing but a *copy* of it. Empathy appears at this moment when an Idea is modeled (when it takes its *form*, in Aristotle's terminology)—it is simply the way in which things can represent other things in an endless fashion. In the Platonic world, however, this *imitation* viewed as *participation* is evaluated and affirmed only in a specific way. *Participation* requires two terms: the *participant* and the *participated*. *Participation* is, therefore, a kind of violence for Plato: If one can participate, one can also be detached, which jeopardizes the whole. The loss of the members of a party, or schisms in a movement, as well as the political, historical and geographical scissions (which we call as *nations* today) or detachments are considered as *violence*, and all such instances are practiced through violence in life—rebellions, revolutions, wars, genocides...

Thus *empathy* corresponds to a kind of participation in the third type: A form of participation that, however, honored and honorable, concurs with what Plato calls the *divine share*—the *theia moira*, which is especially needed for leaders to become philosophers (if philosophers cannot be leaders). *Moira* is used here in the context of *fates* (moirai) that comprise the *necessity* (ananke) mythologically fabulated in the end of the Republic—the 'myth of Er'.[3] This also corresponds to the *divine inspiration* of Socrates that takes place at the end of the Meno,[4] where it is perceived as the source of what we may call *true opinion*. Politicians are perceived as lacking knowledge, insofar as they are not philosophers—therefore they evidently need a divine inspiration for distributing justice, like the *vision* of a prognosticator.

The use of *empathy* as almost reduced to a methodological tool, rather than referring to an *affective state*, tends to be detrimental to the degree that it can apply to any context, loosely and without any clear consequence. Such use is imposed by the idea that *social sciences* are sets of *knowledge* that also rely on *empathetic* relationships. When one talks about *participant observation* he buries a series of *ethical problems* hidden behind the *scientific practice*: observation without experimentation. The *documentary image* is concerned with the imposition of such ethical questions. Even if they do it in a naive fashion, documentarians impose the ethical questions that social researchers never do; such as the question of *how*

---

3   Plato, 'The recompense of life', *Plato's The Republic*, New York: Books, Inc., 1943.
4   Plato, *Meno*, Penguin Books, 1956.

our presence dissolves or modifies the relationships and interactions involved in this social setting, without reducing it simply into a problem of method, or of *metis* (know-how) and subtle arrangements of statistical techniques that try to measure what is called the *bias*. In the case of the documentarist, however, the problem remains sharper and felt already as a burning experience, just because audio-visual media seem to be more powerful than private, often confidential oral or textual records. This is the main reason for us to propose the merging of social sciences' *theoretical* interrogations with what we may call as *documentary* techniques.

The *Affekt*: A Freudian Discharge

Psychoanalysis departs from *affective states*—whether these states are *excesses* or *diseases* is not our concern here. Freud seems to deny the role of certain philosophers of *affects*, like Nietzsche and Schopenhauer (who already seems to have developed a coherent theory of the *unconscious* in his *The World as Will and Representation*), in the process of inventing and developing psychoanalysis and its main concepts: *the Unconscious, the Pulsion, the Ego, and the Will*.[5] He rather recognizes his *scientific* precursors: Pinel who liberated the madmen from L'Hopital Général following the French Revolution,[6] Charcot for whom he worked as an assistant in La Salpêtrière notably on hysteria, and especially Breuer to whom he delegates the merit of the *true inventor of psychoanalysis*. We cannot say that the hysteric (mythically attributed to women in the 19th century) can be considered as a *socio-psychological type*. While common language often pejoratively uses it that way still today for women, the collective work of Freud and Breuer clinically proved that this malady was universal, disturbing men as well as women. Freud recalls in his first essays on hysteria[7] that, evidently hysteria was not perceived as illness during the Middle Ages, but as a devilish *possession*. And in the 19th century, there were different opinions. For some, since the symptoms were singularly varied, unique to each patient and without reference to any physical problems, it was considered as nothing more than a *simulation*, not a real disease but a pseudo-disease that is even somehow due to *exhortations*. Hysteria is considered as a psychosomatic disease in today's psychiatry.[8] Yet, Charcot and Janet, predecessors of Freud, have shown that, on the contrary hysteria was a *real illness*, whose origins were simply *unknown* to patients as well as their attending psychologists—which is the first diagnosis of the *unconscious* (l'inconscient) in psychiatric and medical literature. It should be noted that Freud adopted such meaning of the *unconscious* (*unbewusste* as an adjective) first, before *substantializing* it in his later works, as *the unconscious* (*unbewusstsein*).[9]

---

5   For a detailed critique of this attitude, See: Jacques Derrida, *The post card: From Socrates to Freud and beyond*, trans. Alan Bass, Chicago: University of Chicago Press, 1987 (1980).

6   This event is described by Foucault in his *L'histoire de la folie à l'âge classique*; See: Michel Foucault, *Folie et déraison: histoire de la folie à l'âge classique*, vol. 169. Paris: Plon, 1961.

7   Sigmund Freud, 'Hystérie', trans. M. Borch Jacobsen, P. Koeppel, F. Scherrer, in *Cahiers Confrontation*, 7, 1982 (1888).

8   Harold I. Kaplan and Benjamin J. Sadock, *Comprehensive Textbook of Psychiatry V*, 5th edition, Baltimore: Williams and Wilkins, 1989.

9   Jean Laplanche and Jean-Bertrand Pontalis, *The language of psycho-analysis*, trans. Donald Nicholson-Smith, New York: W. W. Norton., 1973.

Yet, it should also be noted that not only the patient, but also the psychiatrists and psychologists were ignorant about the origins and the *real causes* of the malady: All indicated that the paralyzed arm was *really* insensitive and one could burn it without any sense on the part of the patient.[10] The first interpretation of Charcot and Janet, which was later approved by Freud, was that all symptoms seemed to confirm that the patient *abstracted* a part of her/his body and it was not an act of imitation at all, which proved that, especially for Freud, s/he *no longer wanted her/his arm*.[11] Charcot was using the technique of hypnosis that relied on suggestions, in which he urged the patients that the symptoms would disappear upon her/his awakening. The symptoms indeed disappeared under hypnosis, but only temporarily, since they reappeared afterwards.

We had to wait for Breuer, who presented one of his patients, Anna O., *a very intelligent young girl*, to Freud, informing him that he believed he found out a new method for *cure*. This new method required a form of *collaboration*, if not *participation* of the patient in the process of treatment, which this intelligent girl was capable of doing. This *empirical* method was highly appropriate for the late 19th century medical paradigms Michel Foucault later describes; a *pure* empiricism, a *meticulous reading of symptoms*, *visualization of signs* and a *map of the body*[12]—therefore it was *scientific* enough for Freud. The treatment process was adequately unpredictable and almost improvised. She displayed a severe and insistent cough, long periods of aphasia (although she always understood German, sometimes she could only speak English, French, or Italian), occasional paralysis of her arms, and the presence of two quite different states of mind—that of a dissipated child and of an extremely clever young girl. Anna O. was able to pass between these two distinct states of consciousness, from the abnormal to the normal, by a kind of *autohypnosis*, albeit only temporarily. All these complicated linguistic and somatic troubles (*psycho-somatic*, as we call today thanks to Jacob von Uexküll's work, which appears to us as quite a Spinozist notion) disappeared when she was reawakened, unfortunately always for a short period before they emerged again. Breuer's technique was based on repeating the words she uttered in her hypnosis when she was awake, especially those related with her last and decisively fatal symptom, hydrophobia. In her altered state of consciousness, whenever she wanted to drink water, her mental state was suddenly changing. During these periods of change, when Breuer repeated her the words she uttered under hypnosis, the *patient* begun to recite her dreams, and the images of her past with certain difficulty. But under such exertion she was still telling nothing more than dreams. This Aristotelian *purgatory of soul* is called later, in psychoanalytic vocabulary, as *affective externalization*, or catharsis. The only condition for the definitive termination of a symptom appeared to be an affective burst of feelings, for instance an exaggerated anger or hate (which is an affective state), expressed during hypnosis. So, only after an exaggerated manifestation of anger against

10   Sigmund Freud, 'Observation of a Severe Case of Hemi-Anaesthesia in a Hysterical Male', *The Standard Edition of the Complete Psychological Works of Sigmund Freud, Volume I (1886-1899): Pre-Psycho-Analytic Publications and Unpublished Drafts*, 1966 (1886), pp. 23-31.
11   Ibid.
12   Michel Foucault, *The Order of Things: An Archaeology of the Human Sciences,* New York: Vintage, 1994.

a dog she saw during her childhood while drinking water from a cup in her session, Anna wakes up and drinks the cup of water Breuer gives her.[13]

What can be deduced from this story? That she was blocked at the moment she failed to show her anger against her daddy's *small dog*. Psychoanalysis will explain later that her *affective charge* was not expressed at the due moment for reasons of politeness (today we could also say *for political reasons*, which are not so much distant of the former), and then, once this charge bursts under hypnosis, its repeating symptoms can be forgotten. Psychoanalysis discovers *affects* (*Affekt*) as an inseparable part of its understanding of what is *unconscious* (*unbewusste* as an adjective) in its early beginnings.

It is important to note that the revelation of a past memory is not sufficient for the cure: If this past memory is not accompanied by an actual affective state, in this case the *anger* of Anna O., it could not be *forgotten* at all. We may not immediately discern the specific meaning *forgetting* takes in this context. Can one say that Anna O. *forgets* something that was never revealed to her consciousness, yet which had been the *cause* of her disease? Breuer and Freud seem to say that *forgetting* (the *oblivium*) can be used in two senses: Anna O. forgets her traumatic experience since she was not able to express the corresponding appropriate *affect*, the anger, for reasons of politeness. Yet, her altered state of mind *remembers* it perpetually, as a neurotic obsession, and unconsciously. Once the *problem* and the required *affect* meet each other once again in recollection or under hypnosis, she is able to *forget* this trouble completely.

This means that symptoms appear whenever the patient is unable to express an affect naturally. The cure cannot work unless remembrance is not accompanied by those affects. Affective experiences remain as psychic traumas which are, according to Freud, always determined by *scenes*—such as the scene of the small dog, the scene of drinking the *humanely* offered cup of water.[14] The trauma always seems to be a residual, a remnant, a remanent of a past but concrete event. And traumas have to be the remnants of the disturbing, troubling *interval* between an experience and the corresponding *affect*, or *emotion* in everyday language.

But what happens when such traumas happen to *social bodies*, families, tribes, nations, and to the world on a global scale? Only if there could be an all-powerful State or Government we would be able to figure out the collective traumas of the past—such as the revolutions, wars or even relatively insignificant events that once disturbed the public opinion. No one could *cure* such social traumas without the power to create a general state of *oblivium*, which would be the opposite of what we call *historical consciousness* at least since Hegel. There will always be concrete individuals—*classes* for instance, for Marx—who would remember such *cure* as the trauma itself, as it always happens in the concreteness of the historical experience. We are familiar with the famous notion (which is at least partially adopted even by Gramsci) that *society* is passive (the civil society)

---

13   Sigmund Freud and Joseph Breuer, *Studies in hysteria*, trans. Nicola Luckhurst, London: Penguin, 2004 (1895).

14   Ibid.

while *political classes* are active. Even Hegel, who departs from the *unconscious* of the history, especially with his doctrine of *subtlety of reason*, does not support such dualism.

And Freud would not stop asking the *real* question, following the observations he made with Breuer, which displayed that such *medical* problems were not as *singular, unique* and *empirical* as they seemed to be. They were always part of our ordinary lives, common to all—and that made Freud face the world of the *social* for the first time, but as we will try to show, in a quite inadequate manner. In all these *actes manqués* (the French word for ordinary *oblivia*, the instant forgetting of names, of things to be done, and the like) there is something like a fundamental, primordial *remembrance* at work, he thought. But this was still the *social* in each individual, not a collective form in itself. (Durkheim would have never believed in the notion of *collective unconscious*, which would be developed by Freud's friend—and later critique—Carl Gustav Jung). In other words, if Freud was concerned with such events as *dreams* and *actes manqués*, they were still revealing a self, or an individual, which was radically different from a collectivity of individuals. As such, Freud was able to conceptualize individual as a *social subject* rather than as a superior, sui generis entity, in an exact (yet unarticulated) opposition to Durkheim, who wanted to eliminate everything *psychological* from his sociology.

Freud's interest in wits,[15] actes manqués and especially dreams, is part of late 19th century's wisdom to seriously take into account the things so far remained incomprehensible, superstitious or simply trivial. The first attempt came from E. B. Tylor, who has tried to extract a social structure and a logic of culture merely from the *kinship terminology* of American Indian tribes.[16] Then Frazer came with his huge *Golden Bough*, compiling the mythologies of far distant societies and cultures.[17] Freud followed this interest when he was concerned with wits (*Witz* in German), the trivial things of social life, including dreams.

Freud becomes concerned with what we call as *actes manqués* in one of his essential early works, *Psychopathology of Everyday Life*. These acts are not characteristics of the *ill*, but especially and predominantly of *normal* people. Again, the *dualistic mind* of Anna O. reveals itself in these situations: According to Freud, the cause of *acte manqué* (slips of tongue, losing or insistent forgetting of certain things, like a name or act to be accomplished) has been acts that substituted other failed ones. For example, a meaningless word he utters, *begleitdigen*, could be revealing the sexual intentions of a man, for this meaningless word is the combination of two meaningful words in German— *begleiten* which can be translated as *accompanying* (intentionally and consciously, the young man wants to accompany the young girl to her home), and *beleidigen*, meaning

---

15   Sigmund Freud, 'The psychopathology of everyday life. SE, 6.' in James Strachey (ed) *The Standard Edition of the Complete Psychological Works of Sigmund Freud*, London: The Hogarth Press, 1901.

16   See: Edward B. Tylor, 'On a method of investigating the development of institutions; applied to laws of marriage and descent.', *The Journal of the Anthropological Institute of Great Britain and Ireland* 18 (1889): pp. 245-272. *See also.* Claude Lévi-Strauss, *Les Structures Elementaires de la Parenté*, Paris: Presses Universitaires de France, 1949.

17   James George Frazer, *The Golden Bough; a study in magic and religion*, Abridged (ed), London: Macmillan, 1923.

injury, or lack of respect in German[18]. Freud believes that such lapsus are not trivial and meaningless since we cannot assign organic causes (such as fatigue) to them. In the word *begleitdigen*, some kind of *meaning* is already present, if only as a linguistic recomposition of two words. We need to recall Henri Bergson's study of *laughing*, who was his contemporary, parallel to Freud's work. Bergson looks into a particular kind of *laughing* (*le rire*) which is nothing more than a self-defense in a shameful position one finds oneself in, in order to avoid the laughs of others in that social situation.[19]

Hence, *actes manqués* are really *acts*, always a characteristic of *normal* people, in which two intentions confront each other, one generally approved, and the other always repressed. There is nothing *unintentional* in these acts. Freud interprets the *struggle* of these two intentions as *compromising* in the middle, and one intention is already called as *repressed*, the other as *intended* or *conscious*.[20] All seems to be the struggle between two *opinions* within the soul of a single person. The self-contradictory terms that are firmly established in languages—especially in German—have already attracted certain important philosophers, like Hegel's comment on the opposite meanings present in a single word, or *Schelling*—to whom Freud himself refers in his discussion of *opposite meanings* in his seminal work *Das Unheimliche*.[21] This struggle would continue in the works of Freud's contemporaries, such as Joyce, the first systematic user of *mots valises*—composite words whose sense do not exist yet but are created only through their utterance.

But this compromise between two opposite intentions, according to Freud, is also a contamination—words mutually contaminating each other. Freud prefers to call this *contamination* as *condensation*, which explains all with a metaphor. When two words contaminate each other, since they are not deprived of the affects previously attached to them, they appear to be combined.[22]

For Freud this event is a quasi-repression of an intention filled with an affect, its transformed appearance. Lapsus happens in a social context (to which Freud generally seems to fail to pay attention) preceded by the condition in which the subject feels her/his intention would be indecent, improper, or incongruous. The discourse, always already present there, as Lacan would like to say, will intend to be manifested while being suppressed, by disavowing itself and fulfilling its censorship.

Evidently not all kinds of lapsus are open to be interpreted easily: The level of repression involved determines how symptomatic they appear to be, which in turn determines the ease of interpretation. In any case, the essential condition of a lapsus is always the repression of an expression that is felt by the subject as somehow indecent, or injuring, or again, intolerable. Yet, the repressed tendency that is suppressed in the discourse manifests itself contrary to

---

18   Sigmund Freud, *A General Introduction to Psychoanalysis*, New York: Horace Liveright, 1920, p.21.
19   Henri Bergson, *Le rire*, Paris: P. U. F., 1961.
20   Freud, *The psychopathology of everyday life*.
21   Sigmund Freud, 'The Uncanny (das unheimliche, 1919).' *The Standard Edition of the Complete Psychological Works of Sigmund Freud* 17 (1919): 1917-1919.
22   Ibid.

the will of the speaker, contaminating his or her expression. It appears that sometimes it modifies the manifested, *intended* or declared tendency, or replaces it altogether. Hence the resulting lapsus somehow responds to the self-censorship expected from the subject (the young man in our example, after all, did not surely uttered the offensive word). The contaminating logic of these *portmanteau* words was not only a concern of psychoanalysis, but tainted the avant-garde culture of Western Europe in the beginnings of the 20th century, appearing as an essential *literary* argument in the works of James Joyce, if not emerging from the *Jabberwocky* of Lewis Carroll.

An *acte manqué*, further, is a compromise between two antagonistic intentions that tend to be expressed together, while this common expression remains *impossible* (at least, in the *linear* nature of language) without a mutual concession. Freud often stresses that the unconscious tendency resists to its analysis sufficient enough that the person analyzed (the *patient* for Freud, a *Subject* for Lacanians) tend to deny its value. Freud later reveals such *résistance* in his *Interpretation of Dreams*:

> There are many people who do not seem to find it easy to adopt the required at-
> titude toward the apparently freely rising ideas, and to renounce the criticism
> which is otherwise applied to them. The undesired ideas habitually evoke the
> most violent resistance, which seeks to prevent them from coming to the surface.[23]

This *negation* or rather *de-negation* is quite an important mechanism. For the time, as a pas-sage from a purely therapeutic operation, we should look into the Interpretation of Dreams, probably Freud's most important work on his way to the *invention* of Unconscious.

Freud introduces his *Traumdeutung* at the eve of the 20th century quite pretentiously, as he claims that the 'interpretation of dreams is the *via regis* (royal road) to a knowledge of the unconscious in psychic life'.[24] Now, *unbewusste* becomes *Unbewusstsein*, almost like a substance, if not an essence. If Freud's studies in hysteria and on the *psychopathology of everyday life* still remained as *empirical* (that is, appropriate to the epistemology of the medi-cine and other *natural sciences*) through this *royal road* Freud will now tend to create almost a new domain of existence, which tends to displace the very notion of *consciousness*, if what we understand from consciousness is will, a purely active force of human beings upon their lives.[25] And the *dreams* have already proved their *symptomatic* value in his works on the case of Anna O., as we have mentioned above.

However, the significance of dreams for Freud seems to reveal itself in his therapeutic engage-ment with *neuroses*: If it is true that neuroses revealed the importance of dreams, the study of dreams (empirically, and case by case) gave him the key to the Unconscious. Evidently, Freud was about to leave the ancient technique of *hypnosis* (which, according to him, was difficult to manipulate) in favor of a new treatment method which was based on *free associations*; having

---

23   Sigmund Freud, and A. J. Cronin, *The interpretation of dreams*, Vancouver: Read Books Ltd, 2013.
24   Ibid.
25   Ibid.

the patient lying on a divan with the analysts hand on his head, and expect him to speak and utter those words freely. Even if nothing comes out initially, as long as the analyst would insist, something would necessarily transpire. This insistence would continue until certain *thoughts* could be formed from certain utterances, usually emerging as if the patient says: *'I could tell you these from the beginning, but I didn't think that they were important for you at all'*. For Freud, such non-importance or triviality assigned to a *thought* by the subject himself was symptomatic, and the free-association method was based on the relief stemming from the discovery of the *symptom-thought*. The analyst now urges the patient for freely uttering every idea that comes to his mind, and what follows is typically, almost unanimously, the patients beginning to recite their dreams—and these nocturnal accounts were interpreted by Freud in the same status as other symptoms. Freud's understanding of *spontaneity*, which is conditioned by such *free-flow of utterances* or relief, is interesting. Why is there such spontaneous and recurrent tendency among the patients to talk about their dreams? According to Freud, the dream is not a useless aspect or phenomenon of psychic activity. If it is a *phenomenon* (in its proper Kantian sense, if you will), it is a fully *meaningful* apparition as such, whose apparent absurdity and inherence disappears at the moment we are engaged with it in an appropriately *scientific* method. A dream is meaningful as it always expresses a wish, an unconscious desire that spontaneously suggests its immediate satisfaction. Only the *manifest content* of the dream is remembered after waking up, whereas the analysis reveals the *latent ideas* it contains (its *unconscious* meaning) at the end. Yet, these *latent ideas* never form at the outside of the *manifest content* of the dream—and this is the crucial point for questioning the *status* of the Unconscious. They always constitute the *meaning* of the dream that they are embedded in, as every semiotician would say, since meaning cannot exist without the sign that expresses it. There is not an anteriority-posteriority relation between the *latent* ideas and *manifest* content, except for the sake of presentation.

Hence one could say that the process of transforming manifest content to latent ideas is the essential activity of dream—the *Traumarbeit* (the *dreamwork*) in Freudian terminology. Thus the analysis of dreams is nothing but traversing the same road in reverse direction, moving from the manifest content to latent ideas, or *signs*. Freud notes that only children have *clear and distinct* dreams since they lacked the *depth*, and for them dreaming is simply transforming their wishes into *images*. One could say that children are naturally *naturalists*; their dreams are simple acts or movements, such as falling, flying, or any other familiar daily activity. Yet the *depth* intervenes in the adult, with an entire life-story, expressed in the great gap between latent ideas and the manifest content. Hence the dream is nothing but the *repressed desire* that remains hidden to us.

What will be important for our concerns about the world of images and particularly the cinema, is the way Freud expands his interpretations to *awakened dreams*, which he interprets not too distant from the domain of artistic creation, as he quotes Schiller's letter to Korner:

> The reason for your complaint lies, it seems to me, in the constraint which your intellect imposes upon your imagination. Here I will make an observation, and illustrate it by an allegory. Apparently it is not good- and indeed it hinders the creative work of the mind- if the intellect examines too closely the ideas already pouring in, as it were, at the gates.

Regarded in isolation, an idea may be quite insignificant, and venturesome in the extreme, but it may acquire importance from an idea which follows it; perhaps, in a certain collocation with other ideas, which may seem equally absurd, it may be capable of furnishing a very serviceable link. The intellect cannot judge all these ideas unless it can retain them until it has considered them in connection with these other ideas. In the case of a creative mind, it seems to me, the intellect has withdrawn its watchers from the gates, and the ideas rush in pell-mell, and only then does it review and inspect the multitude. You worthy critics, or whatever you may call yourselves, are ashamed or afraid of the momentary and passing madness which is found in all real creators, the longer or shorter duration of which distinguishes the thinking artist from the dreamer. Hence your complaints of unfruitfulness, for you reject too soon and discriminate too severely.[26]

Schiller belongs to the Romantic German followers of Spinozism (as Goethe and Schelling) and Freud's regard of him is critically important. Departing from the notion of *dream*, Freud and his followers will never cease to apply psychoanalytic notions to the domain of arts: Freud on Leonardo da Vinci, Rollo May on arts in general, and finally Gaston Bachelard's *psychoanalysis of imagination*—which seems to us somehow quite distant from Freud's take.

It is interesting how Freud associates dreams with a certain kind of *tekhne*, and how the fundamental functions of dreams are described in almost *technological* terms—as *Traumarbeit*, the work of the dream. Two small comments on such association are necessary. The first one refers to the domain of philosophy, and evidently to Heidegger, who conceptualized the notion of *tekhne* with a reference to technology (whether ancient or *modern*, artistic or *industrial*), perhaps under the influence of the early work of his friend Ernst Jünger—such as *Der Arbeiter* (The Worker). *Arbeit* (work) is what linked creativity to an aesthetic experience, which can also be said for *dreams*, not only for human beings (Arbeiter). In the same way Heidegger attributes the role of *revealing* (*bringing forth the being*) to technology by referring back to Greek metaphysics, Freud never uses the term Traumarbeit as a metaphor but exactly as the work of the dream. The second is the critical moment in the anti-psychoanalytic device sketched by Deleuze and Guattari later in their *L'Anti-Oedipe*. Their opposition to Freudianism will be based a *constructivist* model of *factory*, rather than the Freudian model they interpret as based on the *theater*, of family mise-en-scènes, and of Oedipus.[27] We are inclined to share this second position, as you will see.

Freud distinguishes between two *techniques* operating in collaboration with each other, as *condensation* and *displacement*—which have been later rendered by Lacan in *linguistic* terminology respectively as *metaphor* and *metonymy*.[28] Condensation is one of the *primitive elements*, as latent, hidden ideas are always much more numerous than the manifest, expressed content. It reveals the *composite* appearance of the persons and

26   Editors note Letter by Friedrich Schiller, December 1, 1788, quoted in Freud, *Interpretation of Dreams*, p. 85.
27   Deleuze and Guattari, 'L'anti-oedipe'.
28   Jacques Lacan, *Le séminaire de Jacques Lacan. / Livre XI, Les quatre concepts fondamentaux de la psychanalyse,* Paris Édition du Seuil, DL, 1973.

objects that are *seen* in a dream, and this explains why any given element in a dream *signifies* a number of latent ideas. Through condensation, a number of constituents are *subsumed* in a single component.

Displacement, rendered in Lacan's terminology as a metonymic process, is the reversal or *exchange* of the values that are present in the scene of the theater of the Unconscious. This means that something extremely important in a hidden, latent thought tends to become quite *useless* or *trivial* in the manifest content of the dream, and vice versa, a multitude of trivial elements in the latent context appears as something quite important to the subject. This *metonymic* process will be exactly what will drive Freud towards his *theory of sexuality*, since it enables the analyst to declare some elements as *trivial*, the others as *important*, depending on the state of Freud's *theoretical position* at a given moment. Hence, Deleuze will object to Freud and his follower Melanie Klein's *abuse* of the metonymic process: A multitude of signs and symptoms are reduced to the Oedipal element, for instance, for restoring Little Hans's *family romance—'This is your mother; this is your father.'*[29]

The concept of *metonymy* also seems be seriously abused by those *linguistically* and *psycho-analytically* oriented cinema theorists later on, such as Christian Metz, as well as feminists like Laura Mulvey, for whom every element in cinematography should (and could) be reduced either to an act of *voyeurism*, to *male gaze*, or to any other psychoanalytic matter.[30] Deleuze denounces this only partially, by simply stating that cinema cannot be reduced to the vocabularies of psychoanalysis and of linguistics.[31]

Following condensation and displacement, Freud also depicts a third Traumarbeit, which seems to be an intermediary *work* between the former two. This is *symbolization* that consists in replacing things, personae and situations with analogical representations, as it happens with playing with words. Through this new concept, the Unconscious really passes from the *adjective* (unbewusste) to a *substance* (Unbewusstsein), expressed now as a power which has already been there, not as something yet to be created. Yet it seems that *symbolization* is the primary function of the dream according to Freud, since only through symbolizing the Traumarbeit can provide the *raw material* for the other functions, the condensation and displacement, as well as the entire mise-en-scène of the theater of the Unconscious.[32]

But why do dreams operate in such tortuous manner, and why *adult* dreams cannot work with Cartesian, *clear and distinct* ideas, affects and images just like the children's dreams? Freud explains this by once again referring to his notion of *repressed desires* which are suppressed by *morality* and unable to appear to consciousness as they are. These repressed desires, according to Freud, can appear to consciousness only during sleep, when moral censorship

29   Gilles Deleuze and Claire Parnet, *Dialogues*, trans. Hugh Tomlinson and Barbara Habberjam, London: Athlone, 1987 (1987).

30   See: Christian Metz, *Le significant imaginaire*, Paris: Christian Bourgeois Editeur, 1993; Laura Mulvey, 'Visual Pleasure and Narrative Cinema', *Visual and Other Pleasures*, London: Palgrave Macmillan, 1989.

31   Gilles Deleuze, *Cinema 2: The time-image*, trans. Hugh Tomlinson and Robert Galeta, London: Continuum, 2005

32   Sigmund Freud, *The interpretation of Dreams*.

is less active. And since censorship is still *active* (there cannot be such thing as *passive* censorship) these intolerable ideas or affects (wishes) disguise themselves through *symbolization*. This explains both the tortuous nature of our adult dreams and why we easily forget—since we have to—our dreams when we awake. According to Freud this is expressed by *nightmares* in which we are suddenly pushed to awake in a very bad state which is soon replaced by a sentiment of relief. These are just excessively *clear and distinct* ideas and thoughts, which somehow escape censorship. Nightmares are unbearable moments of Angst.[33] All that happens in the theater of Unconscious seem to be associated either with a *repressive State*, a *policing* function of censorship, or in a Kafkaesque scene in which all that is *clear or distinct* according to Cartesian logic becomes unbearable and intolerable—whether it is a vision, an image, a wish, a desire, or a thought. The Unconscious, when *substantiated* as a State affair (Oedipus had been a king, after all) tends to become an uncanny *return of the repressed* (*Das Unheimliche*), disappearing forever as soon as it becomes familiar to us.[34]

Why does Freud refer to such a notion like *censorship*, which is clearly a quasi-bureaucratic, quasi-repressive State function, despite living in a modern age. The details of the times he wrote *Traumdeutung* (1899), and the times in which he developed his later theories, can help us identify the presence of *camps* that exist in constant struggle, espionage, and matters of *war and peace*. Unconscious-Consciousness is formulated as a dualistic topic, whereas Id-Ego-Super-Ego corresponds to *compromise* and *diplomacy* between these opposing forces. We can even discern that his emphasis on *censorship* belongs to Traumdeutung, to a *peaceful epoch*, when, however, class struggles, revolutionary and anarchist movements, and evidently a police state with strong censorship were in effect. It was almost an epoch of a *state of emergency* that transformed peace into a discipline. We see the eruption of First World War at a later moment, when Freud's models started to explain everything that relates to war (rather than waiting for the *disturbances of civilization* to end); first Unconscious and Consciousness as a never-ending frontal warfare in trenches, and later Id-Ego-Super-Ego transforming human psyche into a map where tactics and strategies are always at work.

Repression and the Political Topography of Psychoanalysis

What is the true function of censorship? Actes manqués and lapsus already reveal the social nature (politeness, eloquence, and the *civilizing process*) of the forces involved in Freud's fin-de-siècle. This is a society of socio-psychological types, as some of them are described by Simmel, such as the *Poor* (people in need, and socially recognized in this way), the *Mediator* (quite akin to *censors* or *judges* acting as public agents), the *Jew* (and Freud himself was coming from an Atheist Jewish family, to which he seems to return back in his last work before dying, Moses and Monotheism), the *Stranger* (acting both as a Mediator—since he is distant from common *familial sentiments*, and as a source of danger as the Other who threatens our relationships). Jacques Donzelot had described the essential function of the family in this epoch as *policing*. Unlike the *bourgeois* families whose children were confined to the domestic settings of their home and their gardens, or to their schools preparing for the business life to

---

33   Ibid.
34   Sigmund Freud, *Introductory Lectures on Psychoanalysis*, New York: Liveright, 1989.

come, the children of the growing number of proletarian families in this era of industrialization and urbanization were already growing on the streets. The common proletarian family life no longer provided the traditional sphere of *peace* and security, it ceased to be a sanctuary, it just provided an alternative space to the asylum.[35] As Michel Foucault reminds us: The family, the school, the hospital, the military service, and especially the factory (whose institutional difference from prison was unrecognizable) were spatial and temporal enclosures. Hence a certain form of censorship was present in all, waiting for the final war.[36]

Yet, the censorship and repression notions Freud invented appear to be quite distant and highly detached from these social problems, unless we can locate the development of his theory of the unconscious within the transformations of the family, the industry (the coming Taylorism and Fordism), the prison, and the army—in other words, with the emergence of Foucaldian *disciplinary apparatuses*. Freudian notions of censorship and repression has already had their *social* counterparts, which were not merely avatars of a deep Unconscious, but quite complex social strategies developed after the French Revolution. These were Napoleonic institutions: The institutionalized family (modern marriage and family relations organized through the Code of Napoleon), the new, disciplined army, the obligatory schooling system, the *asylum* transformed by Pinel into a medical observation and treatment laboratory, the clinic that also relied on *case by case* empirical observation and medical experiments both as discourse and institution, and the prison system that remained as a source of pride for a while because of the less cruel *punishment* it offered in comparison to the corporeal punishments of the ancient régime.[37]

While dissolving everything in the familial, short-range settings of the dreams, Freud had nevertheless used *socio-political* terms in his work—censorship and repression—although he tried to derive these terms out of his *therapeutic* or *psychiatric* work. He developed the *first topic* during the years preceding the First World War. The word *topic* comes from *topos* in Greek, which means *territory*, or *a place* (*ta topika*; matters concerning commonplaces). The topic of repression already calls for a *conflict* that is to be enacted in the battlefield (just like a reminder of Kant's *Kampfplatz* as the philosophical domain), where opposing forces spread out into strategic fronts. At first, this appears in Freud as an attempt to present the problem, rather than an actual reference to camps or territories. He never seems to refer to physically defined *places* for the localization of these forces and thus, any attempt to try to find a place for these opposing forces in the brain would fail, as they have no *physical-organic supports*.[38]

The First Topic presents the confrontation of the Conscious/Preconscious against the Unconscious: The conscious is already present in our minds, and the preconscious can always be recalled by the memory if we direct our attention in the right way. The unconscious, on the other hand, consists of the psychic contents, which are impossible to be called to consciousness. We learn now that the Unconscious is something clearly substantial; certain sets of

---

35   Jacques Donzelot, *The Policing of Families*, trans. Robert Hurley, New York: Random House Inc., 1979.
36   Michel Foucault, *Discipline and Punish: the Birth of the Prison*, New York: Random House, 1977.
37   Ibid.
38   Sigmund Freud, *The interpretation of Dreams*, New York: Avon, 1980.

forces and repressed wishes. And in the opposite camp, there is our consciousness (a *Cogito*, be it Cartesian or not) which somehow feels the emergence of the Unconscious elements as a threat, more or less in depth or violent, depending on the nature of the desire *repressed* there. This threat already jeopardizes the existence and safety of consciousness (the actual part of our psyche). Freud refers to Angst as the moment in which a *clear and distinct* idea emerges from Unconscious. The symptoms of the Angst can be observed through the power of repressing and denying this idea (*Verneinung*).[39]

Censorship occupies the space between the Ego and the Unconscious, and possesses two main aspects as an agency. It impedes consciousness to reach the Unconscious, as in cases when we try to interpret our dreams by themselves, instead of properly going to a psycho-analyst and paying him. In this case the censorship repels the consciousness—this is called *resistance*. Inversely, if the unconscious elements, wishes, desires tend to invade conscious-ness, they will also be sent back to their place by censorship, and this is called *repression* (*Verdrängung*). In order to understand this phenomenon of *repression* better, we should con-sider Freud's *Pleasure Principle*, which functions plain and freely in the infant, but becomes mediated in the adult. According to this *principle*, all psychic activity aims at pleasure and avoids anything unpleasant—which reminds us Spinoza's famous doctrine of the *Conatus*, but that is strictly different as we will see later. In Freud, the necessity of adapting the *realities* of life partially suspends the Pleasure Principle; one has to tolerate unpleasant events and face obstacle in order to exist. Freud calls the principle that governs such tolerance as the Reality Principle. Reality Principle does not confront Pleasure Principle directly, but, on the contrary, helps it to reach fulfillment in rather tortuous ways.

It seems evident to Freud that, in the domain of necessities concerned with the preservation of life, the maintenance of the Reality Principle at an operational capacity is a priority, and it is not subject to *repression* or *resistance*; real satisfactions are not ignored for the sake of imaginary satisfactions. Yet, such vital urgency does not only apply to sexual matters: The satisfaction of sexual desires are symbolically linked to the punishments, and religions have developed the profound image of Hell as the ultimate punishment. The desires stemming from the Pleasure Principle are rejected (sent to the Unconscious) due to these links, and thus remain unsatisfied. This is why Freud wants to link the entire domain of *sexual life* to an imaginary life: Unconsciousness consists of unsatisfied desires persistently trying to reach to consciousness, which makes it the source of dreams, actes manqués and neuroses.

Yet, later on, Freud also develops a more complex *topic* (known as the Second Topic), as if he faces the problem of the Ego (the Cartesian Cogito and its status) once again—since, because of the process of *repression*, not everything that happens in *I* is revealed to our con-scious. For Freud, a second point of interest was the process of *identification* now, which he primarily associated with the models provided by the parents. Hence one part of Super-Ego corresponds to a *model* image, which is already formed during infancy, and constitute the values of self-regard in the subject. This part of the Super-Ego is formed in infancy for claim-ing the right to self-love (the fundamental problem of Narcissism), and is called by Freud as

---

39   Ibid.

Ideal-Ego. This seems to be the fundamental thematic not only among the psychoanalysts today, but also scrutinized and questioned in the entire domain of social sciences—including film studies, post-colonial and feminist theories, and so forth.

The problem with Narcissism as *self-love* (a primary *Affekt*, according to Freud, as the earliest passion of infancy) is that it cannot be satisfied without conditions or obstacles: As soon as we internalize the *rules* and *interdictions* (parental education), self-love should fulfill the conditions necessary to merit parental love (the love of the Other). The infant loves himself or herself, but just in the same way that his or her parents love him or her. This is a kind of *judgment of others* according to which one will judge himself, as if in a Kantian tribunal. The *imaginary life* of infancy imposes a set of values by which the Ideal-Ego is constituted as an entire system of interdictions and moral judgments, constitutive of the Super-Ego. Hence we have not two but three instances (or agencies) in the Second Topic: the Id (*Das Es*), the Ego (the *I*) and the Super-Ego.

The Id should not be confused with Unconscious itself, since there are unconscious aspects of other instances too. Freud expressly uses impersonal terms in order to show the unknown and recalcitrant nature of the forces involved *there*—or in *it*, as it is expressed in the famous formula *'Wo es war, soll Ich werden'* (where It was, I should be). Id resembles the Unconscious, to which it corresponds after Freud's passage from the First Topic to the Second Topic: Just like the Unconscious, it ignores negation, contradiction, and even time and space, as the desires it comprises never perish. It is utterly amoral, it ignores all kinds of moral restraints and judgments—in a Nietzschean way, it is *beyond good and evil*. Yet, that does not mean that it is entirely chaotic, for it follows the so-called Pleasure Principle. As we will see, it is connected to the body with its reservoir of impulses—it is where *libido* (*I desire*) is reserved. It is essential to note how the Cartesian principle of Cogito (*I think*) is now transformed into Libido (*I desire*), but only as the immoral, fleeing part of the psyche.

Then comes the *control* function: The Super-Ego of internalized constraints and interdictions is supposed to control both the Ego and the Id. Freud associates the formation of Super-Ego with the *decline of the Oedipus complex*, after when one accepts that he could not marry his mother. With this decline, Freud assumes that the child accomplishes his or her Super-Ego. The Ego-Ideal (which is a part of Super-Ego) is not simply an *identification* with the parents—it is an identification with their Super-Ego (which Lacan will equate with what he calls the *symbolic order*).[40] Our morality is nothing but that of our parents; what we forbid to ourselves are things they forbade to themselves.[41] And truly, the Super-Ego *controls* the exigencies of the Id by denying the repressed desires to reach consciousness. But it also controls the exigencies of the Ego: It denies the desires which are not adequate to the Ego-Ideal and repress them. This

40   Jacques Lacan, 'The function and field of speech and language in psychoanalysis.', *Écrits: A selection*, trans. Bruce Fink, New York: W. W. Norton, 2002 (1953).

41   This resonates with Ernst Jünger's abhorrence of *grand moral theories* of philosophers in his *Der Glaserne Bienen* (The Glass Bees) in favor of a strong family guidance, which is somehow different than Spinoza and Nietzsche's denouncements in their peculiar context.
     See: Ernst Jünger, *The glass bees*, trans. Elizabeth Mayer, New York: New York Review of Books, 2000 (1957).

function of control responds then to the exigencies of three things—that of the Id, that of the Ego and that of *reality*. Logically, only those desires which fit both to Id, the Ego and *reality* at the same time are allowed to be realized. Otherwise Angst, Shame, or Neurosis, if not Psychosis, will appear. This means that this controller is at the same time a conciliator, like a diplomat.

Last but not least, we have the Ego, which is our *apparent* personality, already and always inscribed in the reality, and almost like an interface in our contact with the outside world. The real mediator and conciliator (the essential diplomat) is in fact the Ego—it is never a perpetual contradictory force to the Id, but rather the agency which is responsible in realizing the desires of the Id. In a governmental structure it would correspond to the *executive power*.

Only the Ego can take into account the exigencies of reality in Freud, as a *politician* of *real politics*. It should never provoke Super-Ego's reactions, has to act in such a manner that it will not lose Super-Ego's love, or risk to be punished by it. The relation between Ego and the Super-Ego remains unknown to the subject, who may only have an apprehension of it, through a certain kind of Angst (say, anxiety) and sometimes, sentiments of culpability. According to Freud, this sentiment of anxiety is a symptom of a tension between the Ego and the Super-Ego, and Ego's consternation of being punished by the Super-Ego when it becomes complicit in the realization of the desires it forbids. Hence, the situation of the Ego appears as a kind of *diplomacy* and *arbitration* among various sets of *interests*, in the so-called *rationalization* of desires.

And when the Ego feels itself threatened, it can react in two different ways. First is an escapist reaction—under the influence of the Pleasure Principle we have a tendency to avoid any displeasurable effect. Yet, we can only practically avoid it if the thread is external; but if it is internal (such as an impulse, or a pulsion that wishes to be fulfilled while its object is forbidden), then we repress it. Repression can be taken as a form of escape, since repression prevents the awareness of the desire itself. The rational evaluation of danger and obstacles produces similarly rational means to escape them. Freud supposes that the Reality Principle has to be successful in imposing its supremacy, but its domination is always relative and it is often imposed primarily when confronted with external dangers. One of the functions of psychoanalytic therapy is to reinforce the priority of the second mode of *reaction-formation* of the Ego over the first one.

Obviously such *topographic* exposition could never be sufficient without identifying the fundamental chains of causality involved in the Unconscious processes. Thus, Freud begins to consider *forces*, *impulses*, and *pulsions* that equals to some kind of *dynamics*. The major question at that juncture is the nature of the forces that operate in the psychic life in these different instances (or agencies). Freud describes these forces as Trieb (from *treiben*, which means *to push*), which can be translated as *impulse* or *pulsions*—and Trieb should never be confused with what we call *instincts* (unfortunately many commentators fail to see the importance of the difference between *pulsion* and *instinct*). Pulsion is never a hereditary, preformed behavior that could be taken as a characteristic attribute of the species. It is a dynamic process that stems from a *localized* corporeal excitement or stimulation, and *pushes* the subject towards a certain form of activity in order to realize a discharge of tension. This discharge (a kind of *catharsis*, again) is the aim, or the *telos* of a tension, and is always obtained through an object. The infant for instance suffers from an excitation of buccal mucus (which is the *source* of a tension) and is urged to seek the maternal breast in order to reduce the degree of excitation in his mouth by licking, if not, his fingers (the object). Freud really believes that *licking* his finger or maternal milk is indeed a *corporeal* aim for the infant. In any case, the source of a pulsion is somatic (that is, *physical*) and the dynamic movement from physical to *telos*, which is psychosomatic according to Freud, also constitutes the boundaries between the corporeal and the psychic life.

Spinoza versus Freudianism: Logic of Affects and Affections

Spinoza makes a clear distinction between *ideas* and *affects*: An idea is something that represents something—its *ideatum,* according to Spinoza, its object. Anything in our minds that stands in for, represents, or accounts for something—an *object*, is an idea. Whereas an affect (*affectus*, wrongly translated into English as *emotion*, especially in the Elwes Translation) is an event of the mind which, on the contrary, represents nothing. It can be *determined* by an idea, but it represents nothing about that idea, nor about its object. This means that an affect is another *mode of thinking* that involves fluctuations between greater or lesser powers to think, and greater or lesser power to act. In other words, affects (affectus) are the degrees of power of the individual, the ways through which individual fulfills its potential, its singular *essence*.

This creates for us a sphere of discussion in which whole life is conceived as a single *plane of consistency*[42] and anything can be considered as individual. A society (a socius), its environment, the Nature are *individuals* according to a *principium individuationis (principle of individuation)*. The rationalist principle acknowledges the presence of individuals fundamentally and holistically; 'the order of things and the order of ideas are same'[43]. This means that Spinoza's philosophy does not deny the existence of the *individual*. It neither imposes a principle of *community* or *supreme being* in which individuals are epiphenomena, or mere appearances (like in Platonism)—these ideals simply stem from our misconception of the totality or God. And every *single* individual (in Spinozism every individual is single, not only in its existence, but also in its essence) is composed by other individuals, organisms, cells, and so on to infinity. These infinitely small individuals (*corpora simplicissima*) can only be discerned through their modes of *rest and movement* (their *latitudes and amplitudes*) according to Deleuze.[44]

Spinoza warns that we fail to know our bodies themselves, since our body is in a constant interaction with other bodies, human beings, things, landscapes, milieus and objects. This means that we are always individuals within individuals, altogether forming superior individuals or *collectivities*. A society is part of Nature, insofar as it is a particular individual within

---

42   Deleuze and Guattari, *What is Philosophy?*
43   Alexandre Matheron, 'Remarques sur l'immortalité de l'âme chez Spinoza', *Les Études philosophiques* 3 (1972): 369-37, p. 18.
44   Gilles Deleuze, *Spinoza et le problem de l'expression*, Paris: Editions de Minuit (1968): 183–196.

it. And everything that happens to an individual in such an environment is perceived as *modulations* (*affectio*) of the body. What happens (the event) are *occurrences* (*occursus*), bodily actions and reactions, and these can impact the individual in several different ways, due to the complexity of the individual (and human individuals are quite complex bodies, as are the societies they compose). This is quite a different vision of *society* (or rather, *socius*) compared to Durkheim's, who sees *society* as representative of God (or literally the contrary), as a sui generis entity. For Spinoza sui generis can only be considered as the whole, the holistic individual, Nature or God (*Deus sive Natura*), and not as a single individual who is obviously connected to all other individuals in the world. Through the same notion Tarde relates to a philosopher like Leibniz (who followed Spinoza in many respects), in his opposition to Durkheim.

We should not confuse Spinoza's notions of *affectus* (affect) and *affectio* (affection).[45] An affectus is a relation between bodies through any possible means, which causes a differentiation in the powers of the affected body in a negative or positive way. Whereas affectio is concerned with the body that is impacted by affects, they are the remnants of the affects the body becomes exposed to, just like the images that results in the visual cortex as the remnant of the light that falls on the retina. They last until they are replaced by other affections, by being exposed to other images. This is like Simmel's description of the blaze attitude in the modern, urban metropolitan life, in which the individual is constantly *bombarded* by a multitude of stimulations, which results in a forbearing numbness of sensations to cope with[46], or in losing his gestures.[47]

One can always argue that an affect is *determined* by an *idea*. In that case, we have to consider what *idea* means for Spinoza, who still preserves the medieval definitions of the notion. Spinoza defines the idea first through its *objective reality*, which meant for the Medieval Scholasticism he still follows as *something that exists insofar as it represents an object* (ideatum). This is called as an idea's *objective reality*. We have to remember that in the Medieval way of thinking *objective* corresponds to *subjective* in our modern way of thinking, and vice versa. And this is the absolute definition of an *idea*: If there is no object, the idea cannot exist. Ideas can be perfect only insofar as they fit to their objects. What is original in Spinoza, however, is the way in which he defines a second *reality*, a second level of the existence of ideas. He calls this as the *formal* reality (or perfection) of ideas, which is indeed an invention of Spinoza. Since we can form *ideas of ideas*, since we can take them as *objects*, they also have to have a formal existence in our mind. I can form ideas of ideas, since I have always an idea about the fact that I have an idea, and so on. If I compare the ideas of a *fly* and of *God* I have, the latter would be infinitely greater than the idea of the fly, since I experience the idea of God as objectively expressing an infinitely great—and absolute—existence, while the idea of a simple fly is infinitely small with respect to it.

45   Ibid.
46   Georg Simmel, 'The Metropolis and Mental Life', *The Sociology of Georg Simmel*. New York: Free Press, 1950, pp. 409-424.
47   Giorgio Agamben, 'Notes on gesture.', *Means without End: Notes on Politics* 20, Minneapolis, MN: University of Minnesota Press, 2000.

And this is the way in which ideas, in their formal existence, can determine affects. Spinoza has a profound understanding of human mind; he doesn't believe that our intellect only operates through *indifferent* ideas: Our bodies and minds function in such a way that we cannot be neutral or indifferent about the events round us. Every encounter we experience is already an idea, and we cannot experience this idea without experiencing an emotion, or affect. We are really *automates* (automata), but not in the way Descartes distinguishes between the body and mind; we are *spiritual automata* (automaton spiritualis). I have ideas when I read a poem, when I am facing a beautiful landscape, or when I am walking in the street, just encountering people. And these ideas always generate a state of mind in which affects me in certain ways. This is a logic of *continuous variation*, formally expressed by Deleuze.

Affections were *imprints* or *traces* of events upon our bodies. They are *images* in that sense, which can take the form of a sound, a voice, a word, a vision, or even a dream—which would have to wait for Freud's Traumdeutung for being seriously tackled with. In other words, while affections do not directly represent ideas, they necessarily correlate to them. An idea is not something we have, or which we can recall at ease. The important thing is that an idea never appears without *determining* an affect, we are essentially *spiritual automates* even when we simply walk in the street.

This explains why Spinoza carefully distinguishes between *affections* and *affects* on the one hand, and between *images* and *ideas* on the other. These are the elements structuring our intellect, both conscious and unconscious. Images seem to be primarily entities, as they are the *traces* of real affections on our bodies—visions, dreams, everyday encounters with things. Spinoza, in his early-unfinished work *Tractatio de Emendatione Intellectus* (*Treatise on the Amendment of Understanding*, TEI) clarifies the very probable domain in which we encounter images; one has to be able to apprehend images as ideas:

> Further, from what has just been said—namely, that an idea must, in all respects, correspond to its correlate in the world of reality, —it is evident that, in order to reproduce in every respect the faithful image of nature, our mind must deduce all its ideas from the idea which represents the origin and source of the whole of nature, so that it may itself become the source of other ideas.[48]

This total image of the nature would be articulated as the *third kind of knowledge* that is the apprehension of the totality, in Spinoza's later and essential work, *Ethics*. Spinoza already anticipates Leibnizean logic of calculus in his treatment of *affects*, in which everything will no longer be expressed in *geometric* (the *modo geometrico* of Spinoza) but differential terms. An affect in Spinoza is a differential, a *difference* as one would like to say today. It is always a passage, and not a state or a *molar* domain of affectivity. If we believe today that our affective states (emotions or passions) such as love, hate, contempt, sympathy, hope etc. are products of social institutions—such as family, pol-

---

48   Benedictus de Spinoza, *Complete works*, trans. Samuel Shirley and others, Michael L. Morgan (ed.). Cambridge, IN: Hackett Publishing Company, Inc., 2002.

itics, everyday life, aesthetic and moral constructions—that is only true insofar as we can understand them in a Spinozist manner: An affect is a passage, that is, a derivation from other affects.

The Spinozist distinction between *potentia* and the *potestas*, the power-to-do and the power that is *transferred* to the sovereignty (which appears to be an Hobbesian theme) is not onto-logically determined. In fact, only the potentia, the power to do and to act exists, and the potestas—the sovereign power—does not exist in itself, but derived from the former. In other words, for Spinoza potestas is nothing but the separation of human beings from their power to act. The negative connotation of the term potestas, its identification as not a positive ability but with a presupposition of authority, is the key Spinozist notion in treating the sources of *opinion*. But what does *man's separation from his power to act* means? Clearly, Spinoza rejects the Hobbesian theme of the *transfer*: No *power to act* can really be transferred to a sover-eign (whether in the form of Commonwealth or Leviathan) without *instituting* or *constructing* such transferal as a power to do beforehand. Unlike Hobbes, Spinoza seems to evoke the irreducibility of the power-to-act to a given agency of social contract in every domain of life. Like Machiavelli, on the other hand, he is aware of the fact that the sovereign, or the State can appropriate the usage of the collective power, and that this can be a real appropriation. Spinoza's concern with the *subjective* implication of power appears in his unfinished *Treatise on the Amendment of Understanding* (TEI): He mentions that mind is separated from its power to think when what *men regard as the highest good* is reduced to *riches, fame and sensual pleasures*—'With these three the mind is so distracted that it is quite incapable of thinking of any other good.'[49] But the *power-to-reflect*, the primary task of any philosopher (and Spinoza aims to be a philosopher, now), becomes the principle purpose of his Treatise:

1. Having laid down these preliminary rules, I will betake myself to the first and most important task, namely, the amendment of the understanding, and the rendering it capable of under-standing things in the manner necessary for attaining our end.

2. In order to bring this about, the natural order demands that I should here recapitulate all the modes of perception, which I have hitherto employed for affirming or denying anything with certainty, so that I may choose the best, and at the same time begin to know my own powers and the nature which I wish to perfect.[50]

Thereby, Spinoza's project becomes an attempt to discover and nourish the singular power of the mind which would be enjoyed by the philosopher, with two important apparent con-sequences: There are quasi-subjective causes which tend to strip the mind from its powers to think; these are *external* forces (this is the reason why we use the term -quasi) that are nourished by and that can manipulate and amplify these internal tendencies towards fame, sensual pleasures, and vanity. These external forces seemingly belong to potestas as a form of power—to the State or any other kind of theocratic and political powers. Spinoza appears to be the first, and perhaps the single *democratic* philosopher, if we consider the traditional

49 Spinoza, *Complete works*.
50 Spinoza, 'Treatise on the Amendment of Understanding', *Complete works*, p. 18.

orientation of philosophers against the *rule of masses* since Plato. But we should remember that Spinoza's *democraticness* is a claim towards avoiding the obstacles of the political powers that hinder his *power-to-think*. Does it mean that, for Spinoza, democracy is only a less bad political regime that is preferable to others? Certainly not, but we will discuss the implications of Spinoza's understanding of democracy later, in due order.

Spinoza's main concern with the notion of power is thereby associated with the power of the mind, of understanding. Yet, such power to understand (the intellect) should still be established. The Spinozist initial proposition is that, there are too many multilayered experiences in everyday life, which present an excess of affections, and people are generally inclined to select only the essential ones for themselves, subjectively, and filter out the rest. He observes that 'the less the mind understands while yet perceiving more things, the greater its capacity to form fictions; and the more it understands, the lesser its capacity to form fictions.'[51] It is crucial to note that for Spinoza the power of the mind is ambiguous—creating fictive ideas that are unconnected with the reality is also a mental capacity. This means to err is not the refutation of thinking, but a function of the human mind.

At the end of the 19th century, Nietzsche would succinctly evoke and describe three qualities every great philosopher ought to possess: Humility, chastity and poverty. These qualities operate in a quite different manner in the philosopher's humble life style than those structured by moral ideals and traditions. They are not merely adopted as a set of ascetic practices or traditional moral rules, but metaphysical devices that generate a particular *philosophical* will to power, through by which the philosopher constitutes himself and his philosophy. Through them, the philosopher shields himself from the attacks and blows, oppressions and persecutions of theologians, despots, oppressors, persecutors, and the like. They cast the attacker as targeting a poor person living in humility and chastity, and by this way, constitute a protective shield for the philosopher. The act of thinking that brings the powers of thought is shrouded with a certain form of pseudo-powerlessness in its appearance. Philosophers only ask for *toleration*, as in the famous legend of Diogenes of Sinope's encounter with Alexander the Great. Spinoza's *political philosophy* (if he has any) stems from a basic presupposition: The best political regime is the one that tolerates the philosophical (i.e. non-dogmatic) thinking the best—which makes Spinoza the *democratic philosopher* par excellence. Clearly, Spinoza does not believe that the philosopher (as a man living under the guidance of his reason) needs a political regime or State. Besides, no state power or political authority entirely rely on reason, every state requires obedience and unconditional commitment from its subjects.

In the Third Book of his Ethics, Spinoza is engaged in a series of definitions, axioms, postulates, propositions, and proofs about a most challenging subject matter: human affects and emotions. Spinoza distinguishes between sets of emotions—the *primary ones*, internally or externally determined emotions that refer to pleasure and pain, and emotions that are specifically related to the *desire*, which is the *essence of man*, according to Spinoza.

---

51   Spinoza, 'The Treatise on the Emendation of the Intellect', *Complete Works,* #58:3.

Spinoza's philosophy is *practical* in the Deleuzean sense of the term: It is a trajectory through which one can question everything pertaining our nature, and it is practical to the degree that it is largely concerned with pragmatics of affects and emotions. We can find in Spinoza the old idea of controlling ones passions in order to reach perfection and ethical life. We have major systems like Aristotle's ethics and Stoicism, which methodically perfected the theme, vividly describing the power of passions and the pretended ways to control or inhibit them. We can observe that Spinoza's program of ethics radically differs from every moral philosophy up to his time, and probably up to our times. Spinoza develops a unique theory of affects, and the way he describes them is profoundly different from any other treatment of affects and emotions.

Body as Site of Affections

We can find in Romanticism one of the major affirmations of the *affective* world. However, there are too many clichés about the nature of such affirmation of the individual and its problematic opposition to the objective world. We can at least distinguish two kinds of romanticism: the German and the British. (The French had been too absorbed in their new religion of Revolution, followed by the Napoleonic Wars, that they were not able to catch up with the romantic phenomenon, with the exception of a conservative reaction advocated by figures like Joseph de Maistre and de Bonald). I propose to call the German Romanticism as *major Romanticism*, and the British one as the *minor*. These variants correspond to two different kinds of affirmation and articulation of the individuals affective world—the German romantics through poetry and philosophy, and the British through the modern romantic novel, that is interestingly developed by the first women writers like Bronte and Jane Austen.

The German Romanticism cannot be identified with the *Strum und Drang* movement, or even with Fichte's *subjective individualism*, although its birthplace can be located there. Novalis formulates the determination of Romanticism rather decisively; there is no great historical event, a revolution, or a war, no matter how distant it is in time and space, whose pain or happiness we can perceive as *not our personal problem*. This is the way in which the Romantic intends to appropriate history and time—by absorbing the *event* into his individuality, into his *personal*, *private* world.

In Spinoza's works, particularly appearing in some of his letters, we can find an allusion to the idea of *automaton*, which is clearly derived from the Cartesian vision of animalistic body that includes that of human. What remains unclear however, is the way in which Spinoza poses the problem of body-machine, given the fact that he is opposed to the mind-body dualism that lies at the core of Descartes' philosophy. Again there is the evidence that neither Descartes nor Spinoza can be referred as the precursors of *mechanistic materialism*, which would be developed in the following century, in La Mettrie's famous essay *L'Homme-machine*.[52]

---

52   Julien Jean Offray de La Mettrie, *La Mettrie: Machine Man and Other Writings*, Ann Thomson (ed),
      Cambridge: Cambridge University Press, 1996.

This is not the case, however, when a modern sociologist like Georg Simmel was reviving the idea of automaton with a reference to the spirit—'the soul is not able to perceive but the difference of its present movement and stimulation from the ones of the one moment before [...] Our soul responds like an automate to any change in external conditions, and tends to become like those machines destined to keep productivity stable.'[53]

And when the Soviet avant-garde filmmaker Dziga Vertov expressed his preference to film the life of machines rather than *human beings*, this was not a futuristic praise to machinism and automation of life, but an interest in what would become affectively important in the machinic rythms of the modern world. His automaton is an apparatus, the camera, which could show what remains invisible to human eyes through a visual poetry.

These ideas centered around the notion of automaton display parallelisms, and even if we leave aside the historical magical aspects of the automates in Chinese and Arabic civilizations, it is impossible to protest against such deeply rooted notion in Western philosophy in the name of a lost spiritualism.

Spinoza provides us with a candid clue on the significance of the notion; we are not only automata, but *spiritual* automata. We cannot quickly associate the *spiritual* attribute with Spinoza's monism; it should remain as a metaphor of an important aspect of human behavior. Spinoza introduces the notion in the parts of Ethics where he is concerned with the formation of ideas, images, perceptions and affects. Spinoza's understanding of the ideas is manifested in this notion—in order to expose what an idea is, he needs to develop a doctrine of body through a series of lemmas and propositions. As Deleuze would argue later on, Spinoza proposes the body as a model for philosophy.

Ignoramus: A critique of the Unconscious

The adventurous relationship of mankind with the foundational notion of psychoanalysis, the *unconscious*, crystalizes in the question: *Has there been an unconscious before Freud?* It is possible to consider this problem in the intentional context of Claude Lévi-Strauss' answer we mentioned earlier—when asked about *the first structuralists*, Lévi-Strauss had the courage to reply, 'Caduveo natives'. We can even add an astonishingly commonsensical yet paradoxical question to the first one: *How could an unconscious thought be possible?* But we are not interested in repeating this question here; we rather intend to evaluate the notion of Unconscious critically in the way it appears and evolves in various sections and regions of the analytical literature, and posit the problem of *ignoramus* (which literally means '*we do not know*' and refers to *lack of knowledge* in Latin) against it. This very problem leads us to an active force, which the *cerebral thinking* inherent to Western civilization (Needham) necessarily perceives as its limit and the *threshold* of action. Ignoramus differs from the unconscious by not appear-

---

53   Georg Simmel, Bireysellik ve Kültür, trans. Tuncay Birkan, İstanbul: Metis Yayınlan, 2009 (1950). Editors note: The quote is translated to English from the Turkish source by Baker. For the English source, see: Georg Simmel, 'On Individuality and Social Forms', in Donald N. Levine (ed.), *Selected Writings*, Chicago: The University of Chicago Press, 1971.

ing as something to be unveiled or discovered. As such, it emerges as an active stimulant that increases and expands productive powers in all domains of life. The *unconscious* aspect of ignoramus only comes from its status of not *already-being-there*. This status is not derived from a Heideggerian *Vorhandenheit* (*present-at-hand*), nor from an a priori *unknown* out there, waiting to be discovered. The object of ignoramus remains as something to be actively produced, formed, and fabricated through intellectual engagement. In short, ignoramus is not simply the negotiation of ignorance and acceptance of not knowing, but on the contrary, the delineation of what is yet to be known. It is the necessary call for action and production that appears at the limits of consciousness qua consciousness, knowledge qua knowledge, and language qua language. In other words, ignoramus is not an a priori lack of knowledge; it is the state that precedes the acquirement of knowledge, succeeded by action.

Therefore, we will attempt to establish a Spinozist problematization of the *unconscious* based on the notion of *ignoramus*, against the psychoanalytic *unconscious*. Ignoramus does not refer to unexplainable, or the unknown in this sense, it is neither the *incapacity* or *failure* of reason. On the contrary, it is an active force that produces new experiences, desires, and values. From this perspective, what always *negates the negation* is not the content of unconscious that is categorically marked as a *lack* in the psychoanalytic world view, but the generative force of ignoramus.

Thereby, now we need to invert a series of psychoanalytical arguments and rationalizations, as well as the substance of certain psychoanalytic categories. We can begin by looking back on the great *discoveries* of psychoanalysis that compose its success story: The Oedipus complex, Desire, Instinct and Repression... Oedipus complex is like a *Zwangsneurose*, an *idée fixe* that has captured the entire theory, practice and culture of psychoanalysis. It is what demotes psychoanalysis to an assimilating normalization process, and a therapeutic practice restoring the comforts of the domestic sphere. It is evident that a *complex* always incorporates an *imposition*, even an *exigency*. But psychoanalysis will still continue to prioritize its *solution*, recuperate the individual, or assist her/his formation as an adult into the domestic milieu. Today it becomes increasingly more difficult to distinguish between the goals of institutionalized psychiatry as bio-political practice and psychoanalysis as a scientific world-view.

The famous and strange assumption of *castration anxiety* that accompanies Oedipus complex functions as a Trojan horse within psychoanalysis. While proving that psychoanalytic theory and its metapsychology fails to develop a proper idea of the human body, it also characterizes human desire with anthropomorphic and sexist values. Seen from its lens, desire is constituted around a lack, deprivation, absence, or merely emptiness. Satisfaction, the fulfillment of desire, is conceived as its finalization, and at the same time, its absence. In order to posit this, psychoanalysis refers to the categories of *phantasm* and of the *imaginary*, which it disposes under the authority of the totalizing Law defined as symbolic, and regulating the limits between the language and the imaginary. Signifying categories (such as the phallus and the name of father) capture the *real*, as well as the *imaginary* and the already broken apart *symbolic*, into the wider semantic web that surrounds them. Yet, the fundamental question remains unanswered: What to do with these categories—with language, sexuality, labour, and desire in general?

By discarding practical necessities, psychoanalytic theory and culture tend to reproduce the existing relations of family and socio-economic institutions in general, and even the deterministic logic of servitude. Even in its most radical and critical forms (such as Lacan and his followers, French feminism, and post-colonial studies literature) psychoanalysis and other cultural theories address such servitude as a critical observation. Yet, as Adorno elegantly postulates, the power of *criticism* is directly proportional to the power of what it aims to criticize. Thus, such critical observation is never enough to reconstruct, reinterpret, or *deconstruct* symbolic orders in itself. In other words, merely critical approaches are not enough to constitute the logic action that *ignoramus* points to. All that can be achieved by *criticism* is to rely on theoretical and critical foundations, which leads to perpetual postponement of contacting with what lies beyond the domain of theoretical discourse. Criticism is bounded by the faith of its object, whether it adopts psychoanalytic or Marxist framework in its methodology. Once deconstruction is bounded by *structures*, and *intertextuality* by the *texts* they intend to criticize, the criticism these develop will eventually have to comply with their theoretical norms, which impose upon them to remain in the same registers of discourse. Therefore, the communication of these registers with others, their mixture, contamination, recombination, and hybridization (instead of synthesis) has to be facilitated. In other words, a multiplicity of active connections has to be established among these domains.

We will refrain ourselves from listing an account of the detriments caused by the exclusion of *reality* from psychoanalysis here. But we have to note that the most detrimental among these is the withdrawal from the fact that *real* is something to be produced. Symbolic and imaginary are also spheres that have to be produced. The cinematographic apparatus was aware of this necessity more than psychoanalysis: The unconscious in cinema only appears when it is created; it refuses to remain putative. Return of the *production* as such should not be perceived as the same with those modest attempts of establishing a fusion or marriage between psychoanalysis and Marxism. In our view, it is impossible, if not futile, to establish such a union as if each theory would complement to the other by fulfilling what it neglects. Such union could only be possible by introducing production into the unconscious, and the non-purposeful desire into the actual production relations. And what essentially lacks in Freudian psychoanalysis is precisely such conception of desire.

Psychoanalysis has brought its own demise (both theoretically and practically) already in its early beginnings by conceiving desire as lack or absence. Theoretically, some of its fundamental concepts, such as Oedipus, castration, narcissistic self (or *subjectivity*), inevitably jeopardizes some of its central thematics, such as Pleasure Principle and Reality Principle. It is quite possible to consider pre-Oedipal and post-Oedipal societies or cultures today. Even the rebellion of a single individual among all those maddened by the civilization (Nietzsche, Artaud) signifies that the possible should not be left to be defined by social boundaries and limitations. These societies and cultures (such as *primitive* societies, the East, deviant subcultural formations) can operate both at the individual levels (*madness* and psychosis) and in collective, social scale. It seems sufficient to psychoanalyze religious sects and communities themselves today, rather than the individuals or terrorist plots. When the fog of ideological phantasies and blindness is removed, in every instance we see that *group phantasies* tend to become much more important than individual *perversions* and phantasies.

And, at the level of individuals, especially in the artistic-aesthetic domain, phantasies belong to certain creative acts. We can take Gabriel Tarde's main thesis further, and suggest that the individual's phantasy is the creation of the real, an inter-cerebral movement towards the creation of something new—whether it is a dream, an image, or a work of art. Yet, the individual does not exist by itself, there are always *individuals*. Even Oedipus appears to be a badly drawn misunderstanding, or a phantasy of Dr. Freud. Although Freud faithfully believed in the Oedipus myth, he failed to interpret it adequately. For Ancient Greeks myth did not involve a question of belief. While the myth was tied to a tragedy, Freud's conception of Oedipus has never been *tragic*, since it purported to reproduce family settings in an age and geography that was anachronistically different from those of the Greeks. For Deleuze and Guattari the result had been the imperialism and colonialism of the Oedipus, under its pretense to be *universal*.

The privileged notions of psychoanalysis seem to be *narcissism* and *ego ideals* today. These are at least clarified in technical details in their description and more adequately contain the entire empirical domain of psychoanalytic within themselves. Yet, the hopes of reforming or *revolutionizing* the psychoanalysis through these studies still seem to be futile, as they were already aborted, if not distorted, conceptions. Psychoanalysis continues to treat narcissism as a *primordial state*. Thus, its apparition in any individual is perceived as a case of *regression*, a withdrawal from the world. In Freud's writings, narcissism constitutes the foundation of unconscious *resistance* against the therapy attempts. It is the resisting unconscious force against the transfer. From this perspective, *narcissism* is first *individualized*, and then reflected to the historical-societal level, to the proper domain it belongs to. This is truly an extremely long détour. One could as well admit from the beginning that subjectivity is not *information*, something *already given*, but something that is *produced* by institutions like religion, family, and other disciplinary institutions, or by mass communications, or, more deeply, by economic and social structures. This means that psychoanalysis leaves notions such as narcissism or *phantasm* without real substance and correspondence.

Nothing is absent in psychoanalytical theory as the *body*, as psychoanalysis already replaces the body with incorporeal substances or phenomena such as the *ego-ideal* or the *imago*, especially in Lacan, but also in in Freud. One can already feel how any inquiry about this *primordial self* could ultimately destroy the fundamental tenets of psychoanalysis—such as Deleuze and Guattari's discussion towards the notion of *body without organs*, or, first and foremost, the *theater of cruelty* of Antonin Artaud. This is because the *narcissism* in psycho-analysis is not chronologically a *prior* state, but rather a state that is yet to come, belonging to an indeterminate future.

The invention of the unconscious needs to be acknowledged as the fundamental merit of psychoanalysis. Yet this success has subsequently been voided or negated. The unconscious is not something to be deciphered, like a cuneiform tablet, or a divine scripture to be inter-preted. It is especially never an *obscure world*. It should first be cleansed from every Platonic representation as such, and thereby re-conceptualized as an active, creative ignoramus in the service of knowledge, art and philosophy, that remains to be reshaped by them. Yet, the short-coming of the psychoanalysis, along with a series of prejudices, institute major theoretical and practical obstacles against such re-interpretation. These obstacles (or rather *aporias*), neglect, distort or repress actual human experiences, and prevent us from generate the *arts of life*: the arts of love, death, and veracity—in short, the basic arts of the ignoramus and its operations.

Is it possible to *love* through psychoanalysis? This rather bizarre question reflects the practical limits of the experiential merits of psychoanalytic theory and practice. Retorting to sexuality as a predetermined moment, psychoanalysis has nevertheless tried to proceed from its invaluable *family romance* towards *love affair*. But such passage corresponds to a dislocation; certain problematic areas of interest for psychoanalysis—especially literary and art criticism—emerges with these *romantic* references. The intended scope of psychoanalysis (an analysis of the psyche and a technique for therapy) now expands beyond its limits. As a result, semiotic and cultural studies suffer from such psychoanalytical imperialism today. While whether analytical categories could ever penetrate the depths of such areas remains to be a valid question, it seems impossible to ascertain whether such *depths* really exist. Should we believe that the complexity of a literary character is the same with the complexity of a real person? And now psychoanalysis, with a rather fraudulent coup de force, turns towards what is assumed to be the psychic life of the *artistic creator*—as evident from Freud's studies of Dostoyevsky and Leonardo da Vinci. The *creator* is still isolated from his or her real life conditions (in other words, his own *biography*), condemned to the family romance of the Oedipal triangle, and so-called sublimation response. The critical point is whether such *creative genius* really exists. Does a writer like Proust really needs to be *psychoanalytically* interpreted in order to engage with the domain of mundane social experiences, and develop his themes towards a *love affair* outside the family context? And, against the claim that analytical categories can penetrate the deeper truths that are unconsciously present in literature, art, or cinema, we can argue that there are no such deeper levels in a text, a painting, or a film, for they still simply remain as artifacts—and this is the most basic truth we can reach. That is why psychoanalysis eventually turns towards to artists psyche in a swindling maneuver, as in the case of Freud's studies of Leonardo da Vinci and Dostoyevsky. And even so, the *creator* here still has to be assimilated into the Oedipal circle (or rather *triangle*) and sterilized from everything that concretely belong to artist's reality and her/his creative process. It is possible to suggest that the creative process is essential, prior to the psychic state of the artist that embeds process of *sublimation* as a vehicle. Thus the Proustian *love affair* that leads to the outside of family would never need psychoanalysis for being interpreted. It is both an analytics of love and a virtual expression, which we call *life-experience*. Freud's fin-de-siècle cabinet is not superior to Proust's language for analyzing the affective, and even the cognitive life. This is because psychoanalysis tends to reduce affective relations to purely psychic facts or events, which refers to deeper levels of the psyche, to *sexual* and *erotic* experiences that are supposed to be hidden, to be repressed in whatever depths of the human life. Finally, although it had to begin with the interpretation of dreams (as we mentioned, the *Traumdeutung* is perceived as the *royal road* towards the unconscious) and no other practical purpose except the intended therapy, psychoanalysis has never been able to help us to *see our own dreams*. Dreams, we believe, are creative instances of the mind, even when they are analyzed psychoanalytically.

4. WHAT IS AN IMAGE?

Affects and Images

When the psychoanalyst Krafft-Ebing coined the term *sadomasochism* at the beginning of the 20th century in reference to a set of phenomena concerned with certain types of perversions, he was certainly confused about the complexity of human life. His assumption was that *as soon as sadist appears, a masochist emerges to match him* and *whenever there is a masochist, a sadist comes to enjoy...* His master Freud, too, was convinced of a *parallelism* between two attitudes, of the alternating investment of perverse desire in each. Psychoanalysts seemed to be relying upon their *rational* analysis and their meticulous observation of the each psychological type, which results in the theoretical coupling of the two *personality* types. Such theoretical coupling obviously overlooked an entire domain of concrete situations in which such set of phenomena has been invested, and instead, followed the supply and demand rationality of the market model. The masters of psychoanalysis did not read properly the authors they referred to in each case, namely, Marquis de Sade and Leopold von Sacher-Masoch. They were unaware of the fact that, while both were referring to a *landscape of desire and pleasure*, they had quite different viewpoints in these matters. The language of Marquis de Sade, declared by some as the *greatest writer in French language*, was involved in *mise en abyme*[1]; for him writing substituted performing.[2] A Freudian can see here a kind of *sublimation* of a perverse desire, but for our present purpose we should rather invoke a literal device, an absolute literary apparatus invested by Sade in the domain of *political economy* of desire. This was the age of the *political economies* of Adam Smith and David Ricardo, and of the constitution of the modern Subject by Descartes and Kant. Hence, there is *politics* and *economy* in Sade. On the register of *politics*, Sade was able to find a blind spot in the cogito, in the *thinking subject*, as opposed to the body and its passions, as the ultimate philosophical accomplishment of Christian morality. He was able to say 'if you are positing the thought and the thinking subject as a will and a morality which disowns the body, its world of pleasures and pains, its desires altogether, then I can enjoy what you have disowned [...] and no one could impede my right to do this...'[3] If the body becomes an object of Will, one can easily go further, and appropriate it at will, individually or collectively (such as the old idea of collectivization of women). Sade pushed the pure idea of cogito further and further to the degree that it turned against its inventors: he adopted a vigorous *objective* language in describing the infamous scenes of torture and pleasure,

---

1   Editors Note: *Mise en abyme* (French for 'put in the abyss') is a term for a self-reflexive repetition in a text. 'The term has been taken up in deconstructive criticism for the occasional glimpses of the 'solving emptiness' that underlies the endless free-play of meanings in words, the revelations of an abyss of nothingness which is constantly covered and uncovered by the signs themselves.' Gray, M., A Dictionary of Literary Terms, London: Longman, 1992, p. 181.
2   See: Simone de Beauvoir, *Must we burn Sade?*, trans. Annette Michelson, Paris: Olympia Press, 2015, (1951-52).
     See also: Annie Le Brun, *Soudain d'un bloc d'abime Sade*, Paris: Ed. Pauvert, 1986.
3   Marquis de Sade, *L'Histoire de Juliette, ou les Prospérités du vice*, Paris, 1797. Translated from Turkish by Ulus Baker: Marquis de Sade, *Juliette Birinci Kitap: Erdemsizliğe Övgü*, trans. Münire Yılmazer, İstanbul: Chivi Yayınevi, 2003.

a purely descriptive language taking the suffering bodies as objects. It is true, he wrote through *affects*, but these were the affects of a visual lexicon, of pornography of the visual, of the flesh under torture claiming a violent death.

The writing of Sacher-Masoch, on the other hand, is registered to the language of subjectivity, the body is no longer an object, and the scene is no longer visual: All turns into experimentation of the self, of the powers of one's body, through a series of *contracts* made vigorously with the mistress, who profits in turn by experiencing her own powers. It is far from evident that the masochist subject *enjoys* being tortured or suffering, as the popular idea goes, no less than a sadist *enjoys* the suffering of the other. Masochism is putting one's body to the service of the other, but in order to do this, the masochist should make an experiment to discover the limits of the transgression, and every transgression is an excess of certain limits in itself.

It seems like the psychoanalysts (Krafft-Ebing, Freud, and Havelock Ellis—the liberal in matters of perversion) are entirely neglecting the substance and the rationale of Sade and Sacher-Masoch's writings, and notably the extent that they were written in the language of affects, just like Spinoza's *Ethica*. In this sense, Foucault is right when he refers in his *L'Histoire de la folie à l'âge classique*[4] to the *calm and cold language* of Sade Was he trying, like Spinoza in his *Ethica*, to explain the nature of human affects and emotions just like figures, lines, planes, and volumes? Are there any parallelisms between Sade's writings and the *politics* of Machiavelli—who was seeking to ground his notion of political power in the affections of the body politic? Clearly, Sade believes and shows how man is a prisoner of the *theatre of his body*. He says *theatre* since he ultimately disagrees with an apparently similar attitude in Christianity: The body as the prison of soul. The body, or the extension, becomes a spectacle when, in parallel, one recognizes how *the true happiness of man is in his imagination*.[5] His spectacle of horrors is designed to show how we can neither change the way our organs affect each other, nor the laws governing our feelings.

We said that Sade's was a *political economy*: The birth of the political economy, through the works of the contemporaries of Sade, Adam Smith and David Ricardo later, was not far from a new kind of interrogation of the sources of happiness and pleasure. And the libertinage claimed by Sade (he was insisting that he was neither a monster, nor a criminal, but just a libertine) has its costs. The *normal*, *orderly*, and *domestic* life of pleasure was based on the foundational assumption that pleasure was the direct outcome of a normal sexual act. It was nothing but a by-product, a surplus of normal sexual intercourse. What distinguishes perversion is nothing but the sole fact that, here, the pleasure should be a costly outcome of a search for its own sake, and that it should be paid: This is why one has to invest for pleasure—mistresses, castles, instruments, and guardians... There is an entire political economy of libertinage, just like the investment of capital in manufactures, in which the *multidimensional pervert* becomes the *bourgeois* of the *libidinal economic order*. This situation perfectly fits to what George Bataille referred with his concept of *dépense*: The transgres-

---

4   Michel Foucault, *Folie et déraison: histoire de la folie à l'âge classique.*
5   Sade, *Histoire de Juliette: ou les prosperites du vice.*

sion appears when an affect like pleasure is relocated outside of the *exchange cycle*, as an end in itself rather than just a *natural* by-product of the morally approved norms of mating.

In this context, we have to show, first, how the role of affects in social life is generally mis-interpreted by social sciences, and particularly by psychoanalysis and, second, how these sadomasochistic experiences relate to images and visions. Both spheres can generate their own *pornographic* images, yet there are two different kinds of images, two different, but not opposite visions. It is easy to acknowledge fluctuating and accidental world of *fantasies*, but without the concrete images through which these fantasies are connected, the word explains nothing. The elements of pornography are so tangible when the content is expressed in images that everyone can perceive and understand at first sight. We have an entire cinema of erotic images, for instance, from Pier Paolo Pasolini's most direct and explicit Salo, to Robert Bresson, a good Catholic filmmaker's works. In Bresson's *Les Anges du péché* (Angels of Sin, 1943), we can find a visual regime of erotomanic value involved in the sight of a coquette girl praying with somehow ironic gestures, suddenly finding herself under rain. She utters an erotic 'Oh!', which seemingly has nothing to do with the context (as Bresson deploys alternative use of sounds in his cinema) but everything is contained within the image. The metaphor is so powerful that its significance reaches beyond the films plot—the girl is an atheist Résistante, temporarily forced to take asylum in a monastery where she gets close to a nun with some degree of sexual attraction, who is rather devoted to her passionate mission. When invited to pray, through the famous Pascalian motto *'on your knees, pray, you will certainly believe'*, the girl accepts just to be polite to her host, and suddenly, the rain pours ironically. But the image of Bresson crystallizes the entire Christian problem of faith: With drops of water on her cheeks, and the virgins great passion towards the fecundation of the God, centuries of religious history and experience become condensed in one second, in one image. Bresson is far ahead than any sociologist of his time in expressing the nature of faith.

In a similar fashion, Klossowski, the famous pornographer-painter, performs the opposite in his literature, and moves from a pornographic image to a theology of the soul. Through a series of novels, paintings, philosophical essays, Pierre Klossowski develops a model of *identity* and the *disruption of identity*. In his historical novel *Le Baphomet*,[6] he transforms the historical legend of the Templar Knights into a myth 'with a Baroque sumptuosity'.[7] This is a tragicomic situation of the eternal return, when fictitiously applied to *real* individuals, to existing souls, who are *assimilated into cycles of metempsychosis* in a chaotic fashion. Jacques de Molay, the legendary Grand Master of Templars is haunted by the soul of Saint Theresa, while meditating in his cellar. After his initial horror subsides, he complains that his mission in this world is challenged by the fact that *there are too many called, and only a few elected* in these times of great disturbance – wars, plagues, and violent crimes. *What thinks our Lord about this?* The amount of death exceeds that of the births, and the dead souls start pillaging each others left behind bodies in a state of total chaos. As the Day of Judgement is postponed every new century *the most ancient souls are haunting the most*

---

6   Pierre Klossowski, *The Baphomet,* Colorado: Eridanos Press, Inc., 1988.
7   Maurice Blanchot, *L'amitié*. Paris: Gallimard, 1971.

recent ones, and through mixtures by affinities, they compete with each other for haunting the bodies, which results in multiple souls occupying the same body and mix into each other; *and hence, two or three of them, mutually complicated.*

To his tremendous astonishment, the soul of Saint Theresa undertakes a despairing speech instead of consoling him: *O, Grand Master of Templars!* She does not haunt him for debasing his confidence in the divine mission of him and his brothers. But a *cycle of events* occurred beyond this world. His mission is not only difficult, but impossible: The quota of the selected is full. This means that, by this time, the human race has changed its essence. *'It is no longer damnable nor can be sanctified.'* His mind is troubled by such an infinite burst of chaotic, unidentifiable mixtures of souls –the damned are inextricably mixed with the most wise. *'So heavy is the weight of these expired souls that it upsets the equilibrium of the spheres.'* [8] A prodigious amount of spirits are turning onto themselves in vain, and further, amalgams of not only two or three but five, six or more of them strive to enter into a single uterus to reach and infiltrate the embryo, and exert their power of discharging their anterior sins and restore their virtue in an exuberant and tumultuous fashion. And it appears that even she herself, a saint, is among these chaotic *turba* (crowd) of souls. appealed by a young theologian many times to haunt his cupid nights long after her death, she has already entered into a series of bodies, or shared the same body with five, six other souls.

Klossowski offers a profound understanding of religious sentiments here, a Spinozist insight into the *sources* of religious feelings; one needs the assumption that God and the Day of Judgement exist in order to maintain the integrity of the soul, the individuality and the preservation of the self even after death. God is the ultimate horizon that makes possible the feelings of self and identity. A Dostoyevskian theme is evidently present in *Le Baphomet*: if God doesn't exist, all is permitted.

There is one of the oldest theological problems here: Klossowski once again faces the Nietzschean problematic—or challenge: 'God is dead!', Nietzsche said, and that was his *news*, rather than his opinion or a declaration. In the domain of religious sentiments, a central theme or motivation is present: Self requires a responsibility, and its perseverance could only be possible through the assumption of the presence of God. Hence, Klossowski can interpret the Turin period of Nietzsche—to whom he dedicates his book *Nietzsche et le cercle vicieux* (*Nietzsche and the Vicious Circle*—not towards his incidental *madness*, but as a logical consequence of his entire philosophical position: *'I am all personal nouns of history!'*, Nietzsche wrote to Jacob Burckhardt, which means that after the death of God, there is no longer any *self* or identity. As Klossowski puts it, individuality can be conceived as a presupposition of an order and identification with the Self, over space and time. Yet, in another possible conception of individuality, one can perceive a constant variation that traverses through all possible circles of an undetermined zone; a center of indetermination as the trajectory of the self and consciousness.[9] This defines an excess of individuality, expressed in time and, occasionally, in the space of Klossowski's writing—he adopts in *Le Baphomet* a style that reveal

---

8   Klossowski, *The Baphomet,* p. 40.
9   Klossowski, *The Baphomet.*

the *breaths*, their occasional concentrations and ramifications, and a language of rumors, as Foucault puts it.[10] The breaths are like the oscillations of non-substantial particles. Only *images*, rather than words (even when words can reveal images in literature) can afford such oscillations and zones of indetermination. Modern literature turns into a critique of the notions of individuality and identity.

One could attempt, instead of writing on it, to film the Baphomet of Klossowski, and this could be the best definition of *montage-thought*, where distances disappear, and things become detached from each other. This could be the proper magic of cinema, but we rather believe that cinema can accomplish further than fiction. The strength of the image is in its purity, and cinema sustains such purity by detaching the images from words and even actions. Laura Mulvey has tried to show the sadistic-voyeuristic appeal of the cinema, but only in *second rate* films, not in the works of great filmmakers. This is an error inherent to entire film criticism and theory, be it based on narratological, linguistic, feminist or psychoanalytical theories.

Borges: A Theory of Treason and Betrayal

Borges' traitors are conspirators. Naturally, they go way beyond the common clichés of popular detective literature. But the conspiracies they set up evoke some kind of well-cal-culated *fraudulence*, which cannot be defined as *malice* right away. They appear before us sometimes as Pampa's machos, sometimes as sinister members of an international and cosmopolitan civilization in the age of world wars. Their fraud is not the small man's every-day cheats; they belong to a civilization that is reined by chaos, by labyrinths and *gardens of forking paths*: 'I already see people surrendering themselves to new treasons everyday, in the way that only the outlaws and the soldiers will remain in the end.' (Garden of Forking Paths) In Borges's taxonomy, one cannot find small *mischief*, *forgivable* minor everyday conspiracies, ordinary *betrayals* of domestic disputes, children who tie things to cats' tails, or the low indignation and resentment that stems from the *herd being* Nietzsche points at. Our very wise author is not even able to distinguish the difference between betrayal and treason. The reason for that is the way he conceives his scoundrels like those of Poe's, as if they are *heroes*, as if they are actors who are most likely to succeed as long as they do whatever it takes while traversing the unforeseeable labyrinths designed by a superior, anonymous and impersonal intelligence. For him, the design of betrayal has to work in a geometric manner: *more geometrico*. Betrayal is acted out like moves on a chess board, and conforms to only one type in the *endlessness* of the labyrinth: 'He who is to perform a horrendous act should imagine to himself that it is already done, should impose upon himself a future as irrevocable as the past.' (Garden of Forking Paths) As such, his interpretation of Leibniz's *endlessness* is indexed to time. Each story's ending can only be possible with the emergence of a pure and absolute betrayal. No questions will remain unanswered, and yet, in front of the skillfully mastered constitutive intelligence of betrayal, a sad admiration will leave its bitter taste on one's palate. The infamy of Borges is not about execution; it is a form of iniquity that refers to innovation on the one hand, and a universal notion of humanity on the other: 'Whatever

---

10   Michel Foucault, 'The Prose of Actaeon', in Pierre Klossowski, *The Baphomet,* Eridanos Press, Hygiene, Colorado: 1988 *(originally published in N.R.F. No. 135, Editions Gallimard 1964, Paris)**

one man does, it is as though all men did it. That is why it is not unfair that a single act of disobedience in a garden should contaminate all humanity; that is why it is not unfair that a single Jew's crucifixion should be enough to save it' (*The Shape of the Sword*). In this way, there is no difference left between the *scam* that is set forth by the abuse of people's positions in social hierarchy, and the petit fraud of a street seller. Of course, Borges does not pick his scoundrels only from the upper classes: Men and women in the street can also take their place among the famous personalities of the history of infamy. But only on one condition-- forcing the breaches of our common conceptions of crime, treason always has to pass through the labyrinths of a conspiracy, twisting and branching out endlessly, and it has to be able to create a spectacular show of power that can always convey the direction of the accusation and hatred towards the disadvantage of its actual victims. Indeed, at a certain moment, in the very labyrinth he builds with the means of literature, Borges comes face to face with the iniquity he constructs, but only to become its counterpart. 'The idea that history might have copied history is mind-boggling enough; that history should copy literature is inconceivable' (*The Traitor and The Hero*). The end of the story for the traitor is this moment of confrontation and equalization. After all, isn't the story of treason as a narrative a fiction produced by the author? *The disappearance of the author behind his own narrative*, which has been attributed to modern fiction, will appear at the finitude of the long forking paths, and thus surrender itself to the Aristotelian catharsis of affections relating to crime, antipathy and hatred.

Therefore, *A Universal History of Iniquity*, which is among his early works, is neither *universal*, nor *historical* enough. First of all, it excludes the demonic, satanic kind of infamy that we find in the literature of the Middle Ages. As Klossowski demonstrates, *Satan was never a salesman of illusions* or an *illusionist* himself. Quite the contrary, he was a composer, an artisan who blended *mixtures* and *impurities* against the *pure and clean*, against the notion of *beauty* as *perfection*, as *good*, as *truth*, as *essence*, a solely productive force against the despotism of God and his right of possession over the universe. But this productive activity was achieved through *spiritual* materials; it would not be possible for Satan to produce a darkness of the soul that had not already been there. Whereas for Borges, 'No one is someone; a single immortal man is all men. Like Cornelius Agrippa, I am god, hero, philosopher, demon, and world—which is a long-winded way of saying that I am not' (*Immortal*).

Gilles de Rais, or *Blue Beard*, or increasingly *Count Dracula*, closed communities and *compagnonnages*[11], appeared as nothing but peasant cultures against the artisan cults that were organized within secret brotherhoods. That is the source of their phoniness and epic superficialities. But the type of *iniquity* Borges presents takes certain elements from these particular kind of *infamies* that most cultures were boiling with in the Middle Ages, and further, modernizes and redeploys them. Borges desires the traitor he presents to appear in a *devilish* outlook as well. Albeit, in the way that any kind of *illusion* can be perceived as absolutely *real*, an overarching theme that surrounds his work reaches its moment of fulfillment precisely in the *description of the infamy*. Borges's labyrinth is never *endless*.

---

11   Editors Note: *Compagnonnage* is a form of apprenticeship by which a person is trained under the
      supervision of a community.

Yet, there were people who were able to discover an utterly profound kind of treason, one that Borges never wanted to understand and include in his *universal* history of infamy, not only in *modern literature* but also in the heart of modern ways of life: These are the kind of traitors that appear in Gogol's, Brecht's, Kafka's and Foucault's writings. Their difference lies in the fact that their authors never mark them as *traitors*. The sincerity of these grim reapers keeps them apart from all kinds of *demonic* associations, explosive conspiracies and malevolent designs. They appear as simple civil servants, and find '[their] way ahead' through the cracks in the screen of a collapsing society.

Sinisterness also died with God, and its absence breeds a *traitor* who appears to be some-one else. That is why it is not Dostoyevsky, whose protagonists operate under the shadow of the *Big Boss*, but Gogol, who really paved the way to Musil's *The Man Without Qualities*. Gogol's traitor is almost the antidote to the quirkiness of the Hegelian history of the *big boss* (in Russia even Hegel could be unbelievably vulgarized): 'A history of the little man and his innocent betrayals...' The main formula of the Gogolist traitor becomes most definitely visible in *The Inspector*. The fake inspector puts on his *civil servant* disguise to gain a few provisional benefits (such as flirting with girls, and yelling at and humiliating his subordinates) which he would never otherwise enjoy. The surrender of the entire elite of the village to this illusion demonstrates how a very special kind of *mutualism* is the necessary condition of betrayal. He is similar to what Foucault introduces as the nameless heroes of a modern security apparatus, such as the police stooge on the corner, or the superintendent of the building: He is neither the possessor of power, nor its victim; always in between, he becomes its main pillar. Far from being intoxicating, this particular form of power cannot even be *possessed*. This type of power appears in the domesticity of the household, among the neighbors, in the community, in every corner of everyday life. Those ordinary people in every corner, no matter how much they desire to be insignificant and live without any *political identities*, cannot help but become the main *pillars* of authority. That is what Kafka's formula precisely tells us: *Every order a father gives to his son carries a thousand death sentences*.

Love and Hate: Memory Images and Conjured Images

Nature is the domain of the *excess*, which is considered as one of the greatest sins for human beings. We can find such a landscape in *The Waves* of Virginia Woolf, with the image of ocean's waves biting the beach since the time immemorial: a new image of eternity, an introduction of the cosmic into the literature. Woolf needs to write through images, rather than words and symbols; the waves are presented as intensities, or rhythms expressed in her unprecedented *modern* style. A woman should write differently, not in the order of the traditional literature—which she could have done easily since literature can be adopted in its form and structure.[12] This *excess* belongs to Nature, in direct contradiction with the notion of modesty that dominates most religions. The expansion of multiplicities defying the crude conception of individuality occurs in the image of a rain that is not destined to preserve man in this world. The world is no longer the land which has been *promised* to

---

12   Virginia Woolf, 'The waves', *Collected Novels of Virginia Woolf*, London: Palgrave Macmillan 1992, (1932), pp. 335-508.

man by his Lord. From the mans point of view, the Nature is expressed as an *excess*. If we can talk about the *excesses* over nature today, we are responsible as the mankind; this is not only a result of our economic and social modernization, ie. the entire transformation of the city landscape, but also a result of a function inherent to modern literature: the excess of the form, of the rhythm over the content. One writes, composes, or films with the predominance of the *form*, and the form could be filled with any content, although it is not necessary to fill it at all. The classical writing relies upon a form which more or less strictly defines how the content will fill it. In modern literature, on the other hand, the form is not to be filled; it is not necessary to fill it with this or that content. Modernism can never do without a degree of formalism, while Formalism as a movement is nothing but a particular extremist interpretation of it. This is simply the essence of the modern cinema which relies upon a kind of formalism that remains only *stylistic*, as in the case of Bresson who formally denies the coincidence between the hearing and seeing (and not seeing). We may also talk about the extravagant formalism of Tarkovsky in his colloquial, quite personal films: One doesn't need to see in order to understand, and this is especially true when one sees things s/he cannot understand. And this is not simply the effect of the so-called *off-screen* (the French hors-champs is a better term, by the way); it is rather the way in which cinema can formally create images whose meanings are different from what is visible in them every time. But this is also the *transcendental* dimension of the image, since it leaves nothing at its outside. Sokurov's *photographic* cinema is an example: The image contains everything but seeing it requires entering almost into a state of trance afforded by the film's extremely slow rhythm. During the agony of the mother (in Sokurov's Mother and Son),[13] a single movement of the eyes of the dying mother comes with a spectacular violence. This is why images are necessarily *affective* in the Spinozist sense of the concept. In every one of them, the whole universe is already present.

Spinoza's conception of *image* is classical, as it has nothing to do with our preoccupations with the status of images in modern life. Yet, the way he associates images with their causes, and relates them to the power of affects and emotions, is unique in the history of philosophy. The role of the images in his analysis of affects and emotions, especially in the case of *love* and *hatred*, is also unique in regards to the powerful insights involved in his Ethica: Love is the capacity of the mind to *imagine* the things which are not present. Hate, on the other hand, is rather more likely to be a matter of *memory*. While the explicit definitions of Love and Hatred he provides in the 3rd Book of Ethics are so tightly connected to each other, we should note a profound difference between these two emotions; Love is pleasure accompanied with the image of an external cause, whereas Hate is pain again accompanied with the image of an external cause. It is evident that even animals, as relatively simply organized beings can have pleasure and pain as the two fundamental poles of emotions defined as the increase and decrease in their power to act, and in their level of wholeness. But this does not mean that they can have more complex affects of Love and Hate. Such affections remain as the capacity of highly complex individuals and organisms. Surely Love is nothing but pleasure, a passage from a lower degree of completeness to a higher level, and Hate is the opposite. But they involve complex phenomena such as memory and imagination, the

---

13   *Mother and Son* (dir. Aleksandr Sokurov, 1997).

capacity to produce images and remembrances, so that probably only human beings and complex bodies (crowds, societies etc.) are capable of being affected by them. The exact definitions of Love and Hate, for the sake of precision, are: 'Amor est laetitia, concomitante idea causae externae' (Love is Pleasure, accompanied by the idea of an external cause) and 'odium est tristitia, concomitante idea causae externae' (Hate is Sadness accompanied by the idea of an external cause).[14] Spinoza clearly uses the term *idea* (which are defined as the traces of the affections of bodies by other bodies), but the term also comprises the images essentially, since there are no ideas without images. As human beings, we have minds (*mens*) sophisticated enough to be able to form complexly structured images, and these images can be formed in perpetual variations: A peasant, Spinoza will say, seeing horse tracks shoe associates it with the images of cultivation, of the harvest, while a soldier who sees the same horse tracks will think of war chariots and the like. Images are never as neutral as they seem to be. They are perspectival and, moreover, they generate *affects* in our souls. This means that as individuals we are *unique*, and everyone is affected by passions in his own way in a series of encounters with her/his environment. In Spinozist doctrine of Love and Hate, all depends on the ability of *containing the images*.

Is it possible to interpret this towards two kinds of *images* being present in Spinoza's philosophy—*memory images* and *conjured images*? For the moment, we have to be precise: The connection between Love and the preservation of images is rather evident, due to the principle of self-preservation (conatus transposed into the human life); we necessarily tend to prolong an enjoyable stimulation as much as possible. But this stimulation remains more or less ambiguous, since our affections not only involve the stimulated parts of our body, but also the image of the external object. Suppose that the object disappears and the image of this object is preserved in us for a period of time. There is also another possibility: An accidental association can arouse in us the image of thing that has been disappeared since long. The corresponding joy will survive in us for an indefinite period of time, the corresponding image does not: The image can be distorted by other images encountered afterwards, since the images of present things are always more vivid than the images of past things. We may have many present images, which exclude the presence of the thing whose image had affected us with joy in the past. This means that the joy caused by the image of the past object will decrease. But a decrease of joy is nothing but a sadness, which attacks our conatus and forces it to revive the enjoyable image. Our desire is invested in the image of this object now, similar to Freudian *cathexis*[15] of the libidinal energy, and this will be an almost unconditional attachment. Such a positive polarization is called *Love* by Spinoza.

If Love is related with the capacity to imagine, Hate is associated with the Memory in the same way. When we are affected by a painful image, our conatus resists to it as we try to eliminate the pain. This means that we try to restore the state of our lives before the apparition of the painful object enters to it. But this previous state was characterized by the presence of another set of images, that constitute another ensemble of relationships

---

14   Spinoza, *Complete works.*
15   Editors Note: *Cathexis* is the concentration of mental energy on one particular person, idea, or object—
      especially to an unhealthy degree.

between our body and the world. In this relationship, the object of this painful image has been absent. The resistance against the image of the painful object can then be identified as the same with the struggle of our conatus in reviving the images of this older state as much as possible. But, in order to do this, the presence of some traces (images) of these old things is necessary, otherwise, our struggle would just take the form of blind *anxiety*. Hence, we are led to create for ourselves a world constituted by these old, not actually existing images—which is the negative pole, the Hate, for Spinoza. Our Memory is called upon as vividly as possible to keep the present image of the painful object at bay.

Now, we should looking into what *external cause* (or external object as it is) in the Spinozist definition of Love and Hate precisely involves. The externality of an object can only be defined in reference to Memory. Spinoza's assertions that one tends to preserve the loved object, and strives to destroy the object of hate is not a tautology, and has to be argued as such properly. A big portion of the philosophical discourses since Plato and Aristotle can be considered as *metaphysics of love*; human history is full of *appeals* to love, and Christianity sometimes offers itself as the *religion of love*. These metaphysical systems often associate themselves with the idea of Will, and ultimately, as in the case of *Metaphysics of Love* by Arthur Schopenhauer, to the idea of the *primacy* of the Will. The metaphysics of love served two general purposes: the moralization of the affective life, and the institution of *freedom* as the presupposition of any form of moral behavior. Spinoza's position against this meta-physics is quite harsh and clear: If a falling stone had consciousness, it would believe it fell by its own will, freely. Spinoza not only rejects the idea of free will, but also rejects the idea that passions, feelings, emotions, affects (these terms, from a Spinozist point of view, are interchangeable) could ever be *willed*. Love is simply not something that can be called upon, as the religions suggest, as in the principal command of Christianity—*love thy neighbour*. Spinoza affirms this notion in a practically utilitarian fashion; otherwise, affections do not belong to the order of Reason, but to the management of human passions and violence by the states and religions. One cannot command love to anyone; one can only fall into love, practice love, and he is never free in doing so. While Spinoza doesn't have anything partic-ular to say about arts in his Ethica (with the exception of certain arguments in favor of their *utility* for the well-being of the mind), he occasionally takes into account the problem of *religious images*, the image of the God as part of perennial superstition, wrongly replacing *true religion*. Strong passions have always been one of the central themes of every artistic or literary tradition, popular or *classical*, throughout modernity. These passions are no longer *tragic* in the proper Ancient Greek sense of the term; they are rather *imaginative*, based upon a new conception of imagination that came into light with the modernity.

We believe that love is wisdom; but nevertheless it can deteriorate and become (or trans-formed into) jealousy or even hate, which is its opposite. This is the story of the ordinary *romance-film*, the most popular narrative genre in cinema, whereas the way Spinoza pres-ents the dialectics of love largely corresponds to what we call *melodrama* today. What is melodrama after all? It is a large scene where everything, all elements of the drama is represented like a panorama, just like in a musical coda. Melodrama in the 19th century used to consist of a simple play with a rudimentary mise-en-scène, which offered the entirety of all the narrative and staging elements at a precise moment of the play. This was the way in which dramatic cinema established itself, due to its formidable and almost *natural* capacity to present entire scenes of life, which is the worst way to represent life.

This melodramatic element corresponds to what we have tried to demonstrate on the *affect* of love, according to Spinoza. The problem arises with a ménage-à-trois, when the affair of love and hate corresponds to jealousy, and take different roles as sentiments. One now contests the loss of beloved with the other sentiment. This is a quite simple mode of storytelling. But it is universal and present even in the most complex mythologies and primordial literatures of the world.

Spinoza's consideration of love and hate (and jealousy) as *melodramatic* is by no means a misnomer: It is the way these things happen in real life. And cinema and literature cannot avoid such sentiments: deceitful jealous lover and the *bartered* bride as the *go-between*, as in Joseph Losey's famous film[16]. The melodrama is the literary articulation of love.

Benjamin and the Images of Everyday Life

Every sociology is sociology of everyday life, in the sense that once we identify a social type, it is the type's social environment that matters. When a sociologist is engaged in studying the past, there is still a moment that relates to everyday life. The more one penetrates the mundane, the more one's study becomes *sociological* rather than historical. Simmelian apprehension of affective images was unprecedented in its vitality and depth; yet another figure like Walter Benjamin followed it, again as a project of understanding modernity as the apparition of images and details. Bronner points out that, Benjamin's 'interest in bringing the objects of everyday life into the domain of philosophy remained as the key to his method after his conversion to Marxism'[17].

> Benjamin had the quality which was so extraordinarily lacking in Lukács. He had a unique eye precisely for the important detail, for that which lies by the wayside, for the fresh element, which breaks open in thinking and in the world, for an unusual and unschematic disconnected singularity which doesn't fit any preconceived purpose, and which therefore earns a completely private attention that turns one inward.[18]

Such an inwardness constitutes the background of Benjamin's ability to capture the details of everyday life—not only concerning social types but also things and items of mass culture, such as photography. Bronner also notes how Benjamin conceptualizes the impact of modern images, their *microscopic* functionality, and their multidimensionality by quoting Eagleton:

> The thing [...] must not be grasped as a mere instantiation of some universal essence; instead, thought must deploy a whole cluster of stubbornly specific concepts which in

---

16   Joseph Losey, *The Go-Between*, 1971
17   Stephen Eric Bronner, *Of Critical Theory and Its Theorists*, Routledge, 2002, p. 99.
18   Ernst Bloch, 'Erinnerung', *Über Walter Benjamin*, Frankfurt: Suhrkamp (1968): 16-23, p. 17; as quoted in Bronner, *Of Critical Theory and Its Theorists*, p. 99.

Cubist style refract the object in myriad directions or penetrate it from a range of dif-fuse angles. In this way, the phenomenal sphere is itself persuaded to yield up a kind of noumenal truth, as the microscopic gaze estranges the everyday into the remarkable.[19]

An image is never one-sided; it cannot be reduced to a mere *surface*, but we have to appre-hend it in all its refractions, patterns and dimensions. While we are *selective* beings (since an image never shows us all its facets and we have to *select* relationships actively, and images tend to become in-depth *ideas* in this sense) as exemplified in a profound observation by Walter Benjamin:

> Ideas are to objects as constellations are to stars. This means, in the first place, that they are neither their concepts nor their laws. It is the function of concepts to group phenom-ena together, and the division which is brought about within them thanks to the distin-guishing power of the intellect is all the more significant in that it brings about two things at a single stroke: the salvation of the phenomena and the representation of ideas.[20]

Bronner draws attention to Arendt's note on Benjamin's use of metaphors in his writing; 'Met-aphors are the means by which the wholeness of the world is poetically brought about. What is so hard to understand about Benjamin is that, without being a poet he thought poetically and therefore was bound to regard the metaphor as the greatest gift of language'.[21] For him, 'allegory is to language what ruins are to things... It gives power to memory and creates the *horizon* wherein transcendence becomes possible.'[22]

> Allegory is always a symptom that, in a certain respect the Subject-object distance has been sublated (aufgehoben), that the object-world has been transformed in its signification, that it was been worked through by the sub-ject . . . Thus we approach the essence of allegory only then when we recog-nize it as a possibility which lies in the depths of the essence of language.[23]

All these are not only figures of image, or figures to be derived through the act of imagination, but rather the way we experience most of the literary, semiotic and linguistic phenomena that belong to the domain of *high arts* in our ordinary lives. Even the most *popular* arts, pho-tography and cinema in particular, have to be structured on the model of *high arts,* while their technical dimensions and their organization is far from traditional artistic means and techniques, which are generally based on tradition, habitus, subjectivity and artfulness.

19   Terry Eagleton, *The Ideology of the Aesthetic*, Blackwell: Oxford, 1990, p. 328; as quoted in Bronner, *Of Critical Theory and Its Theorists*, p. 99.
20   Walter Benjamin, *The origin of German tragic drama*, London: NLB, 1977, p. 34; as quoted in Bronner, *Of Critical Theory and Its Theorists*, p. 99.
21   Hannah Arendt, *The Human Condition*, Chicago: University of Chicago Press, 1958, p. 164; as quoted in Bronner, *Of Critical Theory and Its Theorists*, p. 279.
22   Bronner, *Of Critical Theory and Its Theorists*, p. 101.
23   Hans Heinz Holz, 'Prismatisches Denken', *Über Walter Benjamin*, Frankfurt: Suhrkamp (1968): 62110, p. 77; as quoted in Bronner, *Of Critical Theory and Its Theorists*, p. 279.

Yet the figurative elements of popular arts also belong to the traditional clichés of the so-called *high art*, and Eisenstein's tracing of the roots of cinema in the melodrama was remarkable: Even a film like *Battleship Potemkin* (1925) (which reveals one of the most striking and universal historical moments) adopted a *melodramatic style*.[24] *Battleship Potemkin*'s melodramatic quality had been the departure of Dziga Vertov's contestation of the dramatic use of cinematography. One of the most remarkable polemics in cinema arose in the context of Eisenstein's *October*, in which Lenin was played by a *worker* (and not even a *professional* actor), a staging device which converts Lenin into an *actor* at the same time. Yet, Vertov thought, there had ben many real *footages* of Lenin, which made such dramatic element unnecessary. This primordial debate in Soviet Union (which was not only confined to cinema but also included the Bolshevik, avant-garde literature and poetry, since Mayakovsky, Meyerhold and Sklovsky among many others, also intervened into the debate from different positions) has been the major questioning of the art of cinema. This was for the ultimate distinction between the images of everyday reality (the documentary) and the dramatic simulation of reality (fiction-film).

The images may not necessarily be mundane; they may show a monarch, a childbirth or, again, a sudden death. All these belong to everyday life but they are not regular or ordinary. Childbirth is part of the *everyday life* of the hospital from the viewpoint of the gynaecologist, but not for the family. The cinema has to consider all these varieties and variations of viewpoints. These *particular* moments don't need to be *extraordinary* either, since they are irregular moments amongst regular, ordinary ones. Metaphors and allegories, emphasized by Benjamin are nevertheless part of the imagery of the everyday life. This is why Vertov could use the most complex montage and shooting techniques in order to *catch life as-it-is* (*zhizn' kak ona 'iest*). But as life is *caught unawares* in the cinema, usually and inescapably giving place to hazardous and unpredictable events, one should refer to the powers of the *imagination* in order to be able to develop a multiplicity of points of view. We need a *monadology* of cinema in this sense.

Bachelard and Modern Imagination

What has been the status of imagination throughout the history of ideas and, more particularly, in philosophy? A general observation is that, while its existence has been affirmed, imagination has been undervalued for a long time in the early history of philosophy, from Ancient Greece to the pre-modern classical philosophies. Not only imagination but also its deeds and products (images and emotions attached to them) have been undervalued, especially since Platonic texts.

Another general observation is that the development of modern philosophy ascribed new importance to the imagination, for instance, the *imaginary* (l'imaginaire) of Jean-Paul Sartre as a substrate for innovation or, as in the case of Ruyer, as a golden path to utopia. One can now discern the power of images in the modern world, the continuous bombardment of social subjects by artificial, representative or *technical* images; an image of the world where imagining tends to become more difficult than the past.

---

24   Sergei Eisenstein, *Film Form*, New York: Harcourt, 1949.

Philosophers devalued imagination by interpreting it as mans blind belief in his desires. We are told to *imagine*, if we want our desires and wishes to become *real*. Such conception prevails in most complex philosophies as much as in ordinary everyday thought. Imagination possessed a privileged place, at least implicitly, as granting access to the invisible layers of a visible reality. Sartre, the philosopher who had enough courage to overvalue imagination, could see in imagination the faculty to negate the reality that is imposed upon us.

Plato, who most clearly devalued imagination, certainly does not conceive it as a faculty in his Republic (Politeia). Imagination offers nothing but a degraded image of reality, and to this extent, it is the principal source of error for Plato. This became a pattern that survived until the *Classical Age* whose *epistemes* were described by Foucault,[25] in the *Essays of Montaigne*, in the *Pensées* of Pascal (where it is depicted as a network of errancy and falsity), and even as a model of madness in Malebranche. For metaphysics, proper job of imagination is to distance us from the real.

Alternatively, this means that the entirety of this traditional-classical cultural context was relying upon the premise of adapting oneself continually to reality, to real life, in some kind of a tradition of conformism. Imagination must then have a kind of power, a negative one, since it is not a faculty but a certain kind of infirmity. Thus, philosophers distinguished between two modes of imagination; one substituting reality (which may be called *reproductive* imagination) and the one which distances us from it, producing chimeras and vain images (the so-called *creative* imagination).

Such negative conception of imagination could only be changed with the spirit of the idea of progress—or rather the quasi-idolatric belief in progress—brought in by the change in the general cultural context. The outcome is the positive value assigned to imagination in cultural sphere that is also revealed in philosophy (for example, the recognition of imagination as a part of the *faculty of reason* by Kant). Not without relation to the idea of of Enlightenment, Conformity ceased to be dominant with the Enlightenment, and reality appeared as something that appeals to change, together with the articulation of great projects of social, political, scientific and industrial revolutions following *Les Lumières*. In any case, imagination in such political-cultural context was stimulating, often to the extreme, from Romanticism to Surrealism. We can even find a call for imagination in Marx's famous Eleventh Thesis, 'The philosophers have only interpreted the world, in various ways; the point, however, is to change it.'[26] A similar implicit reference to imagination as a faculty reappears in Freud, who recognizes the force of desire at work in dreams, but also in the essence of culture; the *principle of pleasure* opposing to the *principle of reality*. At the end of the 19th century, dreams and utopias tend to become serious forces.

When we try to see imagination at work, we can observe one of the outcomes of such a cultural valorization. Liberated from *conformist* ideas, contemporary thought conceived

---

25   Michel Foucault, *The Order of Things*, New York: Pantheon Books 1970.
26   This is the last among Marx's *'Theses on Feuerbach'*. Karl Marx and Friedrich Engels, *The German Ideology*, London: Lawrence & Wishart, 1965, p. 653.

the positive role of imagination, characterizing it as a way of accessing to the new, as an innovative force. Imagination becomes a path that signifies the opening of man to the new, since every project proceeds through imagination. As Ruyer puts it, imagination can now be perceived as a power of utopia, and without imagination there could be no scientific research, no artistic creation.[27]

Surely, this is closely related with the spirit of *positivism* elucidated by Auguste Comte. A scientific theory, before it receives a justified, sustained explanation, is conceived at first as a hypothesis, which is defined as an *imagined explanation*. Charles Sanders Peirce points to a *desiring man* who *burns to know* and *whose first effort will be to imagine what reality could be,* in philosophy (of sciences). Einstein's words echo this: 'Imagination is more important than knowledge.'[28] The domain of art, too, is infused with positive ideas about imagination, as Delacroix redefines art as a product of an inventive activity that finds its source in the imagination of the artist, *opening new ways to beauty.*[29]

Such increasing value assigned to imaginative powers of man continued until the explosion of two great world wars, which seriously damaged the cultural context that brewed such positive conception of imagination. The great 20th century historian and philosopher of science, Gaston Bachelard still invokes imagination as a function of the *irreal*, recognizing it as present '[i]n the human psyche, it is the very experience of openness and newness'.[30] Bachelard denounces the psychological researches dissecting imagination as a plain power of novelty. For Bachelard, there is an essential *etymological* error in these researches that involves considering imagination as *the faculty of forming images*; it should rather be understood as the faculty to *distort images* presented by the perception.

> [...] it is effectively the faculty which liberates us from primary images, which transforms images. If images were not changed, without the unexpected union of images, there is no imagination, there is no imaginative action. If a present image will not force us to think an absent image, if an occasional image will not determine a prodigious number of aberrant images, there is no imagination. There are only perceptions, familiar memories, habituations to colors and forms. The fundamental word that corresponds to imagination is not image, it is the imaginary (l'imaginaire). It is through the imaginary that imagination becomes essentially open, evasive. In human psyche, it is the experience of openness...[31]

Bachelard individualizes images as the *offerings* of perception, as it has been customary for any rationalist philosophy since Spinoza and Leibniz, but he insists on the existence

27   Raymond Ruyer, *L'Utopie et les Utopies*, Paris: Presses Universitaires de France, 1950, pp. 4–5.
28   Albert Einstein, 'What Life Means to Einstein: An Interview by George Sylvester Viereck', *The Saturday Evening Post* 26 (October, 1929): 114.
29   Ferdinand Victor Eugène Delacroix, *French Painter* 1798 – 1863.
30   Gaston Bachelard, *On poetic imagination and reverie*, Washington DC: Spring Publications, 1987, p. 19.
31   Gaston Bachelard, *Air and dreams: An essay on the imagination of movement*, trans. Edith R. Farrell, Dallas Institute Publications, Dallas Institute of Humanities and Culture, 1988 (1943), p. 1.

of an essential faculty of mind, which he calls the *imaginary*. An image which leaves its imaginary principle 'becomes fixed on one definitive form, takes on little by little all the characteristics of immediate perception.'[32] It will soon serve to act, rather than to dream or speak. In other words, if an image becomes stable and fixed, imagination is blocked. It becomes an imagination without images. This is the proof that an image of the imaginary is always something more than itself.

What is interesting about Bachelard's doctrine of the imagery is that imagination reappears once more as an active power of the intellect, which is an active agent even in dreams and discoveries—it wouldn't be a 'discovery' if the image of the thing 'discovered' pre-existed? Hence, in his own terms, Bachelard repeats the profound Bergsonian question of the *new*: How would something new be possible?[33] At this moment, despite Bachelard's hostility against Bergsonism, he joins Tardean and Bergsonian lines of philosophy.

However, one should ask the same question at the level of a *monadology* of everyday life. S*omething new* should appear in the ordinary life and nowhere else. When Leeuwenhoek invented the first microscope and a new *visibility* emerged, his friend and neighbor, the famous painter Vermeer felt himself in full distress. This was not the way in which one sees things, Vermeer most likely thought; millions of bacteria in a tiny drop of water. This was really another point of view, no longer directed towards the macroscopic world of Galileo and Newton, but towards an interiority that is no longer mechanical but organic. This *something new* is expressed in Vermeer's paintings too: The angle of sun create immense effects in the landscape at a specific moment in his *The View of Delft,* which is believed to be created by using an optical device—possibly a camera obscura, or a telescope—to capture the detail. This is no longer the *voyeurism* of Sade, which is based on a mise-en-scène, but a kind of virtuality accompanying modern, post-Renaissance painting in its search for images. This search itself was quite cinematographic since it attempted to create a comparison between two different moments. Cézanne, just like Vermeer, painted the *moments* of an apple, in its own duration (durée), but also under different angles of sunlight.

The Nature-Morte

Stijlleven, or *standing life* (*nature-morte* in French and *still-life* in English) is a painting genre which has its roots in the *memento-mori* (remember the death) of the late Medieval era. M*emento mori* paintings reflected the protest of the painters, who come from humble class of artisans, against the wealthy they were hired to portrait. Foucault's analysis of Velasquez's Las Meninas is perhaps too much imaginative, but it does reflect the general idea: In the early beginnings, a skull was painted at the back of the canvas, reminding that wealth will mean nothing when death eventually arrives. Later, the image of the skull is inserted into the painting, as in Holbein's *Ambassadors*. There was a post-Renaissance tradition in which no wealth and welfare could be represented without a skull in decay. This lies at the roots of the 17th Flemish art of painting called *Stijlleven*, which showed a breakfast table without

---

32   Ibid, p. 2.
33   Ibid, pp. 7-8.

human beings. This is the total objectification of the things, as if one should wait for the intervention of a human hand, as in the case of early still-lives. As in cinematography, there is an *off-screen* (*hors-champs*) in these paintings, and this *hors-champs* has been promoted by Cézanne, the great painter of still-lives, as the *place of the viewer*.

It is possible to trace a polarization of images in traditional still-life paintings in on a semiotic scale; poverty versus wealth are presented in a manner in which some important elements were replaced. In time, the *skull* of memento mori disappears, and boredom, misery and poverty enter into still-life paintings. The hors-champs did not disappear, it has been always there, but in the later moment it is no longer occupied by a *voyeur* but rather by a *thinker*. Celebrating this new form of still-life imagery, Cézanne declares that 'The day is coming when a single carrot, freshly observed, will set off a revolution.'[34] A still life waits for the people to react and intervene. This is the way Van Gogh and Cézanne painted all those *peasant* house corners where mundane life is supposed to go on, with the decay of the rural, as has been lived in the post-counter-revolutionary France. They evoke the futile attempt to interfere to the image, to touch it, and bring it back from its decay.

It could be interesting that the nature-morte and memento mori have been the first interests of the newborn photography, almost tending to become the primary use and main culture of Daguerrotypes. This had been due to technical reasons[35], since photographs has been *technical images*. But, it was also due to *ideological*, and rather cultural reasons, since they also belonged to the order of Protestant phantasms of the dead (and of keeping the dead alive). After all, the memento mori and the still life are still surviving genres, i.e. in television or newsreels, no longer as a form of art, but in the form of information.

The Document Character of the Technical Images

We are now interested in the realm of *technical images*, as Vilém Flusser calls them, as opposed to *representational* images.[36] While we feel distant from his purely *phenomenological* approach, it seems like Flusser's problematization of the technical image as something *readable*, *recordable* and open to transfers and reproduction processes can be fruitful, especially for inquiring upon their *document* status. The technical image is not only a *document*, but it has the possibility of *documenting*, of reproducing other documents by recording them in their *hic et nunc*, in their immediate present and historicity. The camera is a *documenting machine* since it purely records. It is the achievement of a long history of two centuries of modern mechanics, optics, and chemistry—the end of the 18th and the entirety of the 19th century. The camera tends also to become a *thinking machine*, since with cinematography it achieves a kind of mobility, and tends to become another sort of vision, another kind of point of view. These do not mean a painter failed to have a point of view. Points of view are important, especially in the comparative studies of painting. Com-

---

34   Paul Cezanne, *Letters by Paul Cézanne*, John Rewald (ed.), Massachusetts: Da Capo Press, 1995.
35   Editors Note: Daguerrotype photography required long exposure times, which made it suitable for photographing inanimate things.
36   Vilém Flusser, *Towards a Philosophy of Photography*, London: Reaktion Books, 1999.

paring the Chinese and European painting traditions could be quite effective in posing the problem of *point of view* in painting. Yet the *document-character* of the technical image is something quite different, as the points of view it establishes are automatic and don't need the presence of an author who has to figure or represent the image on a canvas or another surface.

Now, we will try to engage with the *document-character* of technical images, in the changing conditions of their nature and cultural role in modern societies, as Flusser's phenomenological perspective concerns with. Certainly there is an *experiential*, and therefore *phenomenological* dimension of the problems technical images impose, and through the question of technology (just to remember Heidegger), in their particular audio-visual world, they reveal an *existential* problem at the ontic level. Truly speaking, the word *technical* does not fit into the deeper meaning intended by Flusser, since there is always a technical element in any kind of human image-making, already starting with the early traits of graphic behavior—marking, piercing, and painting—as André Leroi-Gourhan has pointed to.[37] Flusser rather tries to reveal the *trace* character of the technical images and this character truly corresponds to a totally different psychology of human imagination. We seem to have totally adapted to this psychology, and today everything that surrounds us is simulated through technical images—as Régis Debray points to by proposing the thesis of a *video-sphere*.[38] This new psychology of recorded images also suggests a new aesthetics, which no longer purely relies on graphism, but also to the automatism of the device—camera, print and projection technologies, not to mention the televisual transmission.[3940]

It could be interesting to note how this new aesthetics, at least in the everyday experience seems to *destroy* the traditional conceptions of art, the aesthetics of the beauty and the sublime, and still asserts a counter position vis-à-vis the declaration of Hegelian aesthetics regarding *the end of art* and the *beginning of the age of aesthetics*. Hegel's death roughly coincides with the birth of photography, and this may have something to suggest about the destination of Hegel's *age of aesthetics*.

Our aim is to attempt for a classification of images, not merely alongside the phenomenological thinking of Flusser, but to go further and develop a methodology of the documentation that is not reduced to a mere illustration for social research, but elevated to the level of its *documentary* concerns—the idea of *pure film* as a semiotic, sociological, philosophical research. Corresponding to the *power* of images in everyday life, we have to confront this abusive power with the powers of thinking and imagining, and we believe that this could be the basis for a *sociology of affects*, as we mentioned earlier.

---

37 André Leroi-Gourhan, *Gesture and Speech*, Massachusetts: The MIT Press, 1993. Original: André Leroi-Gourhan, *Le Geste et la parole 1-2*, Paris: Albin Michel, 1964.
38 Régis Debray, 'Vie et mort de l'image: une histoire du regard en Occident', *Esprit* (1994): 57-66. See also: Regis Debray, *Media Manifestos: On the Technological Transmission of Cultural Forms*, London and New York: Verso, 1996.
39 Leroi-Gourhan, *Gesture and Speech*.
40 Debray, 'Vie et mort de l'image: une histoire du regard en Occident'

The theories of photography in general (from Walter Benjamin to Roland Barthes's semiology of the photographic images) share the inertia of the medium and of the apparatus they are intend to discuss: the photography as the frozen moment, an instance. Flusser's *phenomenology* of photography, as we have seen, brought him to the notion of an apparatus, whose dynamism is limited to what we may call *capturing*. André Bazin's important essay on *The Ontology of the Photographic Image*[41] too, brings his reflections towards photography as a defense mechanism against *death* (the *mummy complex* as he calls it) and to a kind of morbid catalepsy —a death mask. We can also invoke the major criticisms of the opponents of *structuralism* (especially Bakhtin against Saussurean linguistics, and those of post-structuralists): positing signs and linguistic codes as *dead* symbolic forms, rather than seeing in language a *living* entity in its dynamic movement. Cinema theories on the other hand, from Rudolf Arnheim to Gilles Deleuze, has co-existed with the historical development of cinema, and largely shared the *dynamism* of their object. Early theories of cinema were part of a popular debate, especially in European countries, and among the questions was whether this new form really carries merits of being considered as *art* —-as simply being a mechanical reproduction of moving objects. With the *mediology* and the *videosphere* of Debray, with the *video-philosophy* suggested by Maurizio Lazzarato, and especially with Jean-Luc Godard's televisual and videographic works, we feel today far distant from these early naive observations that reduced the entire domain of technical images to mere mechanical reproduction of the movement. In this context, one of the earliest cinema-philosophers, André Bazin had written: 'The camera creates an image of the world through a mechanical process. Freed from the confines of time and space, the photograph is an instrumental imprint, an automatic tracing, that directly reproduces and reinvigorates reality.'[42] And cinema became an *added*, supplementary reality (*plus de réalité*, according to Bazin), and today, with interactive images and the general sphere of the audio-visual, the idea of *mechanical reproduction* has been totally eroded.

The Apparata

We have lived through two centuries of photography, one century of cinema, fifty years of television, and two decades of digital images. The common characteristic of all these images is that,-they are technical *images*, if we borrow Vilem Flusser's concept. As technical images, they are produced by means of *generation*, and not *production*, as in the cases of painting and other graphic arts. When we say they are generated and not produced, we refer to the *objectivity* of the apparatus that bring them forth, and this is why photography and film cameras, TV sets, and computer screens are not simply *means* of production, but rather apparata. An apparatus is distinguished from a *tool* by its character of *objectivity*: The producer of the technical images, unlike a painter, works as the operator of the inherent program of the device. Flusser profoundly characterizes the photographic image as a gesture of writing whose historical emergence marked the end of the traditional world of images, where images were seen and writings were read. In their new form the images are

---

41   André Bazin, 'The ontology of the photographic image', trans. Hugh Gray, *Film Quarterly* 13.4 (1960): 4-9.

42   Andre Bazin, 'Qu'est-ce que le cinéma', *Ontologie et langages*, Paris: Le Cerf, 1958. Editors note: The quote must have been translated by the author either from a French source or a Turkish translation.

technically registered, and the polarization of the image and writing is abolished. Now, one no longer *sees* a photograph, but rather *reads* it. This explains how technical images have created a new psychology of image, memory, and movement. This also explains why we refer to camera as an *apparatus*, rather than a tool. An apparatus is defined by a complex material organization accompanying a scientific logic. In this respect, such coupling brings to mind the new machines of Industrial Revolution—such as the steam engine and the thermodynamics, which worked through their own programs, rather than being extensions of human body and energy. The idea of program here is essential, since it is virtually embedded in the physical device, defining it as an apparatus and not as a mere tool. Such virtual embodiment infinitely increases the *information* density of the device; a single needle is much less informational than a house, or a desktop computer, not in its essence, but with respect to the simplicity of its production. Hence one can understand one of the characteristics of modern capitalism. Capitalism produces apparata more than simple means of production today: Work tends to be modulated through the corporate apparata, which extend the *real, material* production to the Third World, and concentrate finances at the programming centers of the apparata. William Burroughs's observation in *Naked Lunch* seems to be profoundly relevant in this context; the drug dealer does not sell a product to his customer, but subscribe his customer to the product.

Today, the collective means of visual enunciation—the press, the motion-picture industry and especially television—operate in the same way Burroughs describes. How can it be possible to sketch out a sociology of *mass media* without appropriating and adopting the modes of operation of such apparata first?

The Ontology of the Image

Ontology is often developed as a later stage of philosophical analysis—the way Hegel ontologizes his phenomenology during his post-Jena philosophy, in his Science of Logic for example, or Heidegger's shift from phenomenology to ontology. Yet, we have many reasons to place it at the beginning: First, the image imposes the problem of *existence* at a primordial level: Man can be considered as mediated by the figure or, if you will, the *face* of the Other (Levinas). Moreover, still in this *existential* perspective, the image can be considered as the most *immediate* human experience, e.g. the *imagery* (l'imaginaire) of Sartre.[43] Every systematic philosophy of modern times encountered the problem of the primacy of the image over any other mental product, while the latter have been treated as *superior forms* of mental activity. Perceptive apprehension or *apperception*, before becoming transcendental, is maintained as the primary and the only contact of man with the outside, especially in Kant. There is no clear-cut distinction between *ideas* and *images* in the classical empiricists like Hume, Locke, and Berkeley. Even in rationalists like Descartes, Spinoza, and Leibniz, the image is that enigmatic, but contestable faculty of the mental apparatus, the sole possibility of contacting world in everyday life. Nietzsche had observed how ordinary/popular knowledge first asked from the scientist and the philosopher the *image* of his invention or discovery. In many systematic philosophies, imagination is evaluated as one of the faculties

---

43   Jean Paul Sartre, *Critique de la Raison dialectique*, Paris: Gallimard, 1960.

of reason (Kant) while it remains, from the standpoint of rationalism, the source of error, confusion, ideology. For classical philosophies, the image occupies an ambiguous zone of primary experience.

Secondly, we have to acknowledge that today the image is more efficient in organizing our mental activities. Each new generation is becoming more adept in thinking through images rather than text. In the sense used by Hegel who invoked a *pedagogy of the concept*, we are today in need of a pedagogy of the image. Even the pre-history of the Paleolithic image (the cave-paintings of Lascaux) forces us to think about their pedagogic function; as the origins of writing usually lead us to pictograms and ideograms before alphabetic structures.

In order to talk about the ontology of the image, however, we have to attribute the image to an ontically defined outside, into the objects. To the degree our contemplation remain focused on the experience of images (imagination) we remain in the domain of phenomenology. Yet in shifting into an ontology, a metaphysical operation seems to be necessary: The images are outside... As we will see, this operation has been explained by the two great philosophers of the 20th century, Henri Bergson and Martin Heidegger, albeit for different purposes and expectations. Heidegger wanted to overcome metaphysics on his path to ontology from phenomenology. In his ontology, the image did not exist anymore; he aimed for *the thing*, *Das Ding*, and the process of the *Thought of Being* itself. Bergson, on the other hand, developed a theory of the image, substantially defying the metaphysical problems related to the play of images one by one. In Heidegger we are living in a world of *world pictures*, while, in Bergson, everything is attributed to a total image of creative thought in a non-teleological evolution. The image is all there is; images are not objects of consciousness that correspond to and represent the objects in the world, for the simple reason that, at a certain level of analysis, consciousness, memory and reason are nothing but images—even the cerebral cortex is an image.

Heidegger, like every phenomenologist, needed to mediate his thought through the image. The world created in Van Gogh's *peasant shoes*, or the character of *tables* in the scientific (scientistic?) imagery. This is not unusual among phenomenologists. Merleau-Ponty cannot outline his argument about *ordinary* perception without referring to the more particular domain of the perception of the work of art, as he passes through Cézanne. While Heidegger transcends the phenomenology through a stronger reference to poetry and the experience of *dwelling in language*, poetry and literature in general never cease to operate through *images*, no less than in plastic arts anyways.

In order to arrive to the somehow strange ontology of image developed by Bergson (well appraised by Gilles Deleuze in his book on cinema), we should first pass through the steps of the metaphysics of the image. Central position will evidently be given to two philosophers— Plato and Spinoza, as two great metaphysical conventions for the possibility of conceiving the image in itself. But this should be left to a further study. The only thing we want to stress here is that such metaphysics of the image has always been an ontology and not a *phenomenology* of the light. From Goethe's famous essay on colors, light still remains the ontological basis of every painting, every view, and every projection. Thus it could be fruitful to discuss the Platonic relevance of this *metaphysics*.

The Metaphysics of Light

We have two series of images that are both part of the life in the *polis*. The first, generated through the private life, constitutes what archaeologists refer to as *ancient iconography* (popular images of figurations), myths, popularly known scenes, wars, things for remembrance. The second belongs to the highest arts of the space, architecture and sculpture; these Apollonian sources of dreaming shape the harmonic space of the Agora. In between, there is nothing but small, popular, quasi-aesthetic objects for rituals, and even just for fun. We can agree with the general proposition of Michel Foucault, that the Greeks were a *society of spectacle*. We can also agree with another idea that Ancient polis was a *society of speech and opinion* (Vernant and Marcel Detienne). There is no incompatibility between these two points of view, in so far as we equate images and opinions. The images of the spectacle, of the ritual and the tragedy are coordinated with the signs of language, with the spoken reality. However, there are many reasons to believe that this society of spectacles or speech and oratory was also a society that has tried to control the spectacle and speech. Language and oratory, as well as the spectacles, could lie, could be abused, and could influence people to act in excessive ways and manners.

It is in this atmosphere that the greatest philosophers of Antiquity, notably Plato and Aristotle, have opposed the domain of *opinions*, contesting the free-floating language of the sophists and orators, in order to provide speech and aesthetic objects with a certain kind of discipline and pedagogy. According to Plato, when doxa dominates the public speech, illusions flourish from the visible, or sensible side of things. The philosopher opposes to the *sensible* with his new invention, the *intelligible,* whose superiority is not a matter of degrees, but of kind. While there are interrelations or *analogies* between the world of the sensible and that of the intelligible, this difference of kind places the intelligible beyond a frontier, or horizon, giving it a heavenly quality, making it the divine sphere of immutable *ideas*. In its earliest Platonic version, the metaphysics of light enters the scene precisely at this moment, while probably coming from older generations of mysticism, or more concretely, Oriental *sun worship* traditions. It is redefined by Plato as a *principle* leading to an ontology: The *sensible light* makes things visible—ontic things like the Sun, Moon, or any other source of light. But light has also an *ontological* existence, as a principle, as the predisposed and immutable one: Light as God. Ideas exist in this sphere, inherently illuminated by the light as principle, or imbued with it as it had been in the Neo-Platonist understanding.

The Platonic model seems to be contested, while essentially being adopted by Plotinus, known as Neo-Platonist with his follower Porphyrius. Their criticism is directed against the Platonic doctrine of light and *participation*. As we mentioned earlier, Plato conceives *participation* in three senses—the first, material-physical kind of participation, the second, daemonic or seductive participation, and the third, the spiritual one. In the first case, two or more things participate into a composition, like parties to the state, classes or more appropriately groups of citizens into the constitution of the Polis, or substances into composite drinks. In the second, I participate to a mixture through being seduced, or *possessed* by a daemonic power, as in the case of Orphic or Dionysiac intoxication experience and communities. In the third, and apparently in the highest form, I participate to the Idea, through imitating its model, as a *dēmiurgós* (craftsman) or an artisan, as a thinker in the life of ideas, belonging to the community of philosophers and of the enlightened. It is important to note the formal and methodological character of these Platonic themes, which allow them to be applied in a wide variety of phenomena, including a fundamental Greek conception of community as association: Through participation, *communities* are generated, as any human group; the demos in the first, the mystic or religious assemblages in the second, and the political foundation of the *ideal* city in the third.

Plotinus opposes Plato in each of these themes: He profoundly conceives the element of *violence* in such Platonic conception of participation. In the first theme of participation, for instance, when one of the elements is retired, the whole, that is the community, collapses. Even in the second and the third, the relationship of the part to the whole remains dyadic. Such Platonic conception of the community and participation still survive in the modern forms and conceptions of integrity, identification and community. Hence, Georg Simmel traces a particular *dyadic* form of social relationship or *association* (*Gesellschaft*). When one of the parties is removed, as it happens with the couple in the family, the unit disappears. Even in certain Marxist traditions class antagonisms are defined in a dyadic form: If one of the classes disappear, the other, the opposite one too is abolished together with the society which is characterized by their tension. This is exactly the element of Platonism that is attacked by Plotinus, who, in turn, proposes the model of a *gift*. Here, the whole, called as the One or the Principle (*arkhai*) has the character of being *imparticipable*; when an element or part is removed, there is something that still remains in the eternal whole. The One, in this early dialectic akin to the Hegelian one, purges everything that could harm its unity and integrity. When we talk about a *principle*, we acknowledge that there is something in it which still remains intact even whatever it implies is broken.

However, if *light* is a principle, it imposes a conceptual problem regarding imaging technologies --photographic, cinematographic, videographic and digital ones, which are all *writings of the light*. Since all these media presents are made visible by the capturing of light, whether digitalized or not, such principle would bring them all into the domain of metaphysics..

One of the most important metaphysical questions is: To whom the images belong? This is not a matter of *property* or *ownership* at all, in the way today's capitalism seems to treat the issue. When captured by a photographer or a filmmaker (this is the critical case of Vertov's understanding of the *documentary*) my image no longer belongs to me. Does this imply an ethical concern, as most documentary filmmakers could (rather naively) agree? Are writing about a person, and filming him/her with a camera, identical actions? This is a crucial metaphysical question should be kept open; whether one's own *image* belongs to oneself, or to its *seer*?

Imagination for Spinoza was certainly the source of all errors. Hence we can conceive how he associates imagination with opinion, as opposed to adequate ideas. Surely, every mind creates images of external bodies in order to modify itself by relating to them. But this is only the source of erring but not the error itself. He expresses it as follows:

> [...] to retain the usual phraseology, the modifications of the human body, of which the ideas represent external bodies as present to us, we will call the im-

ages of things, though they do not recall the figure of things. When the mind regards bodies in this fashion, we say that it imagines. I will here draw attention to the fact, in order to indicate where error lies, that the imaginations of the mind, looked at in themselves, do not contain error. The mind does not err in the mere act of imagining, but only in so far as it is regarded as being without the idea, which excludes the existence of such things as it imagines to be present to it.[44]

This is a quite important conceptualization of imagination, as an image in itself is never an error, nor can it thus be conceived as a pure and ephemeral substitute for a reality. Unlike Kant, imagination cannot be conceived as a faculty of the reason, but as an outcome of sensible materiality for Spinoza. And along the path of associating opinion with imagination, it appears that Spinoza does not entirely dispose knowledge against opinion. We have already seen how complex was the opposition of knowledge and opinion in Ancient Greeks. Yet, Spinoza further complicates the issue by identifying opinion as what he calls *first kind of knowledge*. This is not an error but a kind of knowledge that is gathered only through the affection of one's body by external bodies. And this first kind of knowledge is perceived as *inadequate* by Spinoza, insofar as it is the knowledge of the effects, and not the knowledge of the causes. Hence, opinion is not something that necessarily leads to error, but its inadequacy makes it prone to.

But if imagination is possible, our images *metaphysically* and almost necessarily belong to others. If I stand in someone's visual field, I belong to her/him, and this is not a contract or an exchange, since I can be visible without seeing the eye that gazes at me. This is not a matter of a *copyright* of images, but rather of the ethics of being visible, corresponding to the desire of *seeing*, which should not be contaminated by *voyeurism*. And this has been the way Vertov has developed one of his major principles: *life caught unawares*. It is part of the ethico-political aspects of the documentary filmmaking, and has certain important theoretical implications.

Modernity and the Anticipation of Images

The birth of the cinematographic image was first being marked by strong emotions that we might call *popular* –the fun and the joy of the audiences in earliest films, at the sight of a train moving into a station (first film by Lumière, *L'arrivée du train à la Gare La Ciotat*), a child playing in the garden and the like. The effect of *first sight* of motion pictures was a kind of wonder and shock, operating together with an illusion of reality. Cinema and its audience, in their early stages, were seemingly unequipped with strong passions for dramatic effects or poetic values. Nor there were wonders of exotic places; the documentary as a form would appear soon, but not during this first *simple* stage. The inventors of cinematography, Edison and Dickson in the United States who invented the kinetoscope, and Lumières in France, the inventors of the *cinematograph,* did not believe the probable artistic or scientific value of their inventions in their early stages. Yet, as early as 1904, this new invention was intercepted by both capitalistic enterprise and military organizations. Until the beginning of the First World War, cinematography was deployed as part of national military strategies, with all its

---

44   Benedictus de Spinoza, *Complete works*, trans. Samuel Shirley and others, Michael L. Morgan (ed.), Cambridge, IN: Hackett Publishing Company, Inc., 2002. (The Ethics, Book II, Proposition XVII, Note)

components: the lighting of the battlefield and enemy forces, a representation and *cadrage* of their strength and movement. The battlefield in modern times is conceived as a dynamic field of movement, just as in the classical cinema. The parallelism between military strategy and cinematographic apparatus has been rigorously questioned by the French philosopher Paul Virilio in his *Guerre et cinéma* (War and Cinema): 'War is cinema, and cinema is war.'[45]

Virilio, throughout his analyses of such parallelism, conceives that his formula that identifies war with cinema is not coincidental or purely an importation of technology (cinema in this case) into the domain of warfare: Cinema in itself was a *logistics of representation*. It should be noted that the invention of photography too anticipated the direct representation of movement in the battlefield, and at the exact moment when Eadweard Muybridge, the inventor of sequence photography of movement (the flight of a bird, a horse running) was a battlefield photographer in the late 19th century. One should note here that Muybridge's job was quite different than the paintings of American *war painters* of the Civil War—it was strategic and tactical in essence.

Not only the warfare but also some anticipation of *art* was already present in early cinema, even when most of the intellectuals of the time condemned it as a mere *mechanical reproduction of the movement*. Yet the theme of anticipation is important since modernity seems to be the life-world of anticipations: Hegel, the first great anticipator of modernity, anticipated the solution of the *master-slave dialectics* in the Prussian State, seemingly affected by the sight of working carpenters out his window in Jena University, while the canons of Napoléon hurled around the city: These were the two major powers and experiences of life in its historic evolution —warfare (the value of the Master) and work (the value of the Slave). Later, Marx showed how anticipation works throughout the tentative development of capitalist relations of production: The primitive *putting-out* system anticipating the simple manufacturing, which in turn anticipating the complex manufacture, all anticipating the great capitalist industrial organization in the end. Modernity is really defined by anticipations, which cannot be reduced to causal chains operating through time and history. They are rather *openings*, or possibilities that are actualized or repressed by the historical flux of events. The two great philosophers of the *openness*, Heidegger and Bergson were also great anticipators, while they tended to define the *open* in quite different manners and purposes: In Heidegger; life anticipates death; the *techne* the modern actualization of global technology; the metaphysics the modern nihilism. Bergson, on the contrary, relates the *openness* to the question of the *new*. He is not in search of origins since there is no room to attribute any *beginning* to the time conceived as duration (*la durée*). In questioning the possibility of the creation of the *new*, one cannot simply invoke causal chains deployed in a measurable process of time, since causality requires the division of an abstract time into immobile moments. What is *new* never appears in time, since the duration is exactly the movement of the *open*. Then, it is true that modern life can be characterized by an unrelenting course towards an indefinite future, in which every *moment* can be understood as a *jetztzeit* in the sense used by Walter Benjamin.

---

45   Paul Virilio, *Guerre et cinéma: I. Logistique de la perception*, p. 26.

Again, we can discern the momentum of anticipation in photography. The first photographs (beyond the *Daguerrotype*) of Niepce were long-posed ones, with a still-standing camera obscura, but anticipating the shortening of the duration of the exposure, before being able to take portraits in a few minutes, and later, before being capable to take instantaneous still-shots. This was the moment, in the mid-19th century, that the photo camera was able to shot a passer-by in the street, or depicting urban landscapes as stills. The Barthesian *punctum* too was enabled through this moment.

Yet, this was not the accomplishment of the anticipations of photography, since we can trace a variety of genealogies interacting in modern times: First, it was true that, according to Virilio, there is an anticipation of the rigorous depiction of reality in photography and cinematography, all integrated into a *logistics of representation* worthy for warfare technologies. But, a more complex series of anticipations in the aesthetic and the scientific spheres should be established first: The invention of photography has moved the art of painting into new ways of creation, particularly in the domains of classical and romantic painting, which aimed at creating *resemblances* of the real. We don't necessarily have to believe André Bazin, when he writes that this was an *obsession* of classical-romantic painting which was destroyed by the emergence of photography.[46] We should not overemphasize such chains of causality in history, since the relationships between painting, photography and cinema in the 19th century were far more complex. Aumont draws attention to a particular development in the history of painting that anticipates the birth of cinema; the moment when the draft painting was replaced by *études*.[47] Unlike the drafts that are supposed to precede the final composition in the creative process of the classical painter, the modern painter begins to make *studies*, unfinished drafts that are depicting unique moments of drawn objects —a moment in a landscape, a state of an apple, as in famous paintings of Cézanne. These studies, however, should not be characterized only by their spontaneous or momentary postures, but rather by their *unfinished* qualities. Etudes anticipated the inclusion of the movement into the image by distorting the contours, and thereby avoiding the exact resemblance of the representation to its object. The importance of these *studies* in defining one of the characteristics of modern life —-the valorization of the *affects of the moment*—is far more evident than their role in the development of cinematographic language, which always remains related to the moving images (motion pictures) rather than images representing the movement.

Another important aspect of modernity is the emergence of a particular *visual* style not only in literature, but also in the philosophical writing —-the kind of synoptic writing adopted by Kierkegaard for example, proceeding through drafts, synopses of stories, anecdotes, lists of arguments, bits and fragments. The same can also be observed in Georg Simmel's writings, to the degree that his student Gyorgy Lukacs called him the founder of the *impressionistic sociology*.[48]

46   Bazin, *The ontology of the photographic image.*
47   Jacques Aumont, *L'oeil interminable: cinéma et peinture*, Paris: Libr. Séguier, 1989.
48   David Frisby, *Georg Simmel*, Routledge, 1984, p. xxviii.

Cinema and the Mediation of Reality

Cinema was born parallel to the constitution of modern life, and it is deeply anchored in modern metropolis. According to Deleuze, it was an answer to the crisis in the psychology of perception in the late 19th century related with the perception of motion, before becoming apart of our urban landscape, and shaping the modern *society of spectacle*. Deleuze challenges this old idea of illusion, since cinematography has been the tool to show to human beings that their ordinary perceptions (images, paintings, photography, and real theatrical or natural movement) could be reproduced by mere technological means.[49] The case of the cinema is important here for our discussion, since it was considered as an example, or even a superior form of *illusion*—that is, an inherently unconscious operation of opinion from the very beginning. Yet, cinema further established its own illusory, somehow dream-like world which correlated with the society of opinions that its amorphous audience composed. Unlike the classical arts of spectacle (such as theatre, opera, and dramatic arts) cinema has a global audience today, a mass society that adheres to its spectacle. From its early beginnings, cinema has been an ambiguous form, since it gradually became more difficult to distinguish its aesthetic-artistic aspect from its operation as a superficial, popular form of mass entertainment. Cinema had become the *seventh art* in the early 20s, not only through the dreamworld of Hollywood, but also by the political-economic design of the *first socialist state*, the Soviet Union. For some it belonged to the entertainment industry, whereas for others it has been a proper tool of representing the reality, since it did that more directly than any other medium. Today, the first aspect seems to be victorious if we take the production and imperialistic expansion of opinions as criteria. Actually, in every country, there are national film boards and registries, *golden globes*, circles of critics, reviewers, gossip columnists, film tabloids, Internet databases of films, and department stores, performing the unique task of creating and re-creating interminable discourses about films, tracing genealogies of authors, of images and genres, besides the television. Even Literature, the oldest of arts, was not able to develop such variety of genres throughout its long history: Horror, thriller, science fiction, documentary, Western, romantic drama, comedy, the musical, avant-garde, etc., all appeared in just one hundred years of cinema.

In cinema, like in music, a certain kind of *democracy* prevails. New genres emerge around new audiences, groups of opinion and taste establish *fans,* who are imitated by the films and who imitate the films back in their actual life. The judgments of taste, as in every context of modernity (and as we have seen, even since the Ancient Greece) has established differential norms and identities, a variety of tastes whose overall discernment could only be democratic; everyone lives their own life, as pleasurable as it can get. Cinema generates and reproduces to theoretically endless number of societies of opinion and taste.

However, because of certain inherent challenges, which can only be explained by philosophy and sociology, the cultures of cinema are differently affected than the communities of music. A musical community, such as jazz, rock, hip-hop or metal, is not forced to rely upon

---

49   Gilles Deleuze, *Cinema 1: The movement image*, trans. Hugh Tomlinson and Robert Galeta, London: Continuum, 2005.

a kind of *principle of reality*, whereas in cinema, even in the case of the most avant-garde or fictional productions, a problem of realism and irrealism persists. Unlike music, cinema is representational; it technologically mediates reality.

Godard's Histoire(s) du cinéma

We believe that Jean-Luc Godard has truly invented a *new image*. This has been the video-image that is generated for TV but has never been reducible to that. It is the result of three decades of work, starting from when Godard has begun to produce his first *video-images* —exactly with his departure with Pravda, Cinéma Vérité and particularly the Dziga Vertov Group (Groupe Dziga Vertov)—if not with his *Maoist* inspirations towards an optimistic perspective of *cultural revolution*. His recent *Histoire(s) du cinéma* now, in turn, can be a point of departure for our own perspectives today, as we are interested in conceptualizing videography as an archival device, for reconstituting a methodological tool concerned with both for affects and images. It would be inspiring, for the purpose to envision a sociology of affects, to consider how this neo-Vertovian possibility has been developed over time in Godard's work.

The Godardian formula of *making political films politically* has been uttered, to our knowledge, for the first time in the exposition of the *groupe Dziga Vertov* (*Sur les films du groupe* —an anonymous publication in Cahiers du Cinéma, No 240: Juillet Aout 1972).[50] This formula reminds us that no one can make 'political' films easily. Even Elia Kazan and John Ford made *political films* in a *Pariscope* fashion[51], yet one should go beyond *political film* and ask the question of making *political films politically*. This formula clearly has a Brechtian reference, the *Verfremdungseffekt*, in which the critical alienation effect denaturalizes the events in bourgeois cinema narratives. Godard maintains in his film *Tout va bien* that these narrative events aim to force the spectator to laugh and cry together with the characters on the screen. This alienation effect is not the kind of estrangement we find in *action movies*, where actions and situations are reconstructed in the narrative in a fairly unrealistic, burlesque fashion. In classical realist film narratives, actions are in fact reactions to situations, to milieus, to environments, parallel to the classical sociological model. We can see the same notion at work in pseudo-psychology of American behaviorism as well as Flaherty's early documentaries—such as Nanook dueling with the wild nature. The *anonymous* author not only claims the Brechtian aspect of Groupe Dziga Vertov's works as a *continuation* of Brecht's *critical* distance but as a qualitatively different revival of it—*the fight for opening the critical eye of the spectator*.

This reminds us also what has happened in Soviet cinema, in the triadic opposition between Vertov, Eisenstein and the Stalinist regime. Both Vertov, and Eisenstein had been calling for the *new international language* of the cinematography, but in quite different ways, before

---

50   'Sur les films du groupe', Paris: *Cahiers du Cinéma* 240, (July, 1972).
51   Editors Note: *Pariscope* was a urban guide/magazine published between 1965-2016, which covered the current and forthcoming entertainment events in Paris over the coming week, including theatre, music and films.

both being screwed under Zhadanovism[52] (Zhadanovism is also the point we can understand how Lenin's discourse differentiated from that of Bismarck not only substantially
but also stylistically).

The second Godardian moment can be formulated as *putting everything in a film* (*mettre
tout dans un film*), which we believe, is essential to the way Godard has adopted video since
1975, while considerably reducing the amount of his cinema works. Histoire(s) du cinéma
seems to depart from a non-nostalgic supposition that 'cinema had failed'.[53] Apparently, we
account for the history of something only after its decline: Or we know that cinema is still
alive, and this is exactly the essential problem now—'things are getting worse, both in cinema
and in philosophy' Deleuze would say.[54] The fact that cinema is still alive already imposes a
problem of the past, of history that surely is not Hegelian in its essence. Serge Daney points
to this problem when he reminds that 'Vertov has shown something that had been lived –his
images constitute the past for us, but they are still available, while that 'something which
had been lived' had disappeared'.[55] This was not paradoxical for a Hegelian way of recalling
History—the history of nations, of classes, of wars, of great events. It is still not paradoxical
for a Fernand Braudel, in his project of locating the sediments of the *history* of capitalism. But
in a way, there is an essential paradox in the history of cinema, since the *visible* had already
been passed away, while its images are still present.

We are aware that cinema presupposes the technology—of engineering, of trains, of photography, of scientific revolution and, as Virilio would say, of warfare. Godard sees in this
technological background the basis of a culture that traversed the cinema and invented
television in turn. He maintains that:

> Cinema is an art, and science too, is an art. This is what I am saying in Histoire(s)
> du cinéma. In XIXth century, the technique was born, in an operative (opera-
> toire) sense, and not in an artistic sense (not at the level of the movement of a
> small horologer produced in Jura, but with one hundred and twelwe millions of
> Swatch). Or Flaubert says to us that this birth of technique (telecommunications,
> semaphors) is simultaneous with the birth of idiots, that of Madame Bovay...[56]

Here, Godard seems to reclaim what has been pointed by Ernst Jünger and Martin Heidegger before, especially in the Heidegger's inquiry upon the tendency of *technology* towards
becoming *culture*, rather than remaining merely as *scientific-art*. The only objection we have

---

52   Editor's Note: Andrei Alexandrovich Zhdanov was a Soviet Communist Party leader and cultural
      ideologist who has been described as the 'propagandist-in-chief' of the Soviet Union in the period 1945
      to 1948.
53   Jean-Luc Godard himself seems to claim such failure when interviewed by Serge Daney. See: Jean-Luc
      Godard & Serge Daney, 'Dialogue entre Jean-Luc Godard et Serge Daney', Paris: *Cahiers du Cinéma*
      513, May, 1997 (1988), p. 49.
54   Deleuze, *Cinema 1: The movement image.*
55   Godard & Daney, 'Dialogue entre Jean-Luc Godard et Serge Daney', p. 49.
56   Editors Note: Translation by Ulus Baker. See: Godard & Daney, 'Dialogue entre Jean-Luc Godard et
      Serge Daney', p. 49.

against Godard is about cinema begetting television, since we believe, on the contrary, that television as culture evolved from what Heidegger once observed in his The *Question Concerning Technology*.[57] Modern technology does not produce shoes for a peasant woman's feet, it produces *energy*, it produces *plastic*, it produces *electricity*, it produces *urban heating*, and other completely amorphous things. It is important to keep this in mind, as evident today in the manipulation of opinions, in the *use of pleasures* (if we transpose the Foucaldian understanding of the concept in the Second Volume of his *History of Sexuality*), and especially in the *videosphere* of the images of a televisual and digitized world.

How Can an Image Lie? Magritte and Foucault

How did Foucault, after Spinoza, formulated a new character for what is called *power* in the Western world? First, he developed a new image of power. This image reveals itself in one of Foucault's texts, which is apparently not dealing with the issue of power—his commentary on Magritte's *ceci n'est pas une pipe (this is not a pipe)*. Questioning the domain of language, the art of Magritte, and of the *image*, Foucault seems to proceed onto the blueprints of his analytics of power: The discourse of the executors of power operates in the same way in *this is not a pipe* of Magritte—the judge who sentences says *this is not a prison since we are not punishing, we are trying to restore him to the moral order; we are educating him, we are healing him.* Such *this is not a prison* is part of the modern discourse of jurisprudence, but also the manner in which the modern societies of discipline emerged. The thesis of his book *Surveiller et punir: La naissance de la prison* (*Discipline and Punish: The Birth of the Prison*) is evident—we can call the society which emerges in the beginnings of the 19th century as a *society of discipline*.[58] These disciplines are invested in what we may call Napoleonic institutions, prisons, hospitals, schools, military barracks, and factories but also in specialized discourses—psychiatry, clinic, psychology and even sociologyall pretending to be *scientific*. What is essential of disciplines is that they cannot be *localized* in some specific institutions, but that they are capable of invading the entire life of modern societies during the 19th century. There is no discrepancy between their *physical-historical* reality and the discourses that accompanied them, since the discourses proliferating around their *positivity* are in themselves contradictory. Foucault wanted to show the internal *hypocrisy* of these discourses: *This is not a pipe* belongs to the domain of the discourse of art, to the world of images, and to what Maurice Blanchot formulated as *speaking is not seeing*. When *this is not a prison* uttered by the policeman, the judge or the guardian, it belongs to a similar order of discourse. Accordingly, one can never be sure when everyone talks about his institution in a similar manner; is the hospital really a *therapeutic* milieu whose function is *healing*? Is the factory system really different from a prison, especially during the emergence of the industrial revolution? In short, every institution seems to repeat each other through circular arguments that reveal their *hypocrisy*—perhaps one of the fundamental *aporias* of modernity. Deleuze is right when he sees the essential point of Foucault not in his description of the disciplinary institutions but rather how all these institutions are permeated by an intricate

57   Martin Heidegger, 'The question concerning technology', In: Craig Hanks (Editor), *Technology and values: Essential readings,* Wiley-Blackwell, 2009.
58   Michel Foucault, *Discipline and Punish: the Birth of the Prison*, New York: Random House, 1977.

investment of power, but this is only true to some extent—since Foucault was also aware of the fact that these disciplinary institutions were criticized beginning from (perhaps even before) their birth. It is true that Foucault's analyses are strictly oriented towards the *classical* period and its conclusion in modernity, notably to the Revolutionary and Napoleonic period. But what is essential is not the period of their birth (since we are talking about rather a process) but a specific system of operation: What are the factors that imply a superficial genealogical resemblance among them? The importance is attributed to the functionality which characterizes the disciplinary societies as a linear apprehension of life: There, life is captured, and their specific form is *confinement*. Modern subjectivity passes through a series of segments in which every individual is confined to. Each of them has their specific rules, configurations, and experiences, but this does not prevent them to repeat each other in terms of their implicit presuppositions; every segment seems to reject the preceding one: In the school, we are told 'you are no longer in the family', and when at work, we are told, 'you are no longer in the school'. Foucault's essential question seems to be posed in terms of affects and life-experiences: How come modern institutions repeat each other so manifestly while denying such repetition in every step? How come the entirety of modern life is distributed in such a manner that different life experiences like madness, criminality, learning, having sex, speaking and working, even illness and death are captured in institutions which resemble each other? The reasons for our interest in Foucault's work appear exactly at this point: Societies of opinion enfold what Foucault and Deleuze called *disciplinary societies*—they are societies in which the legitimation and justification of these disciplinary measures are tentatively performed.

The role of the affects in the work of Foucault is evident: He reconstructs the social types corresponding to each stage of his analysis: The mad can never be seen as a *social type* in itself, up to the end of the classical period. It belongs to the order of the *same*; as he is not objectified with the exception of his non-reasonable appearance. Socially, he is still part of the society, and perhaps even bearing magico-religious attributions during the medieval era and the Renaissance. He comes to assume the intricate role of the Other of reason, the impossibility of reasoning in the Classical Age. Even in the period of *Great Confinement*, up to the liberation of the mad people from their chains by Pinel at the beginning of the 19th century, he does not appear as a social type, simply for the reason that they were all confined and thus invisible. The social type of the madman appears only from the moment that he is confined following an investigation into the society, an investigation that encountered and accompanied the process of medicalization of his madness. What Foucault neglects in his own way is the *opinion-based* nature of the modern understanding of madness, as an individuated disturbance.

This *opinion* of the masses, necessary for the social creation of the social type, is much more manifestly analyzed by Foucault in his treatment of a time of crisis when the emerging prison system was not at first popularly justified in the juridical system and the criminal law. This means that prisons are erected, expanding over territories, in the interstices of urban areas, although they remained unjustified in the domain of criminal justice. Foucault gives examples of these early reactions, which cannot be interpreted as *reformist* approaches. The jurists of the revolutionary times were not intending to bring the prison system to the core of criminal justice. We don't know to what extent Foucault's argument that the prison system developed outside the area of the criminal justice before imposing itself in this domain is historically true. But this is the logical consequence of Foucault's way of thinking in which *partiality* is involved in both of its dual meanings; assuming a particular *point of view* on the *present*, and not the *past* (in this sense Foucault is not a historian but a philosopher); and seeing things with a logic of exaggeration of their contours, like the *ideal types* of Weber, to make visible what lies in the background or rather *underground*—this is what Foucault called *eventalization*, creating *events* out of the material, out of the archive.

The *lying image* appears just there, where Foucault notes a scene in Rossellini's *Europe 1951*, where a bourgeois woman sees workers in the factory for the first time, and screams 'I believed they were prisoners'. The magic of the image works in such a manner: One no longer compares two images but just sees one in the other. Like the *énoncés* of Foucault, images are rare, they have to be extracted from the clichés in which they are buried—and this is a creation of ideas. And rarity is their own fashion to appear. This is why we need their derivation through extraction from clichés. Now, Magritte presents his work *ceci n'est pas une pipe* as a cliché, which belongs to the realm of scholarly education and instruction: One of the variants is painted on a blackboard!

Phenomenology of Cinema

If there is a connection from Lumières to Vertov (and thereby to the documentary film) such connection had received certain ruptures in the following history of cinema, until it was apprehended by the televisual apparatus. The beginning was characterized by an epoch where mechanical reproduction of reality was bounded by the limitations of a fixed camera, virtually assuming the eye of the spectator during projection. There are many reasons to believe that during this period, filmmakers recorded the images of life within the context of passivity of screening the film. The cameraman assumed the eye of the public. The aim was hence to represent reality mechanically on the screen. The documentary character of the earliest films was almost *natural*, if such term would be adequate in this context. In this sense, early cinema followed the visual tradition of photography by adding the movement into it. The break with photography comes with the moving and vehicular camera work (the attaching of the camera onto moving vehicles), which introduced relative movements, detachment of the cameras point of view from that of the viewing public and its emancipation. Once mounted on a train, or on a street car, camera can capture aberrant and even disorienting movements, and by this way, it sometimes assume the role of an expanded human eye, and sometimes leave it behind to become almost a cosmic artificial eye. Early inquiries and thematics in the phenomenology of perception historically coincide with the development of early cinema.

Beginning with Husserl's studies on *intentionality*, we notice a general effort in phenomenology to transform (if not revolutionize) the ordinary psychological assumptions about consciousness at the end of the 19th century. What we acknowledge today as almost a banal identifier of phenomenological proceeding, *every consciousness is consciousness of something*, was formulated as an essential and direct attack against earlier postulates of psychology. As an extension of of Kantian philosophy, such formula points to the need for intentionality and orientation of conscious experience. This means that if there is nothing to be conscious about, there would be no consciousness. Consciousness is not something, like a faculty of mind, that precedes the objects of subjects orientation and interests. This formula became a motto of phenomenology from Husserl to Merleau-Ponty, relating the conscious experience to the primacy of perception, and accounting for the orientation of *Dasein* into *this world* in existential philosophies via Heidegger to Sartre.

This principle in fact attacks a particular dimension of the earlier psychological understanding, which extrapolates the mental images we have in consciousness and the things which are outside the mind. Outside, we only have bodies, things, in motion or rest, and inside, as part of the *Umwelt*, we have images, concepts and ideas of these things. Consciousness is thereby substantialized, as a faculty proper, which could therefore be conceptualized as an empty form, while existing individually. With Husserl, the character of this emptiness changes: This emptiness is not formal, but depends on the primacy of the intentionality—i.e. whenever something is *intended* in experience, consciousness arises.

We know that modern Western thought has been aware of the philosophical importance of *empty forms,* at least since Kant. The emptiness of form is almost a characteristic of modernity: The universality of morality was possible only when the categorical imperative was formulated as an empty form, enabling the subject to fill it with any adequate content—a moral rule or *duty*. This means that ethical universality and necessity no longer relies upon the selection of *good* moral rules of the past and present, since the *good* itself is nothing but the outcome of the judgment that defines *duty*. The imperative hence should be categorical—i.e. should apply to all possible empirical moral rules or expressions of conduct. Hence it defines an a priori as an empty form, assumed to be valid everywhere and every time—necessity and universality.

Such an understanding of the *empty form* as necessary and universal should not be confused with the empiricist assumption of a *tabula rasa*, which has rather an ideational character. Tabula rasa does not define an a priori, and thereby belongs to the order of the classical assumptions of psychology. Continental rationalism and Kant's critical philosophy never assumed a tabula rasa that is susceptible to be filled with pure experience. Phenomenology thereby reproduces the continental rationalisms notions of experience. Belief, intention, orientation, being thrown into the world, and the experience itself are phenomena, rather than the substance of human mental activity.

This is why phenomenology challenges the position of ordinary psychology, emphasizing the *orientation* of consciousness. But, there remains an essential problem: If consciousness is always oriented, this means that it could also be *dis*-oriented and distorted. Consciousness, as in the Freudian conception (and there is an interaction between psychoanalysis and phenomenology exactly at this point), has also to be characterized as prone to error. There is an important text by Freud, *The Question of a Weltanschauung*[59], which shows the variety of the errors of the conscious experience. The directly experienced corporeal world is not the

---

59   Freud, New Introductory Lectures on Psycho-analysis, Lecture XXXV, 1933.

world described and explained by science. One of them must err—but which one? A critical answer comes, characteristically from Husserl, in his prominent work *Krisis der Wissenschaft*: The European science errs, since it tries to make its world and concepts compatible with everyday experience. Yet, there is a long history of science since the Renaissance, where the main classical sciences—astronomy, geometry, mathematics, physics and chemistry—have made discoveries that challenged and contradicted with the everyday wisdom, making the invisible in life visible.

Why has cinematography long been a particularly important domain of experience to be studied by phenomenologists? Deleuze and Guattari questioned why phenomenology has always been interested in engaging with the world of art for formulating its concepts—such as Merleau-Ponty being aspired after Cézanne, Freud after Leonardo da Vinci, Heidegger after Van Gogh and poetry? Even when they deal with the most ordinary, everyday experience (for instance, ordinary perception) phenomenologist always feels the need to refer to art—visual, auditory or poetical. 'Phenomenology is forced to transform itself to a phenomenology of art, since the immanence of the lived experience in a transcendental subject needs to be expressed in transcendent functions which are not determined in general experience, but which passed through the here and now of the lived experience itself, incarnating, thereby constituting living sensations.'[60] This is the way Mikel Dufrenne is forced to create an entire analytical system to restore perceptive and affective a prioris that would serve as conditions of the sensation with respect to the relation between human body and the world.[61]

The phenomenological project could not remain indifferent to cinema, and its possible deployment in the world of art. But what was the status of cinema in regards to the art in general, since it occupied a rather ambiguous position between entertainment industry and art proper from its early beginnings? The strict documentary character of the film that followed the tracks of photography—the acknowledgement of the nature of moving image as belonging to something present there and now—could make it impossible to situate cinema within the domain of art. Photographic and cinematographic images belonged more to the domain of opinion, rather than art. Photography was servile to the press during an era where public opinion expanded to cover the entirety of the world, and the earlier exotic images of Lumière brothers were only of general public interest. Yet, phenomenology knew well that art is something quite different from opinion, since it transcends any particularity and singularity it creates. Hence, there were not many reasons for phenomenologists to be interested in this trivial experience, which was not yet at a point where great authors of cinema perfected the cinematographic language.

Yet many phenomenologists, notably Rudolf Arnheim, ventured into developing an expanded phenomenology of cinematic-visual perception. Arnheim's theory of film has been foundational for the future film philosophies. Arnheim seems to be representative of the new psychological research into visual arts which considers the phenomenology

---

60   Deleuze and Guattari, *What is philosophy?*.
61   Mikel Dufrenne, *Phénoménologie de l'expérience esthétique*, Paris: PUF, 1953.

of perception as a general theoretical framework. We have noted that, since Husserl, phenomenology challenged the classical division between cognition and perception. Arnheim assumes this critical standpoint which opposes the actual attitude of Western civilization that disdains perception, that stems from the assumption that perception does not involve thought—a thoughtless perception is helpless against reason in regards to the multitude of perceivable appearances. But is such a valorization of perception sufficient to constitute the *artistic* nature of cinema? Among the contemporaries of Arnheim, there have always been great artists who perceived cinema as a powerful device that is destined to destroy the very notion of art and literature. Even Virginia Woolf wrote an interesting essay against cinema as early as 1926, criminalizing any attempt of transposing the works of literature into cinema. What she laments is not the lower quality of adaptations, but the very idea of cinematographic narrative assuming the form of fiction.[62] She insists upon is rather a critique of cinema's reduction of a full fledged literary personality (a social or psychological *type*, if you will) into a uni-dimensional character with no artistic depth—a perceivable *copy* of Anna Karenina on the screen, for example. The disdain towards early cinema was highly common among the artists and many intellectuals. Hence, Arnheim's task had been challenging and almost assumed a *burden of proof*: How could cinema constitute an art form?

A major thread in the early criticism of cinema among intellectuals of the time had been the reproduction of reality through purely mechanical means in cinema. This is a particularly important point, since it refers to the *naive* and *natural* documentary character of the cinematographic image. This point would become obsolete within the later evolution of the cinema, and the perfection of cinematographic language through development of composition styles and montage would soon outworn the idea of pure mechanical reproduction.

However, varying interests of early filmmakers and cinema publics have already outlined a trajectory for the future of cinema. Its audience embraced the *natural* documentary character of cinema in this epoch. Lumière's *cinématographe* and Edison's kinetoscope films (such as *Dancing Woman*) already presented simple montage. In other words, some of Arnheim's theses on '*why film is art?*' were already present in Edison's device. But the American public was not so much interested in the *mechanical reproduction* of a dancing girl. The fate of Lumière's device was far more a history of success. The reason was not that the cinématographe was technically better and more accessible to the public. In early Lumière films, there was something more, in comparison with Edison's invention: The movement of everyday life without being represented by a painter, and without the stillness of photography. The public of the old continent was no stranger to theatrical representations through projection: We can trace back projections of moving images to Daguerre's Diorama, first publicly exhibited in 1822, in which the spectator was placed in an immobile position and projected lithographs created moving sceneries before her/him through lighting effects. This was followed by Panoramas, in which spectator was moving along the gradually changing exotic sceneries. Walter Benjamin correctly noticed Panorama as the precursor cinema spectatorship; an audience had already

62   Virginia Woolf, 'The Cinema, from The Nation and Athenaeum, 1926', *The Essays of Virginia Woolf: Volume 4 1925 - 1928*, Boston: Mariner Books, 2008.

been formed around moving images and their irresistible attraction.[63] The essential form of the cinema was already present in this experience: Movement was sustained not only on the bodies of spectators, but within the apparatus of the spectacle itself. And, towards the end of century, Emile Reynaud perfected the projection techniques for moving visual theater with his praxinoscope, which had effectively been earliest form of animation film. Lumière's invention, functioning as photogrammes creating an illusion of movement, built upon these earlier forms without the need to tell stories, and showing nothing but slices of movement from everyday life.

There is another genealogical line connecting the cinematographic image to photography besides the synthesis of movement it adds to it. When we discussed the modern categories of images, we mentioned an important psychological factor introduced by the technical images with a reference to Flusser: The passage from the *posing image* to *still image*. With the introduction of instantaneity, moving things could now be photographed as sequences. Such photo sequences were called *chronophotography* by Marey and reached to fame through Eadweard Muybridge's works. Their interest was quasi-scientific: to dissect the motion in sequences of equidistant still images, in order to analyze the mysteries of everyday movements. The still image already created a new kind of perception; a frozen moment, a standstill of moving things, an arrested movement. The galloping of a horse was dissected as such by Muybridge, to show that Géricault was right in painting a running horse with all four legs lifted from the ground. Muybridge himself was interested in projecting these sequences onto a screen, thus making the prehistory of cinema, but the sequences did not serve any serious scientific purposes. The science of kinetics had already gathered everything there is to know about moving bodies, and after the invention of cinematography, Marey did not show much interest in recapturing, dissecting and analyzing the moving bodies. This can be interpreted as an evidence of the absence of much scientific (therefore purely technological) interest in the beginnings of cinema.

There is certainly a prehistory of cinema, but it is rather difficult to ascertain the true genealogy of the cinema. First, there are at least three inventors; Lumière in France inventing the *cinématographe*, Edison-Dickson in United States inventing the *kinetoscope*, and Messter in Germany, inventing the so-called bioscope (Bioskop). For our purposes here, cinema is not merely another domain, which belongs to the technological order of our modern times, but an impure invention, derived out of a plurality of actual inventions, applications and ideas, and coinciding with a certain state of arts and sciences. It has also been an *event* corresponding to a total transformation in perception and in the *ways of seeing*, to borrow a term from John Berger.

In this genealogy, it is somehow useless to invoke the oldest forms of depiction of movement in graphic arts, from the cave paintings of Lascaux to Bayeux tapestry, or from old Chinese shadow theater to camera obscura, or any Arabic-European projection techniques. We know that human beings have always been capable of representing movements and actions, through morphological distortions in graphically depicted bodies. And Lascaux cave paintings, the 20 thousands year old products of an enigmatic art, have still something to do about the

---

63   Jean-Louis Leutrat, *Le Cinéma en perspective: une histoire*, Nathan Université, *Cinéma* 128 (1992).

development of visual representation techniques. However, they do not belong to the *realistic* vision, as it was generally believed at the beginning of the 20th century. Even Lukacs erroneously attributes a *primitive*, perhaps primordial *materialism* and *realism* to these cave paintings. Yet, these pictures without frames (depicting series of animal figures grouped in a syntactic system that relies on a lost tradition) are by no means realistic: As Leroi-Gourhan reveals, they have a symbolic and pedagogic nature that opposes every claim to *realism*. And the Bayeux tapestry in medieval times only *tells stories*, events and facts, which also have nothing to do with any kind of *realism*. Realism, the primary genealogical fact of *technical images*, has never been a naive, primitive aesthetic event. Even in the most developed phenomenological approaches—that of Flusser for instance, cinema belongs to the lineage of photography as the first *technical image*. Yet, motion is essential for cinematography and its *technical* characteristic should nevertheless be treated in a different way.

Arnheim finds the artistic character of film in the movement of images. This sounds rather naive, but if we trace it back to Kantian phenomenology, the aesthetic apprehension of moving images as such creates a series of great aporias. In Kant's construction of the architectonics of the faculties of mind—which forged the modern notion of phenomenon not as an *appearance* but as *apparition*—the act of perceiving tends to become a sequential process of apprehension of parts. The intellect should apprehend something (a house, a landscape) through a *reading* of its parts, but the previous one must be remembered when passing to the next part, or rather be *apprehended* in combination with the next part in Kant's terms. The challenge concerning with this notion is the nature of the apprehension of the last part, in which all previous sequential parts have to be combined—which presents an almost never ending synthesis of mental images. The last image must be *integral*, covering all parts. Kant already seems to be aware of what today's psychology of perception calls *Gestalt*. But he also insists upon the necessity to have a common measure, a unit through which the visible is perceived. In other words, we have to have mental frames, almost like empty frameworks, to be applied a priori to the objects of perception. What he calls the experience of the sublime is related with these; sublime refers to the moments when the object of perception can no longer be contained by the mental frame. If beauty is a result of the perceived harmony among parts of a whole, the two modes of sublime—the mathematical and dynamic—are the results of an a priori inability to attribute categories to the existential excess implied by the encounter. This is the image of an ocean during the tempest, as the dynamic sublime, or the movements of celestial bodies, as the mathematical sublime.

The delight of the first cinematographic reproductions of movement belonged to the level of Kantian sublime, insofar as the sentiment of fear experienced by the first spectators of *La Gare Ciotat* must be that of a movement that escapes from and transcends the frame—a train entering the station. Arnheim's entire paradigm of on cinematographic phenomenology of perception lies in such Kantian context: As an instrument which can show a movement (which necessarily happens in a three-dimensional space) in two-dimensions, the cinematographe can record photogrammes from a particular point of view, with objects of apparent size. For Arnheim, cinema opens the possibility of some kind of bizarre absence as such; the absence of space-time continuum.

An Opposition: Edison-Dickson versus Lumière

Here we have to adopt a sociological approach toward the birth of cinema once again. As we mentioned, we have at least three inventions—the Cinématographe of Lumière brothers, the Kinetoscope of Dickson introduced by Edison, and the Bioskop of Messter. We leave the third to the historians of cinematographic technology and direct our attention to the first two inventions, which approximately occurred around the same period of fin-de-siècle. The continental perspective is clear: Lumière's Cinématographe had become the almost *official* (in other words, sociological) beginning of the cinema as a cultural form. From its very beginnings it has been public, documentary, and oriented towards *storytelling*. Latter, despite the disbelief of its early inventors, would pave the way to popular entertainment industry.

There is a general tendency against considering Lumière and Edison as the two founders of cinema on the basis of the opposition between the documentary quality of Lumière's work, and Méliès's introduction of *fiction* into cinema. It is possible to affirm these two lines not as opposing to each other, but rather as two different aspects of the cinema. If there really is an opposition in cinema, we believe, it belongs to a different order and takes place between the two inventors of motion pictures—Lumière's cinématographe (in which film was projected on a surface) and Edison-Dickson's kinetoscope (in which the viewer watched the film through an eyepiece). The former has also been a form of entertainment, but it always remained as a relatively public device due to the projection. The latter, on the other hand, was certainly capable to project documentaries, but since it operated as a closed device that presented the film through an ocular, it only allowed private watching rather than public screening. It is evident that Lumière's cinématographe has been the winner because the expansion of projection salons. Edison's invention had a very short public/commercial life; it quickly left its place to projection setups. Yet, as Bonitzer puts it, '[...] as every history, the history of cinema has been the history of schisms and divisions, of dehiscences, of ruptures which affected the art of filmmaking, which transformed it and created it as such. This is a history full of noise and furor (not only on the screen but also behind it), of brute polemics, of victims and corpses.'[64] The Lumière Brothers's success should be considered as a limited one now: It seems like television, which has declared its domination over cinema (at the level of culture industry) genealogically belongs to the Edison-Dickson's kinetoscope, with the privacy of the *watching*, open to the voyeurism of the video. Lumière's *care* for the public in their camera work already appears in their first films; they try not to intervene and disturb the passers-by on the streets, carefully frame their shots from a distance. The Cinema was born as a public apparatus, rather than a private one.

Yılmaz Güney and Political Cinema

In order to understand the unique place occupied by Yılmaz Güney in the relatively short history of Turkish cinema, one has to consider the Turkish film industry embodied in Yeşilçam, which emulates Hollywood in form and function. Turkey had its stars, producers and even

---

64   Pascal Bonitzer, *Le champ aveugle: essais sur le réalisme au cinéma*, Vol. 32, Paris: Cahiers du cinéma, 1999.

schools of filmmaking, especially those coming out of Muhsin Ertuğrul's theater. Yeşilçam cinema suffered from its fundamentally theatrical roots. It had its own sub-cultures and genres, and it was not too different from other third-world cinemas in that sense, such as Egyptian, Indian and Iranian cinemas. It has became a mainstream cinema with many genres like melodrama, comedy, and even musicals, not to mention some authorial punctuations of filmmakers such as Lütfü Akad, Metin Erksan, Atıf Yılmaz among others. These authors had been able to avoid the clichés for a while, or rather suspend them at certain moments, to introduce a kind of *social realism* into Turkish cinema.Yet they failed to create a new, *national* cinema, and to become a part of the *Third Cinema* of 1960's, as Latin American filmmakers did. Yılmaz Güney, on the other hand, appeared as a sudden break with the official and traditional establishment of cinema in Turkey.

Yeşilçam films were oriented towards entertaining an illiterate audience, as the film production and distribution expanded with increasing number of open-air cinemas and movie theaters popping up in provincial towns and villages especially during the fifties and the sixties. Such dissemination also implied the proliferation of certain genres specific to Turkey. These genres were shaped by the authorship concerns and geographical differences: Many melodramatic films, having their own narrative and linguistic conventions, culturally belonged to, Istanbul, the main metropolitan urban center of Turkey. This gave certain authors, such as Akad and Erksan, the space to produce films of provincial village life infused with sentiments of authenticity and a sense of social realism. Yılmaz Güney's early films belonged to this cultural sphere, and some of them were made in collaboration with these authors (such as *The Law of Borders* by Lütfü Akad, which was written by Güney who also played the protagonist). These films were not distant from the common clichés of Yeşilçam, but earned so much popularity that Güney became a heroic public figure representing the disintegrating feudal social order, especially in Kurdish regions. Yılmaz Güney was Kurdish himself, born in Çukurova region which had been the stage of capitalistic expansion of industrial agriculture with all its malaises for decades. He soon became a star within the Yeşilçam tradition, and even his unconventional private life soon became a controversial political issue. Adana and Çukurova in general was a place that many Turkish literary figures came from, including some of the most influential authors such as as Orhan Kemal and Yaşar Kemal. Güney's career started in literature with these influences as a storyteller and, later, scriptwriter.

Yet, *social realism* required a new kind of imagery at the very least, which lacked even in the prominent examples of Erksan and Akad's films, such as *Kuyu* (The Well, 1968) or *Sevmek Zamanı* (Time to Love, 1965). Erksan's images were rather extravagant, empty cinematographic clichés, bounded by Yeşilçam's narrative conventions. The orientation towards the illiterate spectator prevailed, but has not been transformed. The experiments made by these directors turned into commercial failures, and they were even criticized by left-wing critics for being distant from social realities. One can consider how these criticisms motivated Güney's later films, such as *Umut, Sürü* and *Yol*.

Yeşilçam clichés were born out of a cinema imitating the banal examples of Hollywood classical cinema with unsophisticated and inadequate means. Turkish cinema was not able to free itself from theatrical dramatization in its early stages, because of a particular influence of the early films of Muhsin Ertuğrul who was not only coming from a family of theatre artists, but also considered as the founder of Turkish national theater. Such consideration of course implies a nationalist perspective and fails to recognize the strong theatrical traditions of Armenians, Greeks and Jews in the late Ottoman era, alongside authentic-popular traditions of representation from Turkish Anatolians. Yet, it is true that the Kemalist Republican regime found in Muhsin Ertuğrul's style its own *official* cinema, distant from the controversies of social realities and closer to restoring the national unity according to Republican ideological premises. Being direct simulations of the low-grade entertainment oriented dramas, Ertuğrul's films had been negligent of their problems with filmic language, representation and thematization. These films aimed at creating national stars in Hollywood fashion, but without any serious investigation into the narrative forms and investment in their production quality. The reaction to Ertuğrul's films did not necessarily intend to create an avant-garde alternative to it, but rather to tell other kinds of stories, those of the provincial, rural life and poverty.

Yeşilçam's narrative forms are still worth deciphering, since the values and the ethos they reflect remain as the backbone of Turkish cinema. Poor in their cinematographic substance, they are still powerful in creating popular images. While none of the great directors seriously payed attention to the problems of filmic language in their work, not even to problems of composition and montage, they did admirable works in creating popular narratives. Within the social realism thread, Erksan was able to disperse the traditional images of Yeşilçam into a fragmented road story, narrating the violence of peasant life and emancipation of a peasant woman symbolically killing her husband. Very close to *socialist realism* trend, Akad's *Law of the Borders* narrated a quite different story while recreating the clichés of Yeşilçam cinema: It offered the image of real life, as the film was shot at real locations rather than in studio. This was quite important since the Yeşilçam tradition even turned certain urban landscapes of Istanbul (such as famous Rumelihisarı and Bosphorus landscape) as exotic background decors for its romantic clichés. Thus, with *Law of the Borders*, documentary element was introduced into Turkish cinema—the village itself as representing the village, and not a landscape to be used as a background for accentuating an affective state.

Already in his early popular films, Güney was able to impose certain anti-clichés upon the directors. For example, a scene of the miserable but honorable protagonist exiting the prison, which is quite a familiar theme in Yesilcam melodramas: Yeşilçam storytelling conventions showed such plan-sequences from outside of the prison, framing the lonely ex-convict from the front, from the street to where he will step in soon, or, from the perspective of someone who waits him outside, a problematic lover, a friend or an enemy. Güney has been the first one to frame the ex-convict leaving the prison from behind, from inside of the prison, as if the outside is no longer the place of relief but an uncanny exterior space, the place of uncertainty, and perhaps suffering and death. Güney would later make a film entirely inside the prison, *Duvar* (*The Wall*, 1983), but only after discovering the *outside* as a prison par excellence in his *Yol* (*The Road*, 1982).

In the pragmatics of cinema, there is no need to frame the moment of release from prison in order to tell the story of an ex-convict. One can simply show him free at the outside, and backtrack his story in the narrative. Yet, the world of Yılmaz Güney has prison bars—internal or external, psychological or social, but ultimately political. Deleuze correctly opposes to regarding Güney's cinema as an example of classical political cinema. The life of contemplation serving as a means of illumination, as a means of gaining consciousness, which has been the main theme of the traditional political cinema, as exemplified in Ford's *The Grapes of Wrath,* or Pudovkin's *The Mother,* is no longer present in Guney's films. The prison serves as the outside, as the place of memories, dreams and reflections, rather than a place of deprivation. It is evident that Güney, who spent time in prisons with a few occasions in his real life was able to see the relation between the prison and the outside from a political perspective. In classical political cinema, militancy—characterized by the *communist* in *The Mother* (adapted from Gorky's novel) or the *communitarian* in *The Grapes of Wrath* (adapted from the novel of Steinbeck)—was essential for preserving the boundaries between the inside and outside, the private and the public, the old and the new. Within the plot, through the complications of gaining consciousness (ultimately a class consciousness), his private affairs or his psychological situation facilitates the means of transition and transgression of the limits for the character. So one needs *political subjects* and great historical events, wars, complicities, revolutions, in order to make a *political film.* This corresponds to the agit-prop of the revolutionary Soviet cinema, and the political criticism involved in Capra, Welles and Wyler's films. In Güney's cinema, the element of *agitation* is present in its fullest strength, but not in the same form: In Yol, the free countryside or metropolis is already a prison, the outside of the prison is the same with inside, and the private is the same with public, and in *Sürü* (*The Herd,* 1978) the *old,* traditional order still coexists with the modern life. And there is an entire world of dreams, of suffering, of misery inside the prison in *Duvar.* The prison is no longer what it is intended to be: As Foucault points, it is nothing but the replication or the ideal model of the modern society, which, unlike the traditional one, becomes a machine of discipline and control.

Hence, as framed by Güney, the modern society is not different from the oppressive model it aims to replace. A hellish prison both of minds and souls is a disciplinary transformative device—the feudal oppression of the minors, of women, of children, of the poor peasants thereby transformed into the concrete oppression of a despotic state. Film compares the abstract symbolism of the agitative idea (misconceived by many as pure *ideology*) with the apparent reality of the image. This is evident in Güney's *Umut* (*The Hope,* 1970) where dried up trees and earth manifest themselves as the symbols of continuing misery and discrimination, which pushes the protagonist towards his hopeless quest. As such, Güney produces *political* and even *agitative* films without retorting to any overt political theme, by simply through the images of everyday life.

Interestingly, Güney's only film that explicitly expresses his leftist political ideas,*Arkadaş* (*The Friend,* 1974) has been generally criticized as his worst film, as its slogans and images clearly corresponded to each other, creating its political effect at a discursive level. Guney's ideas were rather expressed through manifesto-images in this film, without the required cinematographic finesse that we find more powerfully present in the *communist* works of Dziga Vertov group and especially of Jean-Luc Godard in France. In this way, the film attempts to transform its feudal, quasi-maffiatic protagonist into a revolutionary figure. This was a theme that is actually part of the pedagogic assemblages created by Godard, but in Guney's case it retained the clichés of the mainstream Yeşilçam cinema. And the revolutionary figure still preserves the old feudal values such as honor, humility and social status in his transformation.

In Güney's films, there is a type of *minor* politics sustained through the filmic images. In *Yol*, the effects of classical realism are preserved in a dialogue oriented script, with distressed, depressed and symbolic images, such a the dead horse which is presented parallel to the freezing woman in their journey through the snow. Some critics wrongly attribute such parallelism to the *traditional* silencing of women in the Third World context, although they seem to be aware of the ethnological elements in Yılmaz Güney's films[65] On the contrary, what we find here is the test of Nature through which the powers of the woman are assessed and measured—powers concomitant with a mute resistance.

This is because Güney's films were part of the expansion of ethnological concerns in Third World Cinema, followed the model of Latin American cinema, and as such, they were not action but suspense films—or, as Deleuze puts it, *trance films*. Although Turkey's political structures and militant aspirations are quite different from Latin American countries (first of all, by being a Muslim country), the *political* is similarly inflected and intense as a motive. Contrary to the classical political cinema, politics in Guney's films is like an ambient nature which surrounds and suspends every possible action. *Classical politics* as such was non-existent in Turkey anyways—politics in Turkey can only be *official*, and in the case of *opposition*, only moderate or oblique as Yeşilçam cinema exemplifies. Under these circumstances, the reaction Guney's films draw made them illocutionary acts in which politics was inherently present as pure virtuality; although their political criticism was not manifest but only implied, most of these films were banned by the political powers in the following periods.

Political film or agitation? Traditionally, the *political* films account for political events in general—such as revolutions, political complicities, and class struggles. Yet, according to Jean-Luc Godard, what makes films political is the way they are made. It would not be fair to dismiss the *political propaganda* nature of Guney's films, and it is difficult to find such a *clear* political understanding aiming at a *pedagogy of images* in these films. These are not films for gaining political consciousness (or raising it for that matter) but rather films to be affected—that of agitation, rather than propaganda.

What is politics, after all? This is evidently a more difficult question than *what is cinema*, since the latter is clearly a technological-artistic event that is generally used for representational purposes, possessing a recent history whose authors and actors are acknowledged. Yet a particular kind of politics has always been a representation in itself, whether it belongs to the democratic clusters of Ancient Greece (to the polis) or to the historical domain of power struggles. Today the power relations that politics refers to are general and diffused, and according to Foucault, we cannot distinguish the domain of politics from the domain of our private affairs anymore.

---

65   Asuman Suner, 'Specificities: Other Cinemas Speaking the Experience of Political Oppression with a
      Masculine Voice: Making Feminist Sense of Yilmaz Guney's Yol', *Social Identities 4.2* (March 2, 1998):
      283–300.

Yet cinema also has many dimensions—political, ideological, cultural and economic. It can tell us *political* stories, and its birth was nevertheless shaped by political interests of state powers and social classes—an art of mass entertainment for the bourgeoisie, an *opium of the people* in its dramatic-representational manners, according to Vertov. Lenin was the first political leader of the 20th century to recognize cinema as primarily a form of art. Dr. Goebbels, the chief-propaganda minister of the Third Reich ordered this form to be emulated, although he did not wish to raise the political issues as potential subject matters for German filmmakers. Really, what Dr. Goebbels asked from German cinema producers was to propound the empty melodramas—to tell the German people stories. He intended a cinema of embellishment that could function as the *opium of masses*. This is why Siegfried Kracauer sought the roots of Nazi aesthetics in German Expressionist films; with the exception of some propaganda films by Leni Riefenstahl, all great filmmakers were in exile, and no serious films were made.

However, political cinema, properly speaking, appears at the very roots of cinema: Films modeled after Griffith's *The Birth of a Nation* have been shot in many countries in this or that manner, and served to tell the history of the emergence of a nation. Abel Gance's *Napoléon*, as a saga of the Revolution, had been one of those, and in Turkey so many films modeled after the *birth-of-a -nation* were relentlessly shot in different periods of the republic. And in his *Intolerance*, Griffith was already telling at least four stories in a trans-historical political motive—the injustice and the intolerance throughout history, from Babylon to 19th century United States, painted with colors of liberalism. Up until Frank Capra's films, the classical Hollywood cinema offered a model for public and communitarian domains of activity and idealized the tensions between the individual and community. Hence, classical Hollywood cinema remained political only as long as it told stories about political and public issues, and classical political film remained as a thematic if not a pure genre—since political issues can also serve as a background. And the continuation of politics in cinema was always possible and already there: The war film (in the sense of the continuation of politics with different means, according to the classical formulation of Clausewitz) soon became a genre apart, peaking with the American propaganda films produced for recruitment purposes during World War II.

Yet the political was immanent in Soviet cinema. Not to be seen merely as political propaganda, and in spite of Lenin's alleged formula to give priority to cinema among other arts, revolutionary Soviet film tended to become the eminent form of artistic avant-garde with many cinematic inventions and experiments. The works of Kuleshov, Pudovkin, Eisenstein, Dovzhenko and Vertov have been the most thorough and decisive explorations of the means and expressions of cinema, a real conquest for the images as well as their theoretical premises. Even in the context of the agitprop, Vertov's newsreels remained *poetical* and quite complex masterpieces of montage and filmic expression. And the films of Eisenstein proved to be the starting point for the conquest of cinematic language, with extraordinary attempts from the director towards theoretical analysis of cinema. This great expansion of cinema belonged to a highly developed artistic milieu at the same time: Russian formalism, constructivism and futurism, as well as the general communist movement that shook the domain of arts. Many of these movements pretended to embrace the communist cause militantly as soon as they have been banded together in circles like LEF and Bakhtin's Leningrad School of Aesthetics. Yet constructivism (to which Dziga Vertov and his Kinoki movement also belonged at first) never pretended to be an artistic current, but rather to transform the arts, and to become a destructive force towards bringing art at the same level with socialized work, and to the levels of appreciation of the proletarian masses. LEF on the other hand seemed to aspire to become a pure avant-garde, with the Bolsheviks declaration of the birth of *New Language of the New Man*. This was not simply a new model of modernism, since every revolution till now had to be started by some kind of declaration which later took an official form—such as *universal declaration of human rights*, or *the new cult of reason* etc. The one about the *new man* was in fact a part of a wider series of *declarations*, which took a liberal form in United States, yet remained revolutionary in the old continent. The Soviet avant-garde belonged to the second axis, continental, Jacobinist, but aesthetically aware in its fullest.

An artist, a poet, or a filmmaker possesses the awareness of the fact that her/his task is nothing but creating new sensations and perceptions of the world—which is, according to a Hegelian aesthetics, a matter of *particularity*. S/he has to work with *images* and addresses the sensations in an attempt to provide new points of view, and new domains of reality. Paul Klee pointed the direction of new artistic development by reversing the axis of the famous question: *Art is for the people who are yet to come*. This is not purely a matter of aesthetic appreciation.

Leroi-Gourhan, the audio-visual revolution, and the surplus of reality

Our present problem is how André Leroi-Gourhan in the first volume of his *Le geste et la parole* (Gesture and Speech, 1964-65)[66] realized that the audio-visual revolution, the passage to *beyond* writing, in fact happens with the passage from silent to sound cinema. Departing from Leroi-Gourhan's argument, we will try to understand our alleged passage from cinematography to videography. How a video-philosophy could be formulated by Maurizio Lazzarato and Angela Melitopoulos on the grounds of a *videographic revolution* which is not purely an *informational one*[67]. Leroi-Gourhan has demarcated a line of separation between silent and sound cinema (and its *televisual-videographic* hinterland), yet the openings such demarcation points to remain rather unexplored in his works: This signifies a passage to *beyond* writing, and the integration of the sound (including language) into the image that results in common informational content todays audio-visual systems and multimedia technologies.[68] This passage reduces the role of a margin of *imagination* reserved for the individual, and tends to suppress it almost entirely at the level of the full blown *virtual reality*. The question is, then, whether videography constitutes a turning point in the same manner with Leroi-Gourhan's *audio-visual revolution*.

The essential problem was that a certain margin reserved for personal interpretation that provided space for imagination has always existed between writing and the reality it represented. Such margin was still preserved in the phonograph, the recording of the actual

---

66   Leroi-Gourhan, *Gesture and Speech*.
67   Maurizio Lazzarato, *Videophilosophy: The Perception of Time in Post-Fordism*, Columbia University Press, 2019
68   Ibid, pp. 213-214

sounds, since the inability of recognizing the face of the speaking person or the singer is the most playful art for the imagination. The same margin existed for the photographic recording of images: One's imagination always goes further towards the outside of the frame, which belongs to the context of the image rather than the image itself and its form. In other words, the photographic image does not entirely fulfill the reality it represents, its stillness and the pause it implies opens up a margin for interpretation and stimulates imagination. The forms of this interpretation have been categorized by Roland Barthes as the *punctum* and *studium*.[69] Yet, with the audio-visual integration, there are no *stills images* and every image and sound move in time, if not time moves in them and through them. And reality is always constructed in time, which provides it with its forms, constant changes, and continuity, as Leroi-Gourhan associates with filmic and audio-visual processes. As images (and also speeches and sounds) succeed each other, the sound cinema reconstructs the element of time and its rhythms.

Chion calls the sound of radio as *acousmatic*, a term refers to a category of sound in which one hears *without seeing the cause*.[70] It is a term that describes radio dramas and sound events, which are heard by the listeners (and voice actors), but not 'seen'. There is a parallelism between Leroi-Gourhan's point and Chion's conception of acousmatic sound, which he further explains as; 'Radio, phonograph, and telephone, all which transmit sounds without showing their emitter, are acousmatic media by definition.'[71]

We can infer from this one still more important issue: Sound cinema's integration of the visual and auditive media has introduced a *supplementary resemblance to reality*. We can also derive a similar thesis out of the works of André Bazin, with his description of the evolution of the cinematographic language as a developing tendency towards *plus de réalité* (surplus of reality). Bazin's main problematic had been the relationship between cinema and *reality* (which resolves into *surplus of reality*). This surplus is certainly not the *realistic* element but rather the aesthetic-artistic element provided by cinema, since, when he refers to the works of Italian Neorealism, Bazin in fact sees an aesthetic criterion in this expanding realism that distinctly separates Neorealism from classical realism.[72]

In film, sounds and images work together, sometimes in a synchronized fashion, sometimes in counterpoint to each other, and sound adds a vital third dimension to the screen's flatness. Sound helps to extend off-screen space and *widens* the frame, and with the technological achievements of the early 1930s, sound reinforces the reality-effect of characters moving in their diegetic surroundings. But while sight and sound work simultaneously in film and radio, the blind medium is confined to sound alone. The recorded human voice does not refer to a corporeal body, radio does not share cinema's *surplus of reality* and it has even less *presence of an absence*. Radio plays must speak for themselves and create their own sound spaces specific to the medium, uniquely differing from the representation of time

---

69   Roland Barthes, *Camera lucida: Reflections on photography*, London: Macmillan, 1981.
70   Michel Chion, *Le promeneur écoutant: essais d'acoulogie*, Paris: Ed. Plume, 1993, p. 32.
71   Ibid, p. 71.
72   André Bazin, 'Qu'est-ce que le cinéma'.

and space in plays in other media. Dialogue and other narrative devices available to radio drama impose linearity and *real* time upon its diegesis, which allows little or no elasticity.

One can try to understand such argument in this way: The sound cinema (not limited to the *talkies*, as we will see later) has created a *surplus of resemblance to reality* by uniting the visual and auditory media—and one can distill a similar pattern of arguments from Bazin. Yet, the audio-visual integration (largely depending upon the technological inventions in recording and transmission) has given birth to an entirely new apparatus which Bazin seems to neglect at the expense of his analyses about the *device*. This integration was nothing less than the invention of *television*—or of video, while the two are ideologically oriented towards different roads.

Our concern is not the *empirical* reality of the world of television, or involving in an empirical research into the ideological effects of this audio-visual realm. We believe that this reality has never been, and it is unlikely that television *can measure the pulse of the society* or of the public opinion—as it has been alleged by certain liberal views. It is evident that the television reflects and transmits many events, ideas, agendas and the like, and it creates a social memory operating directly through the audio-visual systems—one should better *measure* the *pulse of TV* in that sense. In other words, the televisual apparatus not only provides echoes, representations, and information, it produces the *reality* by forming it. This is not even a reproduction, since in the televisual activity there is at least a *part* of reality which is *consumed* by television, even if we leave aside Baudrillard's notion of *hyperreality* which points to the substitution of reality itself without having any reference to it. Yet it is insufficient to point that television *produces* reality (of its own); we should also add that when television manipulates or reflects opinions, with the same token it produces them as *opinions*. The term deployed by mass communications researchers for approaching to this fact has been *agenda setting*, which still remains as a weak concept. As Godard explains, cinema already started as *agenda setting*—it already functioned as an index, or inventory of images, just because in cinema, as Virginia Woolf once wrote, there was an iconographic simplification of literature, poetry, novel, and theater.

Hegel and the Age of Aesthetics

It is interesting that the birth of photography, invented as the *héliographe* of Nicéphore Niepce coincides with the death of the Great German philosopher Hegel, to whom we owe a foundational thesis on the history of arts and aesthetics. This thesis is a little bizarre and ambiguous despite its Hegelian clarity. It is the continuation of the entire Hegelian system of philosophy. Hegel declares that the age of art has been completed and reached its end, and we now have entered into the age of aesthetics. He already develops his theses on such *end of art* in his *Phänomenologie des Geistes*,[73] which corresponds to a dialectical achievement of history. Since, according to Hegel, everything is the achievement of self-consciousness (that always comes in three formal stages), or rather the dialectical self-development of the Idea, so is the case of the art. Certainly there is a *history of art* which is elevated to a philosophical

---

73   Georg Wilhelm Friedrich Hegel, *The Phenomenology of Spirit (Cambridge Hegel Translations)*, Terry Pinkard (trans.), Cambridge University Press, 2018.

certitude in Hegel, and this development is both historical and evolutionary. Although we are quite distant from Hegel's dialectical conventions in our discussion here, there seems to be a historically important question about *modernity* which should be processed through the bizarre and idealistic assertions of Hegel. This is the ambiguous nature of *modernity; in the* way Hegel declares, that *'now, it is time to...'*

For Hegel, the evolution of the universe is the panlogical paradigm which governs history. The evolution of arts is also part of this panlogic history, and obeys to the same dialectical roots of history in general. However, art is unlike thinking or philosophy, since it is developed through the particular and not the universal. As Kant would say, although art is disinterested, it is still obeying to the general rules of historical development.

And what is this historical development? Hegel invokes the earliest form of art, its *symbolical* stage, when the disinterestedness was not yet fully developed. Art and religion largely coincided, and a divine gigantism prevailed (embodied in Egyptian pyramids, Greek temples, etc.) Yet, everything was reduced to ornamental, symbolic figurations—not only within the small scale, traditional artisanship of Indian, Chinese, and Arab Orient cultures, but also in Europe. Hegel's reasons can easily be understood since the major and dominant branches of art in this first epoch were architecture and sculpture. According to Hegel, architecture and sculpture with their three-dimensional, *topographic* allure is closer to the Nature (alienated in the Nature, in its extension and matter), and although they posses gigantic forms such as the pyramids, they obey to the rules of symbolic ornamentations. Thus, the ornament and its symbolic repetition constitute only a façade, a superficiality and it is part of the tradition rather than reasoning. According to Hegel's formula, this is a stage when self-consciousness is religious, it is closed upon itself, and it operates through a formal self-realization of consciousness as merged with nature (alienation).

Then comes the second stage, dominated by painting. Painting is basically two-dimensional, it signifies the loss of one the three dimensions—the depth. Other branches of art also tend to develop from Middle Ages up to the Renaissance and the Baroque, but fundamentally under the guidance of painting. This two-dimensionality means that the role of consciousness increases, since it involves abstraction and avoidance of pure symbolism. It is certainly more difficult to *understand* a picture than a sculpture, and even the knowledge of symbols has been transformed: Later, Johann Huizinga will describe a late medieval struggle between the Church and popular understanding of the religion of the masses, in which the latter endanger the authority of the Church not with their lack of faith, but their excess of faith expressed in images and icons. It was as if the religion was *crystallized into images*, and this was nothing but the waning of the Middle Ages.

If we return to Hegel's aesthetics, the third and last stage comes when music and poetry dominate: This is certainly the Romantic epoch, when poets like Goethe, Hölderlin and Lessing, and great musicians like Mozart and Beethoven were close friends of Hegel the Philosopher. The consciousness, or the Spirit operating through the *particular* is here in its highest possible level and power. Music is not *dimensional*, it is fully abstract, disinterested and pure. And in poetry, everything is reduced to pure consciousness, to the language which peoples and individuals are born into. This is the ultimate stage of the art, almost its *end* or *telos*. One could even say that this was nothing more than Hegel's courtesy to his poet friends.

Yet Hegel is rather concerned, when talking about the *end of the history of art*. (History, according to Hegel, ends everywhere at his moment—since it reaches to its finalization in Hegel's Prussia—and the age of philosophy starts with him). He poses the question; in what sense the art, as the realm of the particular, should pass into the universal and the general? When he declares the birth of an age of aesthetics and the end of the history of art, he assumes that the philosophical concept of universality will reign from now on. Hence, philosophy is something beyond art, for the latter has always remained as the realm of the particulars—things, perceptions, singular objects, events etc. It is difficult that art *thinks*, since it cannot generalize and universalize. It depicts something particular, and the entirety of the Idea is only revealed in art partially. Thus, the *age of aesthetics* to come is not a higher stage of the history of art, but the lower stage of the age of philosophy, declares Hegel. Aesthetics is philosophical, rather than artistic.

A burning question is always alive throughout our commentary on Hegelian aesthetics. Today, almost two hundred years after Hegel declared the age of aesthetics we are in a historical position that allows us to question what has really happened in this Age of Aesthetics. The subtlety of history has perhaps marked Hegel's death with the invention of photography, which offered an entirely new aesthetic experience, and approximately one and half century later, we are now watching television. How does photography compare with painting, sculpture and architecture as interpreted from Hegel's perspective? A rather strange question haunts the historians of photography: why photography waited for early 19th century (1830s) to be invented, whereas the chemical recording process was already known by the alchemists, just as the camera obscura has been used since Middle Ages by the painters.

In any case, modern art introduced not only *ambiguous materials*, but also ambiguous *ideas*, as in the case of Impressionism and Expressionism, Surrealism and Dadaism. Even the poetry returns back to a Symbolism, which is certainly not the same with what Hegel sees in the art of antiquity. The *age of the aesthetics* is rather a swerving oscillation and conflict of ideas and currents, and schools in constant struggle against each other. This is the very definition of the *modern*. Recursively, we may conceive the enigma in Hegel's perspective: Up until the time when Hegel declared the death of the history of art, artistic currents were defined as *historical periods* (Renaissance, Baroque, Classicism, Romanticism), and from then onwards, the *history* tends to become ambiguous, with the coexistence of many struggling currents and *schools*. This was the milieu in which cinema was born.

The Concept of Pathos: Cinema and Affects

Eisenstein's insistence on the significance of the notions of *pathos* and *ecstasy* (which is clearly part of the Griffithian Hollywood cinema, and dissolved in a dream world) could be taken as a self-contradiction for a materialist Soviet filmmaker and artist. He defines pathos as *being beside oneself*, an ecstatic state whose classical forms he finds and criticizes in Griffithian cinema on his way to develop it as a notion referring to *organic unity* and *teleology* instead. He adopts the Hegelian conception of *modern dialectics* and opposes to the Ancient Greek apprehension of the term. Yet, there is no ambiguity in his understanding of dialectics: Starting from Hegel until Sartre's *Critique of Dialectical Reason* (*Critique de la raison dialéctique*), the idea that there is a dialectics of Nature (provoked by Marx's certain texts and especially Friedrich Engels's unfinished works, compiled as *Dialectics of Nature*) has been denounced, and Eisenstein seems to belong to this tradition: Nature is not dialectical and every dialectic is historical. Dialectics are the laws of thinking and of historical development, and, in the case of Eisenstein, it gives us the general laws of *artistic composition*.

Still, the problem only shifts to another controversial stage now: Where is Nature, then? As a filmmaker, Eisenstein should now propose that, unlike theatre, Nature is present everywhere in cinema, in the way André Bazin will later insist upon.[74] One can only show people and their actions in a landscape—or a desert or a forest, if not the artificial urban environment in that regard—which constitutes the settings or the milieu of the film. Even Sartre shows how, in opposition to theatre, the trajectory of movement in cinema is from Nature to the eyes, irreducible to the *theatrical contract* between actors and spectators. The cinematographic image is already in Nature.

Hence, in order to solve this problem, Eisenstein develops his sophisticated concept of *non-indifferent nature*. 'Let us assume we are to present grief on the screen. There is no such thing as grief *in general*. Grief is concrete, thematic.'[75] These words clearly brings Eisenstein closer to *phenomenologists* according to whom no empty consciousness existed: Every consciousness is consciousness of something, according to Edmund Husserl's famous formula. And, if an artistic composition is nothing but an exchange that takes place at least two conscious persons, each having sentiments, ideas, thoughts, it simply appears that '[grief] [...] has a vehicle when a character is grieving; it has a consumer when sorrow is presented, so that the viewer also grieves.'[76]

Yet the Spinozist element of *automatism of affects* (the automaton spiritualis) is evidently present in his analyses: 'The enemy's grief after suffering defeat evokes joy in the viewer, who identifies himself with the victor...'[77] This element is still present in its simplest form, and it leads to a more complex issue: In cinema, the *viewer* is not a child, a set of intellectual and affective network of relations are already at work in the cinematic automaton.

Cinema was born parallel to the formation of modern landscape, the metropolis, and it is deeply anchored in it as its life-world (or rather its dream-world). According to Deleuze, cinema had been an answer to the late 19th century crisis in the psychology of perception in regards to the perception of motion, before becoming an integral part of our urban landscape, and

74   Andre Bazin, *Qu'est-ce que le cinema*.
75   Sergei Eisenstein, *Nonindifferent Nature: Film and the Structure of Things*, Cambridge University Press, 1987, p. 3.
76   Ibid.
77   Ibid.

before shaping the modern *society of spectacle*. Deleuze rehashes and challenges this old idea of illusion, since cinema has been the means to show human beings that their ordinary perceptions (images, paintings, photography, and theatrical or natural movement) could be reproduced by mere technological means.[78] Cinema is important for our discussion, since as early as its birth, it was considered as an example of *illusion*, that is, an inherently unconscious operation of opinion. Yet, it further established its own dream-like, illusory world that is correlated with a society of opinions, consisting in its amorphous audience.

Documentation and the Dreams of Others

We have stated that the *documentary* film fulfills its mission whenever it goes beyond merely *documenting*. Documents may as well be archived from the viewpoints of state, bureaucracy, academicians (especially historians and sociologists), or capitalist enterprise (the *book-keeping* reappears several times in Weber's account for the birth of capitalism, almost like the ultimate form of documentation), as well as documentary filmmakers. But such classification and archiving involves a montage that presuppose a logic, a pragmatic reason, and assumptions implied by that particular viewpoint. Such documentation appears to be merely technical, but Foucault's work shows us how *classification* assumes an epistemic order of seeing and reading, which are the historical a prioris of the discourse. The difference between documentation and the documentary is key to our concerns towards drawing parallelisms between the *theoretical* powers of social sciences (which, as we mentioned earlier have been considerably lessened in the course of the *academization* of social sciences and the emergence of the *sociology of opinions*) and the *imaginative* powers of documentary filmmaking (which, again, has surrendered to a *society of opinions*), and merging them together in a proposal for a *visual sociology*.

The answer to the question concerning whether *social types* irremediably withered away or *objectively* disappeared (not only in social sciences based on a doxology now, but also in other domains, as in literature and cinema) is that social types are still present at least in *history*, and remain still as both *analytical tools* and *events* for understanding the conditions of modern life, or cluster of life-experiences in modern times. For example, Michel Foucault was able to recreate them through his conceptions such as the *dangerous individual*, who was really a *social type* during the 19th century. Regarding the question whether historians are still able to create social types in general, however, we have to answer negatively, with very rare exceptions, such as Georges Duby and all those *private* historians—including the so called *oral history* attempts. Without binding with an upper (psychological) or lower (social) level of individuality, a social type cannot be created or made visible. Sociological imagination cannot operate without such a *social bond* since, as Simmel would argue, a socio-psychological type cannot be *sociologically* described without first being viewed, labeled, and *named* as such in a complex field of social exchanges, by a considerable amount of social interactions, discourses, milieus, environments.

We cannot return back to Simmel's (or any other founding fathers') conception of social types, since these were derived from experiences that had a socio-aesthetic nature. They revealed

---

78   Deleuze, *Cinema 1: The movement image*.

themselves in gestures and repetitions, and they were both *visible* and *affective*—as the *lover* somehow tended to become a *social type* in the very context of the late 19th century. A melodramatic or morbid environment was involved in the *lovers* milieu, sometimes representing him as a *dandy*, but also a *suffering* (that is *affective*) being. We have seen that this theme was essential to the literature at the end of the 19th century. This was not only concerning the *high literature* of the great Naturalist, or Realist novelists (or the *Russian novel* which we had to take apart) but also the *popular* literature and general culture; the main formula is everywhere the same—in Gogol and repetitive melodramas—, and can be stated as follows: A lover is essentially a sufferer, for the simple reason that s/he does not reciprocate love when it was available to her/him—an essential delay that envelopes the beautiful melodramas of Vincente Minelli.

Does the withering away or the demise of social types in contemporary social sciences reflect their *objective* disappearance in life under today's modern and post-modern *social conditions*? Nothing exists in the societies of opinion that we live in without already being questioned, represented, and rendered to a *simulation*. We have, however, kept our distance from the dangers of Baudrillard's or Kristeva's theses that *reality* itself withered away—simply for the reason that, although the Gulf War did not happen for us apart from its mediatic representation[79], a lot of people really died, and suffered from its consequences.

Freud taught us to take dreams seriously; but for him dreams reflected ones own lived experiences. His critic, Deleuze, pointed that *to be captured by another's dream, means nothing less than a catastrophe.*[80] When a corporeal subject becomes the object of another's dream—of his plans, ideas, mythologies, and in his media, that dream produces certain forces that decomposes or destroys its corporeal object.

Hence Edward Curtis's work on the *photographic world* of the *dying culture* of Native Americans was a Western Dream, but it had the capacity to destroy, if not suffocate or push into decay the entire Native American population. Edward Said's work—his *sociology* of texts and interpretations of Orientalist literature—attempts to detect the effects of Orientalism on the *Orient*, on those who have been dreamed about, but who nevertheless have actually corporeally existed *there*.

But sometimes, on the contrary, the East dreams the West. It is evident that the Orient was a dream or *ideological theme* of a Western, Eurocentric discourse, searching to legitimize itself as *progress* or as *accomplished* and therefore *emancipated* way of life. But it is also true that the West was, for a long time and still today, a dream for the East, as in the case of Dostoyevsky's *Idiot*, or *Young Turks*. And if the West and its social, cultural, economic and political manners are aspired in Third World, the West remains as a *model* or as a *dreamworld*—which are, from our perspective, just the same things.

---

79   Jean Baudrillard, *The Gulf War Did Not Take Place*, Indiana University Press, 1995
80   Gilles Deleuze, 'What is the creative act?', French Theory in America, ed. Sylvere Lotringer, Sande Cohen, Routledge 2001, p. 103.

The problem is that one can never escape the dreams of others. It was unlikely that all those dramatic philosophies of the Other (Levinas, Martin Buber and so forth) could *awaken* the Other from its dream. Today dreams are substantialized—they have institutions, like cinema, television and *public opinion,* they are *engineered*, *distributed* and *disseminated* (Derrida). But the question is not dreaming, but how to emancipate from Other's dream.

Kusturica's Dream in *Underground*

In his film *Underground* (a quite *popular film* as Slavoj Zizek would say), Emir Kusturica creates a dream-like world behind which we have the images of a naive and robust Balkan fighter, in a rather blasphemous (but still naive) cooperation with a disguised *conspirator* who will be his persecutor in future. He shows the two-sided *vampirism* of such a collaboration—a naive one that is *acceptable* in Kusturica's eyes, and the subtle other that appears to be a *radical evil*. Yet this a dreamed evil—and the film will continue as a dream in due course, with all kinds of archetypes, Fellini Effects, nostalgic scenes, festivities, traditional ballads, a collage of axioms on the ex-Yugoslavian conditions. Kusturica still claims to be a Yugoslavian, a country which no longer exists in substance, only through a dream dreamed by the Other, by Europe. A kind of *primitivism* emerges fundamentally and in a primordial way in his film, which becomes contested by Slavoj Zizek: that the Balkans is the primordial place of *suffering*, of *vampirism* (according to the *mythos*), of *violence* and of the *continuous war of each one against everyone*.

Yet this is a lie that cannot be openly whispered to European ears, but can only be conveyed by images. Kusturica's lies could be accepted by Europe only in its *artistic form*—the audio-visual world of *dreams*. Hence Kusturica, utters his *performative sentences* only twice in his entire narrative: 'Once Upon a Time There Was One Country ' and 'we cannot say that this is a real war when brothers don't strangle their brothers.'[81] If we didn't know that Yugoslavia itself was a country of *dreams*—Tito's dream was fundamentally different from the *American Dream*, which was a European disease according to Heidegger—Kusturica's film could mean something to us.

And once he choose the images of Bosnians applauding the incoming of Nazi troops, he *lies* at the level of *documentation*: We historically know that Bosnians, Serbians, and Croatians alike, all conspired with the occupying Hitlerian regime. But there were also those who resisted, some of them Serbian (the resistant's leader Tito), some of them Croatian, and some of them Bosnian and Macedonian. This means that the use of the *documentary* quotations in Kusturica's film are nothing more than an *aesthetic alibi* for lying, or transforming and distorting real historical events. While we believe in the *artistic freedoms*, such freedoms should not become an excuse for distorting the experiential truth or its *documentations*. Our last thesis already proves this: it is not that *documents* can lie (this is a well-known banal fact of the documents provided by *official* registers, like the Nazi documents examined by Lanzmann during his researches for *Shoah*) but that or a scene in a fiction-film as an audio-visual document, should only be used in a perspective that conspires with the demands of the reality, that is, the context in which it was shoot, and not with the demands of fiction.

---

81   *Underground* (dir. Emir Kusturica, 1995).

Lanzmann's *Shoah* and Sublimation of Images

Lanzmann's terrible interview-film about Holocaust imposes a number of complications, and once again haunts us with the problem of *existence* in Pascal's wager. Adorno urged us before: 'Is it possible still to write poetry after Auschwitz?' And Blanchot, asked again: 'And how, in fact, can one accept not to know?'[82] It is possible to distinguish the two levels of existence—the ontic and the ontologic—philosophically, but we are still unable to account for what happened there. We obviously do not have anything like a *sociology of the extermination camp*, we have no *proofs*, no *documents*—everything seems to have been suppressed by the Nazis upon their defeat, we practically have nothing. And we still watch the film in horror, while we hear already at the beginning of the film the voice of a survivor from Chelmno, in Poland, where the first gas extermination camps was erected: 'One can not speak about it. Nobody could represent what happened here himself. This is impossible. And nobody has been able to understand this.'

How this film *works* then—when it could *represent* nothing? *Shoah* (which means *disaster*) is a film successfully composed on the true *nothingness*, a nothing which is no less powerful than Sartre's, and Heidegger's. This is almost an *obsessional* camera, turning around the blind spot, around the invisibilities of a series of *absences; absence of the images,* as proofs of existence; absence of words, since no one can speak about *what just happened there; absence of documents* since they are effaced; absence of archives; absence of *witnesses*... We really believe that Lanzmann had created a new kind of *imaginary* shadowed by the grandiose *pratico-inerte* of what remained from these extermination camps—images of now emptied places, innocent forests (similar to Heidegger's), faces of oblivion, confusion and horror (especially that of the old railroad worker, on a train entering through the gate of Treblinka). We have nothing more than the confused accounts of *witnesses*, often *off voice* with a shoulder camera which is blindly in search of what is no longer visible—forever.

All questions relating to *images* suddenly reappear, no longer as purely *theoretical* problems, but also as fundamentally ethical series of questions: What is Kinopravda? What is filming the *real*? What is *fiction*? What is a mise-en-scène? How can one film death, and give its account, within morally based responsibility? Blanchot stated that 'Concentration camps, annihilation camps, emblems wherein the invisible has made itself visible forever'.[83] The terrible question is the fact that Jews were condemned to death simply for being Jew, and camps were simply modern *machines* of extermination. At this moment, we are facing the archaic figure of the *homo sacer*, in Agamben's excellent work that tries to measure the close *interval* between what we call democracy and totalitarianism.[84]

Homo sacer (sacred man) is the one who, although being condemned to death, could not be *ritually* executed. Not a *social type* but, left undefined by the *rituals of law* and the Sovereign power, anyone can judge him and condemn him, and kill him. But the major monstrous appearance of homo sacer is that in case he is killed, his killing is not considered murder.

---

82   Maurice Blanchot, *The Writing of the Disaster*, Nebraska: Univ. of Nebraska Press, 1995, p. 181.
83   Blanchot, *The Writing of the Disaster,* p. 178.
84   Agamben, *Homo Sacer: Sovereign Power and Bare Life.*

Agamben reads an entire tradition of *sovereignty* into this, where passages from totalitari-
anisms to democracies (or, pseudo-democracies) and evidently, vice versa, and a logic of
sovereignty that *delegates* its responsibilities to a community (or *civil society*) consisting in a
mass of *homo sacers*. In Lanzmann's film, there is a scene where the wife of a Nazi teacher
is asked about how many Jews were exterminated there. She states between the numbers
40,000 and 400,000—'all I can say, it was a number beginning by ...4'. Everything seems
to be horribly reduced to numbers—and there is the horror when we hear a witness uttering
'Germans forced us to unburry 240,000 corpses in order to burn them'. The film's obsession
turns around this very particular *lapsus* based on numbers—no longer a mysticism of numbers, but operating in transforming numbers into *images* and therefore, qualities... The main
problem seems to *incarnate the number*. This number could only be treated by the film, which
becomes a *document in itself*, somehow beyond documentary. Social sciences also deal with
numbers, in order to quantify opinions and intensities in the same way governments and state
bureaucracies—or, capitalism—needs *numbers*. *Shoah*'s obsession with numbers aims to
give them a new character, a quality, a quantum power: The difference between the two
moments of woman's hesitation is expressed in the great gap between two numbers—and
here, quantities become images or qualities.

What is an obsession? *Shoah* and the *written* or *oral* accounts Lanzmann provide on his experiences with the film are quite controversial, and have been denounced many times: He was
first *obsessed* with his *film, the Ultimate Film* as he calls it, since it is about the Holocaust,
the major *event* in history which remains without *documents* or even *traces*.[85] But Lanzmann
certainly wanted his film to become *the last word* par excellence—and he even admits that
if he had found a *real document* proving what has happened in the extermination camps,
'he would destroy it at that moment.'[86]

We have already talked about an *obsessional camera*, a tempting way of creating images
of the invisible, of the nothingness, of complete negation. It seems that Lanzmann made
his nine-hour long film with implicit ideological presuppositions: that only the Jew was
the victim—whereas we know that workers, peasants, gypsies of so many countries were
were also exterminated by the Nazis with the same token. And this was also the age when
Israel (which seems to have financed and promoted the film) is the oppressor of Palestin-
ians. According to Spinozist formula talking or thinking about the *bad* was bad, talking or
thinking about hate was hate. Lanzmann needs something almost like the Kantian *sublime*

---

85   Alain Finkielraut, a Jewish public intellectual, retorts: 'Claude Lanzmann considers himself as the
      exclusive commissioner of the Extermination, attempting to invent a new definition of Antisemitism:
      The Antisemitic is the one who does not pay his devotions to his 'Film Unique'. This auto-idolatry is
      grotesque and disgusting...' (['Le cas Lanzmann'], *Le Nouvel Observateur* (31 janvier 1991), p. 118).
      And Tzvetan Todorov the linguist believes that 'Shoah, a film on hatred, is made by means of hatred and
      teaches hatred' (Tzvetan Todorov, *Face à l'extrême*, Paris: Le Seuil, 2013, p. 255). There are evidences
      that Shoah was financed by Menahem Begin's government, and Lanzmann, an assimilated French Jew,
      has previously made a film apologizing Israel's politics (and even its military stance) against Palestinians
      (Israel, Why / Pourquoi Israel, 1973).We believe that all these debates about the film belong to a sphere
      of *opinions* around it, and we prefer to concentrate on the substance of the film instead.
86   *Shoah*, (dir. Claude Lanzmann, 1985).

instead, that is capable of creating *positive* affects out of *negative* ones. The *unnameable, the unaccountable, the invisible* have to be present in his film. And the name of the film, *the shoah* (which literally means *catastrophe* and refers to Jewish Holocaust in Modern Hebrew) is akin to, and perhaps copied by Kusturica in his popular action film—the *Underground*.

This essential ambiguity, causing many *political* and *ideological* debates over *Shoah* in our view should be the point of departure for discussing the *powers of visibility*. As we have postulated, Lanzmann's film does not only betray the pathetic force of the *time-image* (which is described by Deleuze as a kind of image which no longer shows an action against a situation that reveals a challenge to the actor, but constitutes pure sounds and images of life, crystalizing and revealing the temporality of the image—the memory-images), but Lanzmann also seems to force upon his interlocutors a *humanistic* and *existential* ideal: they were infinitely indebted to the world, to account for their *existential experiences*, and this debt imposed the responsibility to speak, for the benefit of *humanity* or *potentially* of Israel. This debt to speak however, is not only imposed (obsessionally) upon the victims and the survivors, but also indiscriminately upon the old Nazis and old polish peasants, like the wife of the Nazi teacher. Lanzmann wildly insists on calling for his subjects to speak, which they are not capable of—*Shoah* turns into an Existentialist film in this sense, a torture, an obsessive and often paranoid investigation and claims. The pratico-inerte is present everywhere, not only in the discourse, but also in the now empty spaces of Treblinka and Birkenau. The Kantian *sublime* of the image creates horror rather than *understanding,* and Lanzmann seems to expect a miraculous dialectics to suddenly starting to work.

Yet the *sublime* is nothing but an *idea*. It is the incommensurable, it cannot be imagined (by being outside our powers to imagine), and as Heidegger commented, it gives a *nooshock* to us just to reveal that even *understanding* could not be a adequate.[87] Understanding (*Verstand*) for Kant was a faculty in need of *concepts* yet incapable of *conceptualizing* (which could only be provided by the faculty of *Vernunft*, the Reason), thus surrendered to the world of *ideas* that it perpetually categorized.[88]

Cinema has a long historical experience with the sublime: Flaherty has already provided an excellent example of it in documentary filmmaking with his *Nanook of the North*. But this is still a *mathematical sublime* revealing itself in the *situation* provided by an hostile environment, infinite *whiteness* of nature as a milieu, where the Inuit *socius* is represented by a single individual (through staging nevertheless) who becomes an *actor* in the documentary. Vertov had reasons in urging that the documentary don't need *names* (like Nanook, since all Inuits are the same in their social and collective life experiences) and *persons*, but only *life as it is*.[89] And Deleuze had reasons for at least partially recognizing Flaherty's merits: Flaherty's films are constituted by two *ideologies*; if the first is Hollywoodian, the second belongs to the Anglo-Saxon way of viewing history (especially Toynbee, but later by Pitirim Sorokin. . .).[90] The

---

87   Gilles Deleuze, *Cinema 2*, p. 152.
88   Kant, *Critique of Pure Reason.*
89   Vertov, *Kino-Eye: The Writings of Dzigo Vertov.*
90   Deleuze, *Cinema 1: The movement image.*

classical Hollywood film, beginning with Griffith imposes a regime of images mainly based on the presentation of *situations* (social, natural, dreamful and so forth) against which an *individualized* hero should react, whose actions create small changes in the previously given situation. For instance, Simmel's Stranger reappears as *mediator* and *judge* in classical Westerns—coming from the wild with his savage soul, he enters to a community in which he appears not as someone 'who comes today and will leave tomorrow', but one 'who comes today but will stay tomorrow'. The American *community* is purely a community of *good* or *evil*, of *peace* or a Hobbesian *war of all against all*. And the Stranger appears here either as a *mediator* or *intruder*: He will help the community stand against its enemies who appear in the form of untamed external threat (such as Native Americans, or the outlaws), restore the peace and the communitarian sentiments of *home sweet home*. Nanook is not far from such western narrative, but it is quite remote from Simmel's Stranger. He is in a constant struggle with such a strong and imposing *Nature* which is his life-world, that he does not appear as an actor who can change the situation he falls into, his milieu or his environment.

Recapitulation of the Theory of Images

In our attempt to classify images, the first principle had been Flusser's distinction between *technical* and *representational* images. This was, however, a quite broad categorization that can only reveal at most the possible reasons for the *fascination* of masses encountering popular images (photography, cinema) for the first time. Bazin, on the other hand, on a similar line, has tried to base his philosophy of cinema in contradistinction with an *ontology of photography*—a kind of memento mori and a religious logic of *survival through images and effigies*. Peirce the logician and semiotician gave a much more detailed account of an adequate classification of images: When the optical character of certain signs was *intentional*, one could discern them as *opsigns*[91] that can convey meanings without the aid of *language* as a totally symbolic medium. In such Peircean sense, we are today living almost in an *imagosphere*, where all meaning passes onto images and *recordings*. This is almost the state of *panimagism*, which we would like to attribute to Bergson's, and following him, Deleuze's notion of the image.

For Bergson matter is an image, and it is perceived in a similar fashion to Vertov, for whom the fundamental task of the newborn cinema was to *translate* perceptions (percepts) into things themselves—and this is a positive attempt to abolish the Kantian-phenomenological distinction between things-in-themselves and things-as-they-appear-to-us (phenomena). Montage for Vertov was part of the classification of images, and what mattered were not images themselves, but the apperceptive link, almost the empty space which connects at least two images. This was his theory of *intervals*, in which the space between two images had not been perceived as a distance that separates two entities or events, but a connection, bonds that bring them together. Thus, through images and intervals, Vertov was able to link two distant things in the same sequence—the metropolitan and the nomadic, death and birth, labor and entertainment, as exemplified in his film *Man With The Movie Camera*. In his *Enthu-*

---

91   Gilles Deleuze, *Cinema 2: The time-image*, p. 39: 'The relation, sensory-motor situation: indirect image of time is replaced by a non-localizable relation, pure optical and sound situation: direct time-image. Opsigns and sonsigns are direct presentation of time.'

siasm, one can understand how, through the work of intervals, images are cumulative—as they accumulate towards creating intense powers and emotions, a revolution is on its way.

Eisenstein has been the one who, through his polemics with Vertov and his *Kino-Eyes*, understood the play of such an accumulation of images—first and most simply at the level of associations, secondly at the level of what he calls as the *pathetic*. This is the Hegelian *leap* in a process of accumulation, a moment when the accumulated images of hope are transformed into images of victory, the images of misery into images of revolution, the images of pain into those of anger, and therefrom leaping into revolutionary joy and enthusiasm. Vertov's and Eisenstein's' classification of images was truly quite different, but they belong to the same revolutionary parlance. As most of the early filmmakers (those of Deleuze's *movement-image*), these Soviet cinematographers believed in the world of *actions*; not that of the individual as in the case of Griffith and classical Hollywood cinema, not just a psychological landscape as it was the case with German Expressionist cinema, but just as wisdom integrated into the image, faces, events, facts, and realities. Actions were always collective (the *one* necessarily becoming *many*, following Eisenstein's dialectical rule), and Eisenstein criticizes Griffith while finding in him the founder of his own cinematographic doctrine based on the powers of the montage. Griffith (and the classical Hollywood cinema with its genres and *non-social* types) is an empiricist; the ideas and contradictions having their own value in themselves—there are the poor and the rich, woman and man, young and adult, white and black, the individual and the community, and they are empirical, factual, entering into a dialectical relationship in a classical, almost Platonic manner. This is because for Platonism a man is a man, but not a father at the same time—it has to be reported to another idea, that of the *father* (a good father) in order to become effectively a model or type of father. The traits which create and reproduce the *typical* are here nonetheless *empirical* since they are *given*. Griffith's films fail to explain in what ways poverty is related to exploiters who become richer through others' poverty. In fact, that psychological depth never existed in early cinema, we had to wait until the Shakespearean and Nietzschean style of Orson Welles.

Deleuze argues that a crisis appeared in classical cinema at a point when life ceased to support the images that intended to represent it. The image of the action was now unbelievably futile, the logical-perceptive and sensory-motor links between images (actions against situations and vice-versa) were no longer evident, and somehow they failed to correspond to actual reality. In old, revolutionary cinema, the *shocking* percepts were evidently working: They had their own place in social life, in Americanism and its individualistic-communitarian value systems, in the European political settings (Weimar in Germany and the Front Populaire in France). In American culture, one believed in the effectiveness of actions. Now, in Europe ruined by the war, Rossellini no longer believes in *actions*, but rather to *testimonies*, to *witnesses*, to the strangled voice of the victims of war, terror, and poverty. Deleuze does not sufficiently develop the *sociopathetic* influence of these events on cinema. A generalized state of crisis reigned in the post-war period: German cinematographers did not exist anymore (they had all migrated to the United States), and as Godard points to since the French failed to organize a real *resistance* with the exception of communist militants, they also failed to valorize the imaginative cinematographic values of witnessing. Only the Italians, in the form of neo-realism, had made substantial attempts to film what is *ordinary* about the disastrous post-war period.

Deleuze calls these new images *direct images of time*, instead of the time given as an indirect function of movements and articulations of shots. His distinction between the movement-image and time-image is genial since this is a *logical* rather than *historical* distinction. Yet, Deleuze was searching the motives for the development of time-image only within cinematography and the new subjects of modern cinema (neo-realismo, Welles, American Independent Cinema, and the continental cinema with Nouvelle Vague and the New German cinema). Yet we believe there are some important social changes that are still concomitant with the evolution of the time-image. First, we have to notice how the post-war political life was reconstituted on the basis of mourning for the victims, in a ruined landscape where people no longer believed in their capacities to act and transform the world with their actions. And this motive, also prevailed in the Third World cinema during their revolutionary periods, as declared by Solanas' famous manifesto for the *Third Cinema*.[92] It seems that for the first time, human activity and individualized action (even in its collective forms) have fallen into a general crisis, and this did not affect not only the cinema. This is why the time-image is important for our discussion towards marriage between social sciences and documentary filmmaking.

It is evident that the crisis of the movement-image occurred right in the center of documentary filmmaking too, while Deleuze observes it only generally in the domain of cinema at large. Such a crisis imposed general disbelief in action and to the powers of *thinking*, which enveloped the modern societies of opinion in general. The *old cinema* had believed in human actions and intentionality. This belief was *empiricist* and *individualistic* in the case of Griffith (in accordance with Eisenstein's criticisms towards him) or *dialectical* and *collective* in the Soviet cinema. Thus, from a sociological viewpoint, the classical Hollywood cinema was based on community-situations to be transformed by the actions of human agents, who were mainly individuals or detached persons: Social relations were always determined by a line of tension. Soviet cinema on the other hand was concerned with the *collectivity* in general, the *mass* as the subject of the action, as in the films of Eisenstein. Even in his later films, those historical *sagas* like *Alexandre Nevsky* and *Ivan Grozny* (*Ivan's Childhood*), the hero is not the *person* or any individual, but a collective in which these great historical sovereigns were encapsulated, as if in a network of historically transcending situations and relationships. This is far more interesting in the case of Vertov, who even rejects filming *human beings*, preferring to use his intervals as detached from the machine-life, the electrified zone declared by Lenin (*electrifikatsia*) and out of which the *new man* will emerge. Vertov even believes that human beings are not interesting for filming; they are unworthy facades of the electrified-constructivist life, who can only operate within their networks. It is almost the ideal expressed in the context of *desiring machines* in Deleuze and Guattari's *Anti-Oedipus*. We have to closely examine what had just happened in the Soviet cinema, at least until the Stalinist period and thereafter, with eminent *modern* filmmakers of the *time-image*, as Parajanov, Tarkovsky and particularly Sokurov.

Eisenstein's critical engagement with the founding father of the montage, David Wark Griffith is a good start. His criticisms are not only formulated in his writings and papers, but also in his films, such as the *Strike*, *October*, and *Battleship Potemkin*. Eisenstein seems to believe in

---

92   Fernando Solanas and Octavio Getino, 'Toward a third cinema', *Cineaste* 4.3 (1970): 1-10.

the *truth* of the cinema as the art of masses. The same idea also prevails in Griffith and in the logic of Hollywood's spectacular productions: It is an art for masses. Yet, these are evidently *different* masses and are imagined in quite different forms, somehow obeying to the norms of Deleuze's movement-image. The *masses* or *communities* of Griffith were empirically given, as if they were already there, passive both as audience and representation. Under revolutionary conditions, on the other hand, Eisenstein believes in the ideological reality of masses, their collective actions, and reactions. The strength of the image comes from the active presence of crowds, of the proletarian masses in the unified act. This unification is dialectically structured through all kinds of devices subtly invented by Potter and Griffith—the alternating montage with moments of suspense and tension, a logic of the duel between the good and bad, good and evil, individual and community, man and woman, and the like. Contradictions are particular and empirical, failing to show the deeper causal networks of dialectical relationships. It is the montage-thought of the bourgeois ideology. Eisenstein, on the other hand, further develops the idea of automaton spiritualis: The film is this powerful medium that can stimulate the brains of masses and provide them with the will to act. And if his understanding of dialectics is strictly Hegelian (there is only a dialectics of history and of human consciousness and not a dialectics of Nature), his *tekhne* of mounting his *cine-fist* (as opposed to the *cine-eye* of Vertovians) still relies upon Kantian aesthetics: There is a constant and relentless move from the image to the affect, and from the affect to thought (ideas), and this is exactly the way in which the Kantian sublime operates. All are caught almost in a Spinozist divine Nature, and ideas are following each other not only from a logical point of view but also according to the rules of the affective chains. The *fist* works as the *pathos* (which is the term he uses), and the pathetic is the definition of cinema par excellence. As in Kant's experience of the sublime, the abyss of thought appears as a psychological motive in the already futile attempt to *measure the measureless*, to measure the incommensurability of being (Spinoza) and history (Hegel). Kant suggests that whenever our schemes of imagination fail to work in measuring the affects of a landscape, or of whatever-phenomenon, the mind is forced to create Ideas (*Ideen*) in order to cope with it. These are not *representations* (*Darstellungen*) but *presentations* (*Vorstellungen*). Contrary to Spinoza, in Kant ideas are presentations, or gifts, as they are given by the conflict of faculties—Reason, Understanding, and Imagination. And this is exactly the cinematographic conflict imagined by Eisenstein: Without conflicts, no idea could arise in the minds of masses and multitudes. And Hegel replaces the role of the Kantian sublime with his idea of history: The only history is capable of the dialectical movement, as it should develop the idea in the mind's attempt to measure the immeasurable by ordinary schemes. What is transcendental is History since it paradoxically appears to us as an illogical series of events and phenomena, while it is never like that, as it finds its own trajectory rationally, by using individuals with the ruse of reason. Such transcendentalism is almost aesthetically founded in Eisenstein's doctrine: The movement from the image to the affect leads the spectators to think, the logical consequence of this process is the production of ideas in minds through montage-thoughts.

This is the way in which Eisenstein confronts the problem of the *power of images*. The power of the image has to traverse pathos, the dramatic emotional explosion, pass from one passion to another, from sadness to anger, from misery to hope, from repression to revolution. The pathos presupposes an accumulation of images and emotions, growing according to the dialectical rule of evolution and growth, and this accumulation is founded on montage. Eisenstein provides the example of Nonindifferent Nature through his films, by comparing *Battleship Potemkin* and *The Old and the New* (*General Line*)—the first one used *powerful images* of the ship, whose canons create the emotions of fear and suspense by themselves, condensed as a revolutionary hope. These images almost automatically impose emotions and affects in their spectators, since they are *images-in-themselves* that do not require an emotive supplement or signifying procedure. Affectively, they belong to the automatism of the mind, at least with the help of what is called Kuleshov Effect.

We have to note that most textbooks misrecognize what happens in the Kuleshov Effect, and connect it with a mere association of ideas. In this superficial conception, the Kuleshov Effect is reduced to an operation in the mind through associations of ideas produced by the sensible images in connection, which constitute a language of film. The best examples are mostly a face *without expressions* connected to another image of a scene, a helpless child, a funeral ceremony, or a scene of entertainment (it could be a face watching TV etc.). And in all these various connections, spectators attribute different expressions to the same face. Yet we believe that the mechanism of the Kuleshov Effect is much deeper, it is almost neurological. This can be explained with an experiment that is designed to induce vertigo with images; the sight of an empty moving landscape or an image of abyss shot from the top will not cause vertigo, whereas an image of a person at the edge will. The feeling of vertigo is fundamentally a physiological-neurological state of the brain, and it is not distant from the cinematographic experience. Physiological depth is somehow more relevant to cinema than psychological depth.

Eisenstein seems to be aware of this in his essays on Pathos in the first chapters of in his *Nonindifferent Nature*: He argues, quite simply and in a Spinozist fashion, that there are no emotions or feelings *in general*—every feeling, every affect or sentiment, every emotion is and should be presented as a concrete situation. There is no anger in general, without a particular object that creates it. And sadness turns into joy when faced with the sight of the defeated enemy. This complies with Spinozist derivation of affects from each other, and ultimately, from desire, sorrow and joy.... The necessary materiality of the image is essential here, and Eisenstein's Hegelian-fashioned dialectics leads him to develop the rather bizarre concept of *non-indifferent nature*: that, in cinematography and through montage, nature is not without passions and emotions—there is the sad sunlight in fog, with the empty landscape of the docks of Odessa port on strike in the morning, which *mourns* for the victims. The white unusually turns out to be a mark of terror in *Alexandre Nevsky*, while the black becomes friendly in the sight of the Russian peasants led by the Prince Nevsky, the men of the land. The filmic representation of milieus and environments is by no means a *non-affective* or *signifying* event, it is rather a profound factuality of sentiments and of the passionate life. And this is the great magic of cinema and its automatic seduction on the spectators.

Yet, such automatism of feelings and affects complicates things: such as *The Old and New*, which offers the images of rural transformation in the Soviet Union. It is no longer the time of revolution but the period of the *peaceful construction of socialism*, the introduction of agricultural machinery, and the propaganda for the establishment of cooperatives. Unlike the *canons* of *Potemkin*, none of the *images-in-themselves* are strong enough. 'How the tranquil peasant life could provide such powerful images' asks Eisenstein. We have only images of a milk-cream machine, incomparable to the images of canons and soldier's massacres of people. Only montage and purely montage could create the affective images the plea for cooperatives require. We have images of a young girl, tentatively used to introduce the milk-separator to the peasants. And the richer and more *traditional* peasants are skeptical about the new invention, while more helpless ones are looking at the machine with awe and hope... Hence, Eisenstein creates one of the most pulsating image-sequences of the entire history of cinematography: The suspense is extreme with the accumulation of faces, the insistent close-ups of the milk-separator, and the fearful face of the young propaganda-girl. Yet, what is the significance of this plan-sequence, whether if it worked or not? It is not a matter of life or death, evidently, but nevertheless, it is something more from an intellectual, economic, historical perspective. The indirect image of the time, which does not simply *pass* but *accumulates* now, provides us with the context of the complex set of relations within the rural transformation of Soviet Russia. Yet, in cinema images ought to tell further than that, and the way in which Eisenstein solves this problem is wonderful: At the end of the suspenseful scene, the milk separator explodes in close-up with all kinds of sparks, the white liquid splashes on the face of the young girl, and in almost an orgy-like fashion, an erotic element suddenly enters to the frame with all its imaginative powers. This is one of the most powerful metaphors in the history of cinema. The orgy-like element had been merely connoted, would say film semiologists, but we believe that this is a purely metaphoric power that signifies not through analogies but rather through a *lacking image*, an unseen image that can only be conceived in its absence: It is the impregnation of the soil, the birth of Dionysus, and a kind of divine eroticism.

Eisenstein mostly used metonymic tropes in his films: This had been the conception of what he calls as *montage of attractions*, distilled from his earlier experience in theater. Attractions were analogies that appealed to the cognition, to the intellect, rather than solely to sensibility. Only the mind's eyes could perceive them and their intentionality since there is no room for a comparison between the massacre of strikers and the scene where a cow is strangled. This is really something more than platitude if we consider how the Eisensteinian principles of montage are deployed by advertisers today.

Cinema: Production and Reproduction

In the lexicon of cinema, a series of technical terms refer to a set of economic relationships—the film is a *production* and it is produced through collective labor processes of somehow individual workers. In its final form the film is a *product*, it has owners (who are called *producers* in films lexicon) who sell it, and it enters the market as commodity. In other words, it tends to have this *mystical* character which has been attributed every commodified product and described by Marx in the 3rd Volume of *Das Kapital* as the ultimate effect of the detachment of the product from the process of production.[93] One can object that it is the same for every product that emerge as a commodity or transformed into one in the market, and such character is not specific to cinematic commodities in an age of absolute and total commodification.

93   Karl Marx, *Capital*. London: Penguin Books in association with New Left Review, 1981.

However, in a sense, *commodification* is not the same for all. For cinematographic or aesthetic *production* in general, the quasi-mystical character of all commodities seems to appear more naturally, as different from other commodities. In other words, the mystical character fits to the object of art far more than any other commodity, if not valued by the culture differently.

This is a point where Marx progresses from his position in the famous chapter of the First Volume of *Das Kapital, The Fetishism of Commodities*. At that point, Marx seems to understand that the process of labour mainly *re-produces*, rather than *producing*. And *Das Kapital* is a work which needs to be read retrospectively and interpreted from the standpoint of *reproduction*. Althusser and the other authors of *Reading Capital*[94] (Lire le capital) were aware of this necessity, but we are not sure whether they were able to fulfill the potentials of such awareness.

The *mystical* character is never too distant from the cinema productions by their nature. After all, the product is a work of art, or carries the attributions of it. These cultural and motivational values attributed to it render it as a *creation* rather than a mere *product*. In its process of commodification, the work of art is integrated into a realm of re-production, which can only be analyzed by a new set of concepts. It does have a producer who introduces it into market, but here, neither the process of production, nor the process of circulation and distribution carry the characteristics of a product for consumption. A painting and a dish can be introduced in the same way into circulation in the market; yet societies interpret their process of circulation and marketing in different ways. In the case of the products of collective memory (artisanal products and antiques) this cultural attitude is evident, and it is affirmed in any *cultural theory* proposed in Anglo-Saxon world since the end of the 19th century. As Tylor's anthropology exemplifies, these theories have wrongly reduced every human product and institution to *cultural artifact*.[95] But this reduction or unification carries the risk of neglecting the importance of the differences of nature among different products. In spite of its *ambiguous* nature, cinema productions (among many others) enter into circulation as works of art even if they are actually popular entertainment rubbish.

In short, we still have to depart from Marx's attempt of explaining the process of *re-production*. The possible paths of such analysis have already been studied by Frankfurt School scholars in particular, and more technically, in Joseph Schumpeter's studies of political economy. Both have been on the trajectory of privileging *production* over *re-production*, while they have been aware of the fact that the latter should analytically come first. It is evident that a film requires an investment. But what kind of investment is it? An author can become an author only insofar as she or he writes novels. No one can interfere her/his work, or create obstacles for writing—paper and pen, a little patience and imagination, time and labour are necessary but sufficient. Yet, unlike a literary work, a film can never be produced without making a serious investment. In earlier stages of cinema, the scriptwriting already became a separate literary device. This is the very core of cinema's fundamental and also foundational *ambiguity;* the history of cinema is full of scripts without success, aborted projects and cor-

94   Louis Althusser, Étienne Balibar, *Reading Capital*. Verso 1998
95   Edward Burnett Tylor, *Primitive Culture: Researches into the Development of Mythology, Philosophy, Religion, Art, and Custom*, Cambridge University Press, 2010.

responding tragedies, and failures, while it is hardly tragic in itself. Yet, none of its projects could be realized without opposing the circle of *re-production*, since cinema always has to create a difference for gaining a culturally recognizable value. In its essence, Gabriel Tarde appears as the unique scholar who attempted to analyze such a *psycho-social* problem, that is, the broader cultural meaning of the processes of production and of reproduction. We have to remember how Tarde was insistently trying to substitute a broader frame of (or *variants* of) *economic psychology* to the narrow, economistic and reductionist field of classical political economy.[96] And without such a psychology, we believe it is impossible to recognize how a cultural product should distinguish itself from any other commodity.

One of the practical theses of Tarde refers to the repetitive, therefore *boring* aspect of labour in general. This *boring* nature of work was already contested by early Marx and his followers, under the heading of *alienation*. Yet in Tarde, the boring character of the labor process is not reduced to the consequences of *alienation*. This character necessarily belongs to the production process in general. Labour, in its ordinary sense, only re-produces, since it simply involves *imitation*. This does not mean that *imitation* is not a fundamental concept of Tarde's philosophy: It is readily at its hard core, since everything, every human activity is always open to imitation, and without imitation, nothing could survive in the realm of life. Without becoming taken as habitus, before its expansion and routinization, the labour process is never a part of invention or creation, which could ultimately satisfy the requirements of innovation. And if we consider the *habitus* of labour, learned from the antecedents, parents and masters, this refers to a kind of artisanship, beyond mere *labour*. On the other hand, we can understand how the re-production is essential in the modern industrial-capitalist (or the so-called *post-industrial*) milieu, since the system fundamentally works through a pre-programming of the re-production (as it is the case in many sectors of advanced economies today). The *product design* for mass-production tends to become essential today. Reproduction always comes before the production, since the latter should be reserved to innovation and creation (and not necessarily the *artistic* or *mental* one).

This means that production should always be a part of innovation. According to Tarde, novelty is always a coincidence, or an encounter between two series of imitations and *reproductions*. Events of invention, before being expanded, can be historically and culturally imperceptible. After all, Nicéphore Niepce had not been driven with a *superior* motive towards his invention— he was simply a bad painter, and was trying to prepare a device to help his son, an equally bad painter. And the cinema emerged from the reunion of his invention with the capacities of the human perception of movement. In these inventions, no supreme scientific or artistic motives were present, but still, they were beyond mere circumstance or chance.

The element of chance and lucky encounters are already present in the earliest cinema, in Lumière's *views*, and the montage-thought is articulated as emotive expressions through them, which provides these earliest images their document-character. Was this not a strict problem of the early *thinking* cinema, once exposed in theoretical clarity by Sergey M. Eisenstein? He reports that it had not been challenging to create the *pathos* (hightening of emotions)

---

96   Gabriel Tarde, *Psychologie économique, 2 vols.*

in Battleship Potemkin; transforming the growth and dialectical accumulation of emotions (grief) towards a dialectical leap (revolutionary anger) were already powerful images in themselves—and visually expressed in the canons of the battleship, as we mentioned earlier. He writes about being commissioned a quasi-propaganda film on the transformation of *peasant life* into *socialist collectives* during the period of *peaceful construction of socialism*, that is:

> At the same time, the theme of industrialization of agriculture could not be appealing in itself. One must keep in mind that in those years the imagery of industry was one of the most popular with the artists of our generation [...] and this, no doubt, is because priority was given to the *pathos of the machine*, rather than to the social analysis of those profound processes, which our villages experienced in their transition to forms of collective farm economy [...] It was our film The Old and the New (with a variant title, the General Line, 1926-9), which acquired its fame by heralding the *pathos of the milk separator*.[97]

The *numbers* already appear there, in this film, not as symbols or even signs but as pure *images*; such as the ecstatic arousal when the *milk separator* works—the scene we mentioned earlier. Eisenstein clearly departs from a past when agrarian life is still perceived as *life in nature*. Unlike Vertov, Eisenstein the Hegelian never believed in the dialectics of this past life; a peaceful life, but oppressed under the exigencies of semi-feudal regimes, with the *pratico inerte* of dependency upon nature, the seasons, and seemingly condemned to the *inertia*—so well perceived by Marx. And the image that is used for expressing the Pathos, of the sudden *leap* the socialist *calling* was nothing more than that of a simple *milk separator*. We should concede that this is not an image *powerful* in itself, in comparison to the canons of *Bronenosets Potiomkin*. And the solution to this problem comes from his montage-thought, transforming the *attentive*, *ironic*, *hopeful* faces of peasants (and of the young militant girl who is responsible of introducing the machinery of progress to them) into a cascade of orgiastic, seminal images.

The Kino-Glaz of Vertov and its Implications for the Documentary

The movement of Kinoki, led by the Soviet filmmaker Dziga Vertov, emerged in the context of Russian revolutionary process. The main idea of the Kinoks collective was to contest the capitalist production of images and representations, which seemed to transform the aesthetic desires of masses into an entertainment technology, into what Adorno later baptised as *culture industry*. As Maurizio Lazzarato argues, the movement of Kinoks can be seen as a political project, *war machine* against the ideological frames of bourgeois world vision. In more than one sense, Vertov's ideas sketch a deeper critical formulation than Guy Debord's *situationist* movement of the sixties, which relied upon the denunciation of the *societies of spectacle*. It is possible to argue that Vertov's position is still more relevant today than Debord's criticism of the spectacle.

Vertov develops a materialist conception of a movement against spectacle—for him, it is more appropriate to attack the *machinery of the spectacle* rather than its outcomes, rather than

---

97   Eisenstein, *Nondifferent Nature*, p. 39.

its ideological effects. Here he adopts a Spinozist approach; one has to attack the *causes* rather than effects. The Situationist position, on the other hand, limits itself to the critique of the spectacle, rendering the problem to a separation or detachment of reality from its representation. Can we still believe in the old Marxist interpretation that the world is represented upside down in its image? Vertov argues that the mere discovery of the discrepancy between the image and representation, the alienation of the immediate lived experience, is not sufficient by itself to relieve us from the magical world of images and representations. As Virilio notes, we need a Foucauldian genealogy of the cinematographic apparatus in itself.[98] Vertov's slogan here seems to be uncompromising: 'Neither the scene, nor the spectacle, nor representation—there is only a machine.'[99]

It is evident that the machine Vertov identifies is immediately and simultaneously semiotic, technological, collective-social and aesthetic, while it cannot be reduced to any one of these. To attack *the visible world organized by capitalism*, one has to take into consideration all these dimensions as if they are inextricably related. Throughout the 20th century, the complexity of this apparatus seemed to lead to partial critiques—aesthetic, politic, economic or social— which remain inefficient. Nowadays, with the development of ultra-modern technologies of representation and manipulation of images—video and digital image processing—all of these previous critical formulations are being revisited altogether at the same time, regardless of their incompatibility with each other.

Vertov interpreted the Russian Revolution not only as the political destruction of power in Russia and the simultaneous destruction of capitalist institutions, but also as the disinte- gration of *man* and *his world*. In this context, the seventh art, the cinema was taken as the *machinic* expression of *external forces*, which could be incorporated into man's internal faculties: seeing, feeling, being affected, perceiving, thinking... These external forces were at first sight technological inventions of capitalism, adapted to the interests of the bour- geois world. Their pure expressions were revealed in the organization of time (including labor-time and the time of entertainment and leisure) and of the virtuality embedded in vision machines (the strength of images). These cinematographic machines were capable of *crystallizing the time*.[100] Yet, the camera mechanically liberates perception from the human body it is bounded to. The *Kino-Glaz* (Cine-Eye) is a machinic eye that reveals a new matter and new affections make the uninterrupted movement of things and bodies visible. Hence, the earliest forms of the cinematographic images already shook the tenacity and the stability of the world, despite the full potentials of cinema were yet to be actualized. The cine-eye was able to inject into the images not only the movement but also the time. Thus, it could capture the intensities of the bodies beyond their corporeal presence. The aberrant movements of the camera and of the montage could lead us to a direct experience of a non-anthropic time, of pure time, in a variety of speeds.

98   Paul Virilio, *War and Cinema: the logistics of perception*.Verso, 2009.
99   Dziga Vertov, *Kino-Eye: The Writings of Dzigo Vertov*, trans. Kevin O'Brien, forw. Annette Michelson, Berkeley and Los Angeles: Univ of California Press, 1984.
100 Gilles Deleuze, *Cinema 2: The time-image*.

As Deleuze puts it, this is the *de-territorialization* of objects in the world, their revolutionary instability at that moment, their becomings... Cine-eye captures the virtuality of such a deterritorialized world—it is as if cinema envied a new body and a new thought. Individuals are transformed into perceptive, visual, and cognitive *mutants*. Vertov conceived this transfiguration as parallel to the transformation of the individuals in factories, who had been irremediably impregnated by thermodynamic machines. Thereby, man recognizes that he does not think with his consciousness but through machines. At the early stages of cinema, a new kind of rationalism had to be invented, not without direct reference to Spinoza's and Leibniz's *major rationalism*: The concept of *spiritual* had to be redefined to include the *spiritual automaton*. This was a novel form of sequential thinking—a visual one, which had been able to concatenate the images *beyond* or *below* consciousness. Kinoks's new rationalism exhibited a new kind of realism of images, which had been conceived as an experiential ground in the domain of class struggles.

It has long been said that capitalism is forming a new kind of *visible* whose subject is no longer constituted merely psychologically. This means that the social form of this visibility cannot be reduced to the spectators. Vertov anticipates a new, collective, and plural subject that transcends the *naive and zealous client* of the dark movie theaters. The *'I see'* of the Kinoglaz is, on the contrary, a singularization of the collective body of the proletariat in the process of its formation. There is no room for an ideological reference in evaluating Vertov's position: This is a paradigm for an aesthetic and productive agency. His motto is *factory instead of theatre*—and a *cyborg*, inter-dependency of man and machine, as a collective worker.

Vertov does not believe that the traditional aesthetic positions and arts could be able to decipher the *visible* anymore: Literary, dramatic or graphic techniques are not adapted to the crystallization of time and its reproduction. This requires the cinematographic machine. Hence, from the perspective of the working-class struggle, it is necessary not to *close* the cinema upon itself; the *temporal* specificity and the immediate social nature of these machines have to be taken into consideration. In fact, the filmmaker, the producer, and the spectators more or less consciously cooperate in the sustainment and reproduction of their roles. Each develops its subjective functions inherent to the cinematographic apparatus and commitment to their parts. *Mass production* attribute of cinema also has to be considered in this context; cinematographic communication imposes a mass production process designed for the mass spectatorship.

According to Vertov, the closure of the cinema upon itself means the sacrifice of a new and different mode of production to the established *commercial* and *artistic* forms. 'There is nothing in common between what we are doing and the cinema that is conceived as a commercial activity, or as a branch of art.'[101]

By rejecting commercial and artistic cinema, Vertov clearly aims to destroy cinema in its own domain, since commercial cinema is nothing but a capitalist machine deployed in

---

101 Vertov, *Kino-Eye: The Writings of Dzigo Vertov.*

the production of the visible, of the perception, and of thought. The mere utterance of the order-word long live the class perspective does not refer to a more moral, more political, more aesthetic vision of the world, but to another corporeal, technological and linguistic agency which will re-organize all functions of cinema. Vertovian conception of cinema was different in its nature, rather than its social, political, or economic thematic content.

Vertov was aware of the fact that the class struggles of the fin-de-siècle, which coincided with the invention of cinema, have engendered new ways of perception and thought. However, the virtual parties of these struggles were still trapped in the framework of spectator-film-maker relationship in the context of representation. What was the function of cine-drama after all? With all its actors, scenarists, studios, script-writers it served to the reduction of the new modes of expression to a form of spectacle for the amusement of a collective body generated by the world-revolution that itself is reduced to the masses. Vertov was evidently unaware of the capacity and the future of this mutant and generic industrial proletariat that he perceived as a collective body, but he knew very well that the cinematographic cognizance was one of the most urgent political problems.

Hence, the strategy of Vertov's Kinoks aims at the destruction of the division of labor technologically imposed by cinema. According to Vertov, cinema can do two things: It can either show us the images our consciousness demand, or it can be engaged in the conquest of the chaos, bring in front of our eyes the events of the world, by means of a camera that is free from the movement of our bodies. The second option is the Kinoglaz: 'I am Cine-Eye, A mechanic eye. I, the machine, I show you the world in the way only I can see it. I am now totally liberated from human inertia. I am within the uninterrupted movement... Liberating myself from the passage of 16-17 pictures at one second, from the frames of space and time, I bring together every point of the universe I recorded...'[102] This idea of absolute, pure cinema based on camera and montage is immediately imbued with a secondary idea of the Kinoks, the serendipity of the filming process—speed-shots, microscopic shots, moving-camera shots, the most extraordinary or aberrant shots. Cine-eye becomes a system of visual clinamen in its entirety, which can reveal us time through montage: 'Cine-Eye is the microscope and telescope of Time...'[103]

Vertov, then, had many reasons to denounce the use of film-scripts and scenarios. For him, these function as normative agencies within the cinematographic division of labour, which are destined to neutralize the entire span of incidents in the film-making process. In its attempt to predispose everything, the script freezes all the contingencies arising from camera's contact with the reality at large. The definition of Cine-Truth (Kinopravda) is derived from such refusal; 'This also means that Kinopravda doesn't order life to proceed according to a writer's scenario, but observes and records life as it is, and only then draws conclusions from these observations.'[104] Scripts do not help us in our meeting with a world we don't know yet: 'Proceeding from material to film-object, and not from film-object to material, the kinoks are seizing the last (most tenacious) stronghold of artistic cinema in the

102 Ibid. p. 17.
103 Ibid, p. 41.
104 Ibid, p. 45.

literary scenario. The scenario, whether in the form of a fascinating short story or a so-called preliminary editing sheet, must disappear forever as an element foreign to cinema.'[105]

In addition, in this doctrine of Cine-Truth, the representation of the event by the filmmaker is only of secondary importance to the *real time* actualization of the flow of life. If the camera is the machine-eye that enables us to the uninterrupted movement of the world, and the perpetual variations in the constant flux of things, montage should not obey the demands of human perception and prejudices. Certain basic needs and demands of the spectators are supplied and satisfied by the entertainment technology of cinema, through a psychology of the eye and the fetishism of language in the Nietzschean sense. Yet, montage aims at the *organization of the visible world* by taking into consideration the temporality of the world: 'Attempts in that direction have been made. And it must be said, with some success. Editing tables containing definite calculations, similar to systems of musical notation, as well as studies in rhythm, *intervals*, etc., exist.'[106]

Through such a Constructivist methodology, the movement of the Kinoks prefer the factories, trains and boats, rather than the projection salons—the *electrical opium of cinema halls*: 'I am guiding a cine-wagon, we give a spectacle in a lost station...'[107] We can trace two series of movement—the series of modern transportation which transport us in space, and a parallel series of transportation in time that is assembled by the cine-eye. This is a new mode of perception, a new means of *deciphering* an unknown world.

The function of the cine-eye is to see and to show us: 'It opens eyes, enlightens the gaze...' Cine-eye gives us the possibility of joining a movement or image at one point of the universe with another movement or image at another point. These images or movements are not commensurable from the viewpoint of the human eye, which cannot see them in the finitude of its prejudices: 'Kino-eye is the possibility of seeing life processes in any temporal order or at any speed inaccessible to the human eye.'[108] Cine-eye should relate to the invisible layers of the 'daily life and its organization', and extract the 'resulting vector of the essential movement' out of its chaotic movements.

Vertov's project would not reproduce the division of labour of commercial cinema. Vertov suggests a process of production, which develops in six *series*. Only the first *series* seems to be accomplished through the works of the Kinoks; the other stages remained tentative before the oppressions of the Stalinist regime took effect. This is the serie called 'life through improvisation'...

> In this series, the camera prudently enters into life, selecting a certain little vulnerable point, and it is directed in the visual milieu it deployed. Through following series, with the augmentation of the number of cameras, the space placed under obser-

---

105 Ibid. p. 39.
106 Ibid, p. 100.
107 Ibid, p. 29.
108 Ibid, p. 88

vation gets larger. The juxtaposition of different places of the earth and of different pieces of life forces us to discover the visible world. Each series add clarity to the comprehension of reality. Millions of workers, having reconquered the vision are putting doubt on the necessity of sustaining the bourgeois structure of the world.[109]

Here, the same visual material is moved into a more profound analysis and a reorganization, to acknowledge the relationships among the treated subjects, using every technical means at disposal, including cinema's formal technics. For Vertov, *the fabric of events* is reconquered by the *cine-observers* who produce *cine-observations* and *cine-analyses* in a poetic cinematic context. Apparently cinema had abandoned such a possibility after Vertov, and we had to wait until Jean-Luc Godard's invocation that 'Cinema... can make history visible.'[110] It is possible to see the same anticipation in the works of a few video-artists today.

The entire polemic of Vertov with the Hollywood ideology (and with some differences, with Eisenstein) is organized along the *revolutionary* necessity to relieve cinema from representations. The critical idea that the *image is the reification of the visible* holds true in Vertov, but he also transcends it: The visible is not reduced to images and movements. Vertov calls the true genetic element of the visible as the *interval*. Intervals take place *in between* the images, in the form of rhythms and aberrant movements, and create another dimension, which allows us to see more than images. 'The school of cine-eye expects that the film should be built on 'intervals', that is, on the movement between the images... The intervals (passages from a movement to another) constitute the materials and the elements of the art of movement, not movements themselves...'[111]

The theory of intervals is at the core of the Vertovian philosophy: An interval is a *suture*, a shift, a pause or a transfer. It is the *background*, the pure plane of the whole that resists to be defined by only the flux of images themselves. The interval cannot be reduced to images and movements it connects; it is their source or origin. It is something like the absolute eternal attributes of Spinoza. Within the domain of the visible, the interval cannot be reduced to any discursive or figurative entity.

The *major rationalism* of Spinoza and the minor rationalism of Bergson (intuition as a method) can now be seen as keys to understanding the notion of *interval*. In Spinoza, one should go beyond pure images, beyond the inadequate knowledge of the first kinds, beyond the notions of affections. The knowledge of an attribute (a thought or an extension) is to comprehend the plane upon which every idea, every object are linked together through the mental eyes of the intellect. Bergson too, through his intuitive method, wanted to go beyond the mere representation of things through their images, which appear to the consciousness as *immobile sections* of becomings and interrupted processes—the movement and duration.

---

109 Vertov, *Kino-Eye: The Writings of Dzigo Vertov*, p. 39.
110 Prairie Miller, 'For Ever Mozart: An interview with Jean-Luc Godard', *Cinema=Godard=Cinema*, June 1996, http://cinemagodardcinema.wordpress.com/interviews/for-ever-mozart/.
111 Vertov, *Kino-Eye: The Writings of Dziga Vertov*, p. 39.

The Kinoglaz tends to become, through the doctrine of intervals, a machine for contracting and arresting time. The time crystallizes by being made visible: 'The mechanic eye of the camera leaves itself to be attracted or guided by the movements and thus opens the way of its own movement or of its own oscillation. It experiences the tracking of time, it dismembers the movement or absorbs time in itself... The cine-eye is the concentration and decomposition of the time...'[112]

It is crucial here to compare Vertov's perspective with the Situationist position, especially that of Debord's who state that 'The entire life of societies in which modern conditions of production reign announces itself as an immense accumulation of spectacles. Everything that was directly lived has moved away into a representation.'[113] And if '[T]he spectacle is capital to such a degree of accumulation that it becomes an image'[114], one should nevertheless go beyond the image as a commodity. Marx was already aware of the role of the crystallization of time in the process of the enigmatic capitalist relationship constructed between time (of labour in this instance) and subjectivity—the commodification of the time as labour-time into capital. The cinematography and the philosophy of Vertov shows us another aspect of *crystallization of time*—the invention of another type of machine that can encounter the mechanic and thermodynamic machines; a machine that can reproduce the time of perception, sensibility and thought.

It is essential to note that cinema practically shows that thought can be formed beyond consciousness just as images can be formed beyond pure, natural perception of human beings. With cinema, man has lost the certainty of being the producer of the images and thoughts. Therefore, in the epoch of the separation of *man* from his world, what is at stake is the *power of thinking* (remember Spinoza), the image of thought and the process of its creation. The *visual thought* of the cine-eye leads to automatic production of images, corresponding to the *spiritual automaton* that we are. It stimulates the *cycles of thoughts* that are dormant in our memory, and make ideas 'fall directly from the screen to the brain of the spectator.' Therefore, what is central to Vertovian cinema is not the representation, nor mediation: 'Thoughts should directly flourish on the screen, without the trick of speech. This is a living contact with the screen, a transmission from the brain to the brain... Each of us penetrates into a circle of ideas which agitates in us our own consciousness...'[115]

Today especially structuralists and cinema semioticians affirm that *cinema is a language*. Yet Vertov presents that it is not a narrative language at all, but a *visual one*: This visual language can be opposed to the spoken or written language, since it is deployed in the network of complexity of forces and signs that stimulate the production of thought. He evidentially avoids words and narration in his documentary film *Tri Pesne o Lenine* (Three Songs on Lenin). He deliberately tries to adopt other ways to capture the interaction between the sound and the

112 Ibid.
113 Guy Debord, *Society of Spectacle*, trans. Fredy Perlmanand Jon Supak, Detroit, MI: Black & Red: 1970 (1967), par. 1.
114 Ibid. par. 34.
115 Vertov, *Kino-Eye: The Writings of Dziga Vertov*.

image, *with the resulting vector of multiple channels* in his words: 'Hereby the sound, thereby the image, or in the inter-title; hereby the internal framing of the movement, thereby the stroke of darkness to the light; and sometimes with noise...'[116] His method is to pass by 'subterranean paths sometimes leaving some sentences or words to reach the surface'.[117]

Vertov points that *only some sentences*, certain bits of words coming to the *surface*. It is important to note that what he denounces here is the entire *imperialistic* signifying regime which imposes the fetishism of subject and object in the production of thought. When their primacy is avoided, the written or spoken words in film can be reorganized in a system of rhythms and counter-points. By this way cine-eye produces another image of thought.

Guy Debord insists that 'The spectacle is not a collection of images but a social relation among people mediated by images.'[118] This also means that the forces captured, manipulated and exploited by the spectacle are the same forces that can actually constitute social relationships in other ways. While Situationists denounce *cine-sensation*, Vertov, transcending the mere critique of the spectacle, endeavors to liberate the forces it captures to reorganize them in another way. He interprets the *cine-sensation* as the totality of the powers of seeing, feeling and thinking—not a top-down domination by the spectacle. By means of cinema, these powers are expressed in their machinic nature and become appropriated by a collective will. Vertov introduces the notion of 'the establishing of a class bond that is visual (kino-eye) and auditory (radio-ear) between the proletarians of all nations and all lands.'[119] Such community of sensations and class bonds among the proletarians of distant nations could not be imagined without seeing through intervals. Hence, the cine-eye should be defined as 'an appropriated space of visual bonds between the people of the entire world' and founded on *cine-documents*, uninterrupted exchange of the facts seen by each—which stands against the mainly commercial exchange of cine-theatrical representations, and spectacles that are inherent to the entertainment culture of capitalism.

Vertov imagines the passage from *cine-sensation* to *cine-bond* as a simultaneously ethical and political process which leads to the organization and constitution of social body, destined to compose and augment the creativity of multitudes through the 'machines to see, to feel and to think...' The ethics of Vertov is not concerned with the individual responsibility of the film-director against the images themselves or the viewers/public. It is rather concerned with the encounter, the composition, the augmentation of the power to be affected and to affect of bodies through *cine-sensation* and *cine-bond*. The constitutive force of the cine-bond is somewhat of a telematic oscillation that can work through distances. We can find a similar articulation in todays debates about the possibilities of the new information and communication technologies.

---

116 Ibid.
117 Ibid, p. 118.
118 Debord, *Oeuvres Cinématographiques Complètes*.
119 Vertov, *Kino-Eye: The Writings of Dziga Vertov*, p. 50.

The non-human perception the cine-eye provides thus brings to mind some sort of a Nietzschean *Übermensch*, or a revolutionary *new man*. Vertov does not attend to the kind of *communist humanism* we find in his contemporaries such as Charles Chaplin and Sergey M. Eisenstein. We don't find any opposition to the hybridization of the man with the machine in Vertov: Man already assumed the *second nature* imposed onto him by capitalism and this is an irreversible reality, therefore *transcending the man* is bound to take place under this condition. The *cine-eye*, the *radio-ear* and the *tele-eye* (and the brain-computer of our times) are hybrid machines by which the collective subject of the revolution can see, speak, hear, and think. The machinic body, the cyborg being generates vision, perception, and thought as such, without delegating the task of producing the visible and the sensible to anyone in particular. This means that a micro-politics of the cine-eye that implies the socialization of the cinematographic know-how, and the miniaturization of the technology, would necessarily challenge the technological and financial concentration of the cinema under capitalism. In this sense, Vertov anticipates todays video technologies: 'We have absolutely no need of huge studios or massive sets, just as we have no need for *mighty* film directors, *great* actors, and *amazing*, photogenic women. On the other hand, we must have: 1) quick means of transport, 2) more sensitive film, 3) small, lightweight, hand-held cameras, 4) lighting equipment that is equally lightweight, 5) a staff of lightning-fast film reporters, 6) an army of kinok-observers.'[120]

The organization of the Kinoks would 'distinguish amongst 1. kinok-observers, 2. kinok-cameramen, 3. kinok-constructors [designers], 4. kinok-editors (women and men), 5. kinok laboratory assistants'[121] The main project is to 'teach our methods of cinema work only to Komsomols and Young Pioneers; we pass on our skill and our technical experience to the rising generation of young workers in whom we place our trust.'[122] In this context, the *mass character* of the cinema should not only be limited to the diffusion-distribution of films and to their reception by the audience, but it should also involve the imperatives of *production*—since otherwise, the power of expression would necessarily become *expropriated*. Vertov anticipates what Godard had later appealed: 'We need a pedagogy of the image...'

Vertov's rejection of *cine-drama* is the necessary outcome of his criticism of the concentration and control of the means of production and redistribution by the capitalist cinema industry. From this point of view, the Soviet regime was reproducing the organization of work socialism attempted to criticize, and retorting to propaganda through entertainment films and dramatic works. Such *leftist* engagement with cinema is also disapproved, through a form of *micro-politics*, which appears to be the only way to provide the Soviet workers with the alternative of not becoming the subject of films. For instance, for him, Eisenstein's cinema was only admitting the masses as the formal, but not real, subjects of cinematography. For Vertov, masses should become not the subject of films but of the entire production process pertaining the visible and the sensible.

---

120 Ibid, pp. 74-75.
121 Vertov, *Kino-Eye: The Writings of Dzigo Vertov*, p. 75.
122 Ibid, p. 75.

Hence, Vertov appears to be the only author to conceptualize and organize cinema as not the *art of masses* but as a mass activity, as a constitutive activity, as collective work. Vertov unveils and evaluates what was already implicitly present in the technological apparition of cinema as a constructive force. One can easily consider today's post-Fordist accumulation through computers and networks similarly generating a new kind of intellectual and affective activity. Vertov rejects the idea of working like an *artist*, and pretends to become a relay in the network of correspondents throughout the entire Soviet Union instead. He works within a flux that resists to be reduced to and controlled by any frame of division of labour. Such a conception of work denies any reference to the distinction between *manual* and *intellectual* labour and thus prohibits the emergence of the *artist*, author, or intellectual as a self-contained agency... Therefore, the work of Kinoks cannot be simply reduced to artistic work; its machinic and collective form and character objectively and subjectively connect it to labour in general: 'The Goskino kinoks' cell should be regarded as one of the factories in which the raw material supplied by kinok-observers is made into film-objects.'[123] Vertov acknowledges and establishes the universality and generality of the creative work: 'The present film represents an assault on our reality by the cameras and prepares the theme of creative labor against a background of class contradictions and of everyday life.'[124]

We should also note that Vertov's position has nothing to do with the anti-intellectual and populist vision of a *proletarian artist*. What he affirms is the fact that the agencies beyond those of the author and the artist can open unknown territories, and generate becomings open to the virtualities of other aesthetic, social and productive paradigms.

We have already stressed how Vertov anticipates the video, if not the television—which remains today as the unilateral agent of a flow of images from the screen towards the viewer. He used the technological apparatus of cinema effectively with such anticipation—the anticipation of a *tele-emission of images and sounds*: 'From the human eye's viewpoint, I haven't really the right to *edit in* myself beside those who are seated in this hall, for instance. Yet in kino-eye space, I can edit myself not only sitting here beside you, but in various parts of the globe.'[125] It would be absurd to create obstacles such as walls and distance for kino-eye. In anticipation of television it should be clear that such *vision-at-a-distance* is possible in film-montage. Hence, according to Vertov, the television is not only a technological device more appropriate to the *circulating eye*, but also an apparatus more convenient to the social and collective dimensions of the production of life, which has already been presupposed by capitalism: 'The procedure of the radio-transmission of the images that come to be invented in our epoch could help us reaching what is essential more and more... To establish a visual bind of class (the cine-eye) in parallel to an auditive one (radio-ear) between the proletarians of all countries, on the platform of a communist deciphering of the world.'[126]

123 Ibid, p. 70.
124 Ibid, p. 34.
125 Vertov, *Kino-Eye: The Writings of Dzigo Vertov*, p. 125.
126 Ibid, p. 50.

The common perception of our times that cinema is an *artistic* medium and television is a *cultural* one is irrelevant for Vertov's position—since technology of television was not yet invented in his time, and he did not anticipate the mode of television as a unilateral machine for the manipulation of opinions under capitalist conditions. He is not a *futurist* of machines, a technology fetishist fascinated by the imperialism of the technology and the cult of science. Vertov always believed in the priority of the social and collective machine over technological machine: 'Even in technique we only partially overlap with so-called artistic cinema, since the goals we have set for ourselves require a different technical approach.'[127] This reference to *another conception of technique* is here essential, since Vertov's *war machine of Kinoglaz* has been crushed under the Soviet regime in thirties, which adopted Eisenstein's *cine-drama* mode penetrated by Hollywood's commercial mentalities and structures as *socialist realism*. Yet, the movement of the Kinoks remains remarkable not because of their persecution by the regime, or the evident victory of Hollywood cinema as an entertainment industry, but in its power to anticipate new technologies and agencies of social communication, and their attempt to create a new conception of technology. They were aware of the fact that machines were not only external appendices of man—men and their collectivities could also be conceived as machinic assemblages.

It is evident that the Nazi aesthetics, as revealed in the works of Leni Riefenstahl, had somehow moved on to imitate the experience of the cine-eye, under the form of a great spectacle of power, with guidance from the propaganda minister Dr. Goebbels. Yet, the Nazi regime of truth was far distant from any understanding of Kinopravda. Riefenstahl was asked to organize great scenes of Nazi demonstration, during Nurnberg rallies in 1933 and 1934, and and 1936 Berlin Olympics, but not to build a collective cine-eye that can bring the masses into creative labour process of cinema. Her films had been conceived as pure propaganda, that of a totalitarian society of spectacle. Jean-Pierre Faye discerns the *totalitarian language* of the Nazis as the one which makes what it says, as different from the language of Italian fascism, which was deployed to justify the deeds afterwards. There is no cine-eye in Leni Riefenstahl's *The Triumph of the Will*, since the dramatization of the event comes first, before shooting and editing. Riefenstahl did not produce images in a process of discovery or in contact with truth. She was expected to compose the entire *mise-en-scène*, as the primary author of the ceremony, transforming life into a grandiose decor.

Yet, as Godard puts it in the videographic *comparison* he did in his *Histoire(s) du cinéma*, it is impossible to see the *same smile* in the faces of Soviet worker girls of Vertov and in the German youth represented in these films. This distance or interval is what we mean by the *power of the image*; sometimes *transcendental*, but sometimes indiscernible from its own *reality*—a reality which could trace the trajectory of a new *sociology of affects* through the means of *documentary* filmmaking.

127 Ibid, p. 74.

5. TOWARDS A NEO-VERTOVIAN SENSIBILITY OF AFFECTS

Our study has been based upon the criticism of the mainstream sociology, a *sociology of opinions* whose methods have been shaped by the basic assumptions of the corresponding *societies of opinion*. As we mentioned in the beginning, leaving aside the old epistemological argument about *knowledge*, sociology becomes the work of collecting, filtering, and classifying constantly changing opinions. The productive model of a major approach in mass communications becomes the condition of all *scientific* claims in social sciences. It is believed that *information societies* in which we are supposed to live require and justify such a model that has been developed during the academization of social sciences, parallel to the erosion of imaginative-affective formulas of early founders of social sciences (such as Tarde, Weber, Simmel and even Durkheim). This is the demise of *social types,* the last examples of which can be seen in the works of certain historians, and an array of microsociologists or critics, such as Charles Wright Mills and, occasionally, Michel Foucault. A further tendency that arises today is the *textualization* of the sociological work and criticism. It is no longer based on the experience of everyday life, except for mild phenomenological observations and arguments, but rather on the interplay of texts and contexts, paving the way for meta-theoretical discussions in semiology, cultural studies, postcolonial studies, cultural criticism, deconstruction, and even hermeneutics. The last method too is nothing more than a *sociology of opinions*, attempting to derive out the *intentions* behind texts and words. We are far from Marx's early tenet today: One cannot understand people or an epoch by asking them what they are thinking about themselves.

Evidently, we do not oppose the attempts to recover the domain of opinions, texts, and cultural artifacts: We are rather suggesting an *affective sociology*, a sociology of affects, which could enlarge the methodological toolkit of social research and of humanities at large. Considering opinion as a certain kind of *affective state* which arises with modernity, it is important to remember Tarde's works, who has been the founder of what we would today call *sociology of opinions*. The *monadological* work of Tarde and his criticisms directed against the Durkheimian conception of sui generis society have been an essential starting point for our debate. This is mainly due to Tarde's foundational microsociology, which has later been misinterpreted by American sociologists as *social psychology*. Also lying at the roots of the Foucauldian conception of *power*, Tarde's *microphysics of the social* is founded on a fundamental premise: The small is more complex than the big, the individual is much more complex than society—so there is no room for perceiving them as the opposites of each other, as Durkheim, his followers, and the structuralists did.

Thus, we try to develop a tentative critique of the notion of opinion, from the standpoints of Ancient philosophy—the tension between *episteme* and *doxa*—and from the standpoint of the modern *societies of opinion*, whose political institutions largely depend on the controlling and manipulation of opinions, such as today's parliamentary democracies.

Our main interrogation is about the way societies of opinion coincide, in both historical and logical contexts, with what Foucault labeled as *disciplinary societies* and Guy Debord called *societies of the spectacle*. As our purpose was to establish a *marriage* between the social sciences and documentary filmmaking, each having its own merits, it became essential to reconstruct the connections between these concepts. This should pass through a critique of the societies of opinion with respect to their ontological reality, a point at which Frederic Jameson also hints.[1] In other words, we had to question whether the social sciences, conceived under the title of a *sociology of opinions* really coincide with the historical development of the *societies of opinion,* or whether the methods guiding and restraining the actual practice of social sciences to become *opinion of opinions* are a methodological failure and have to be corrected and criticized.

We believe that the keyword here should be *social types* and why the creation of *social type* is no longer within the capacity of social sciences, save for some lucky exceptions. For Simmel, *social types* (in contradistinction to Weber's *ideal types*) are mainly analytical tools to conceive, including the powers of intuition, concrete social formations and events. This means that a social type has a *figure*, and a *formula* which can be visualized for the imagination of the laymen, and is constituted by a bundle of traits, characters, and affects which are mainly attributed to them by the community in which they are a part of: The *Stranger*, the *Poor,* the *Jew* are examples of *social types*, only by being recognized by the community as such. Early social sciences and their founders were capable of creating such social types. This has been a fundamental characteristic of their individual work: Simmel has a veritable gallery, and Marx invented the *Lumpenproletariat*, Weber the *Protestant* with his *ethos* being constitutive of the *spirit of capitalism*, Sombart the *bourgeois* whose formula is the *first man detached or freed from the conditions and rhythms of the Nature*. One can add to this list the *flâneur* of Walter Benjamin, the *conservative* of Karl Mannheim and *Der Arbeiter* of Ernst Jünger.

Yet we find that the creation of social types is not restrained to the domain of social sciences. Since Balzac, the literary form of the novel had particularly created them with concrete elaborations and formulations. Modern literature means creating social types rather than *individuals*, as Lukács would have put it. As a rule, we maintain that a social type should have a *formula,* and one can find such formulas in the 19th century novel, from Stendhal to Dostoyevsky's *Idiot*. Moreover, the birth of cinema has given us more *visualized* accounts of social types. Major *genres* of cinema and the novel correspond to social types they create in this sense: film-noir, gangster films, family or love romances, and especially the burlesque films with their gags. Under the cartoonish figure of the *Tramp*, Charles Chaplin *formulated* the eminent social types of his epoch: the *Migrant*, the *Flâneur*, the *Poor*, and so forth. *Dr. Mabuse* of Murnau is a social type in transformation, throughout his fantastic move from Germany to United States... Bertolt Brecht had formulated Hitler as an Al Capone-like Chicago mobster in his *Arturo Ui*. This means that *affects* and *traits* that constitute the social types are much more easily presented (or *represented* if you will) by cinema, and this urges us, even at this level, to suggest a marriage between the documentary filmmaking and social-scientific research.

---

1   Fredric Jameson, *Late Marxism: Adorno, or, the persistence of the dialectic*, London: Verso, 1990.

Finally, the inevitable question is that: Does their loss of ability to create social types signify a failure particular to social sciences today? Or, is it the peregrinations of mass culture in modern society that lead to the disappearance or dissolution of the social types? We are by no means nostalgic about *social types*; yet we can observe that they have also been deserted within the domains of cinema and the novel (in their postmodern variations) today. These critical questions should be further developed and elaborated on, but we can only suggest at this point that the disappearance of social types does not only take place in the social sciences but also in the domains of other representative practices such as cinema, theater, literature and even psychoanalysis. Today's *yuppies* or *hackers* are not *social types*, because they lack the necessary *formula*, or their formula is only provided by journalistic *newspeak* if not by governments.

Thus, in the second chapter on *affects*, we have intended to look deeper into the domain of affective traits, through Spinoza's rational yet empirical doctrine of affects, passions, and emotions. This could only be achieved through a criticism of psychoanalysis, which unjustifiably seems to monopolize the analysis of subjectivity today, even the *juridical* one, as the Lacanians aim to. This critique is mainly concerned with the absence of analytical considerations in psychoanalysis, except the *therapy*. Psychoanalysis doesn't serve to dream, to love, or to act; it only restores life in the Oedipal triangle of domestic sphere, as Deleuze and Guattari have convincingly shown. We believe that the analysis of affects, which are essentially ethical and political, could tell more about such practical matters. This is why we needed to develop the notion of *ignoramus*, the notion of the *ignorant*, instead of contending ourselves with the psychoanalytical theme of the *Unconscious*. We have tried to develop a Spinozist conception of the unconscious which cannot be conveniently reduced to the quasi-mystic internality of the Id (*Es*).

Positively speaking, such a form of *Unconscious* is something to be produced and assembled. It needs to be created rather than being given, being already-present-there. It does not lie in the depths of the psyche but at the surface, while it is difficult to see it thoroughly. It has to be constructed at a socio-political level rather than on a personal, individual basis. Economically, it is an investment of desire rather than a constant search for satisfaction. Our critique of psychoanalysis tries to reach the point where Spinoza (and occasionally Tarde) elaborates on the passionate life not only at the level of the individual but rather on a *plane of consistency* where societies and individuals are thrown—for Spinoza, societies enjoy or suffer from affects, emotions, and passions too.

This is against the Cartesian architecture of the mind, which had been a great revolution apart from its *cerebrality*. The revolution of the cogito-situated *thinking* as a form of human activity, hence paving the path for claims to the *rights* of *thinking, having opinions,* and *professing conscience*. However, we choose to uphold the Leibnizean, Spinozist and Kantian critiques of Descartes: The first relates to the development of the *point of view* as a theme, which is necessary for our discussion on *ways of seeing* and *making visible* in the last chapter; the second relates to the *emancipatory* nature of ideas; and finally, there is the Kantian search for the *creation* of a world based on subjectivity.

We believe that a sociology of affects cannot be founded without the aid of these three funda-mental philosophical considerations. Spinoza was aware of the fact that everything is a play between the *power to act* (potentia) and the *sovereign power* (potestas); the former being the way in which we enjoy life, production and creation of pleasures, and the latter was the way in which we are detached from our power to act in sadness, fear, terror, etc. Liberal democracies, even (and perhaps particularly) social-democratic ones, absorb individuality into fictional *potestas* that promise to solve the problems in the name of the people who are assumed to be *helpless* and thus has to be *governed*. Governing is perceived as a *service* from the position of *sovereign powers,* which create those problems that require solutions themselves, whereas people do have the potentials (powers to act) for governing themselves. This is the fundamental Spinozist definition of democracy that he has declared as the *most powerful political regime*, in contradistinction with any liberal definition of democracy.

Spinoza was concerned with affective life at every possible level, ranging from individuals to groups, from collectivities to classes, from nations to societies at large. He was aware of the fact that *nations* too had affections, ideas, symbols, superstitions. He believed that *individ-uality* is plural, subject to *fluctuatio animi* (emotional fluctuations), just as the society that is defined as a *body*. Thus, the best political regime (democracy) for Spinoza is the one that promises the maximum joy for all, and those that are based on fear, terror, and even hope (such as *utopianism*) are to be avoided.

Yet there remains an architectural problem to be solved, in the context of Spinoza's doctrine of affects and images. This has been our point of departure in suggesting the *realm* of image (or *imagination*) as the basis of our proposition for a possible *sociology of affects*. We needed an excursion into *documentary* film and cinema in general, alongside some contemporary forms of recording and modifying what we call *thought-images*. We have the entire realm and archive of document-images, which lacks a proper theoretical discussion, but is equipped with an ethico-political dimension due to the power of images they contain. The social sciences, on the other hand, seem to have developed a theoretical-methodological toolkit for substituting such ethico-political concerns. The documentary lacks what the social sciences have developed in their own textualized and academized domains. Hence we were forced to suggest a marriage between the social sciences and the possibilities of *images*, of audio-visual forms, and of the powers of the *document-image*. Cinema is not something to be semiologically, sociologically, or psychoanalytically analyzed; from its earliest beginnings (for instance, since Vertov) cine-ma had been analyzing social facts and their rather *invisible* associations, articulations, and events. Cinema, video, and digital images today are destined to make visible the invisible, identify relationships, and constitute *ideas*. The eminent danger of the world of images is not their power and domination over every domain of life. The real danger has been the television and its digital offspring, transforming images into clichés and repetitions, as part of their *management of time*. However, television and other digital communication technologies still continue to be the most developed means of expression. They not only form an actual *society of the spectacle* (Debord) but also a *videosphere* (Debray). Television is a *society of opinions* in itself, interpreting everything that passes through it—photographs, films, paintings, speeches, dialogues, and all kinds of documents. We believe that it is essential to liberate images from their ordinary televisual form, in which they become clichés of themselves.

The material we work with is hence audio-visual, and not only a collection or classification of opinions, but also of images and affects. Like Michel Foucault's proclamation, we believe that they are rare, and rarity is their mode of presence itself. Clichés and opinions are everywhere, they form the sphere that surrounds our lives, but they are *senseless,* people look at them indifferently. This is the *rise of non-importance*, as Castoriadis argued. Only through a criticism of television, which incorporates combatting it with its own means, one could develop a *neo-Vertovian* sensibility of affects, images, and in the Deleuzean sense, *affection-images*.

6. ON CINEMA AND ULUS BAKER

The interview below was conducted with Aras Özgün after Baker's death by Can Sarvan, an independent filmmaker who lives and works in Cyprus, and was published in EMAA (European-Mediterranean Arts Association) Journal, No: 7, Nicosia, Cyprus, December 2007.

Can: I think that, the common element in Ulus Baker's perspective on both philosophy and cinema is believing in the belief itself. By referring to J. L. Godard, he mentions, the politicization of cinema, and as a consequence, the only way for the emergence of belief, could be done by dealing with matters which are not yet politicized. What do you think about the potential to raise such a belief in cinema as a filmmaker, although, at the same time, in Baker's own words, cinema is the most characteristic 'industrial design' of our times, which brings the loss of gestures, and precisely the medium through which subjective and objective melt into each other?

Aras: Your question certainly calls for the discussion of what is avant-garde? But, from another perspective, believing in belief itself is an important point which should not be dismissed as a rhetorical statement, but should rather be taken as a philosophical break and discussed in depth. 'I believe' is a different claim than 'I know', and totally different than 'in my opinion'. Believing implies the subjects' active participation. The believer participates in the object of his/her belief, to the degree that the object of his belief exists only through such participation (as in the case of believing in God). As such, the object of belief is performatively embodied within his/her participation; believing drives the subject into action, while embodying its own object precisely through this action, with desire. Believing is a constitutive form of knowledge armed with desire. Therefore, doubt and belief should not be considered in contrast to each other, but rather as complimentary to each other—we can doubt about certain things as long as we believe in certain others.

If we take the notion of belief as a form of knowledge requiring participation and engagement, we can see that it is almost in contrast with the forms of knowledge established through modernity. Believing has been taught to us as the opposite of reasoning; thinking has been seen as an active of questioning by keeping oneself at a certain distance from the object/event, without participating to it and being indifferent to it. In modernity, the fact that thinking as such requires a certain belief in itself has been disregarded. The form of modern knowledge, which has been rooted in the Enlightenment Philosophy, aimed at placing the knowing subject in the center of the universe by separating him/her from the event of which s/he acquires knowledge. The death of God announced by Nietzsche, the world picture coined by Heidegger, all refer to this new form of cognition; with modernity, knowledge refers to a set of relations expressed within the distance between the subject and the object of knowledge. At this moment, the awareness of what happens in the world starts to mean looking, watching, and recording the events from a certain distance. Through these recordings, we reassemble the representations of these events, and we can analyze them. Through these representations, we investigate our life-world. The form of modern knowledge is quite a specific form of relation with the world in this sense. As Jonathan Beller, Gilles Deleuze, and others mentioned, cinema on the one hand constituted a perfect model of modern industrial production style (with the studio system already highly developed in the first half of 20th century, along with the sophisticated mechanisms of production and distribution); and on the other hand, it presents us a brilliant model of this form of cognition since its birth. In this respect, we should consider not only the techniques and technology Etienne-Jules Marey and Eadweard Muybridge developed even before the birth of cinema for analyzing the moving images, but we should also consider the evolution of documentary and ethnographic film from the Lumière brothers to Flaherty and Gardner throughout the old 20th century.

That's why, while discussing cinema as the mirror of reality, we shouldn't undermine what kind of a specific relationship it establishes with reality. In this sense, cinema establishes a new ontology and circulates the forms of representations it produces with an idea of realism through the narrative clichés mastered by the culture industry. Cinema has been engaged in producing realistic narratives by utilizing various techniques of realism within a production system that is modeled after industrial factory production, and at the same time, it cut off its relation with everyday reality by concealing such production process entirely—precisely on the same ontological ground which it helped to consolidate. That is to say, cinema paradoxically produces a spectacle proper on the one hand, and intro-duces this spectacle as illusion of reality (that the psychoanalytic theory associates with the identification process) on the other, and such paradox is related with the ontological construction of modernity.

So how can we recall belief and doubt as such in cinema, how can we sustain perceiving, and gathering the knowledge of life, by participating to it at the same time through cine-ma? In short, how can we desist cinema from being a representation system and make it a participation machine? How can we abandon cinema as an instrument of spectacle and observation, and make it a cognitive apparatus? Ulus' intellectual occupation in regards to cinema was mostly focused on this question. He produced lots of resources around this question, and attempted to relate the philosophical lineage passing from Spinoza, Tarde and Bergson to Deleuze with the cinema of Vertov, Godard, Güney and others.

Can: Since you mentioned Vertov, can you talk about your ideas on the political cinema of Dziga Vertov, to whom Baker often referred?

Aras: As a political form of cinema, Vertov's filmmaking was not staging the images of power, or simply a stupefying rhetoric like Riefenstahl's. Riefenstahl was so ignorant about the expressive potentials of cinema that she couldn't realize the simple difference between the images of power and the power of the image, and moreover, she was clueless enough to claim that she didn't realize what was going on when she was asked to explain the part she took in the Third Reich. Whereas, when we look at Vertov, we not only recognize a very strong determination about what he was trying to achieve, but we also notice that his determination originated from a lengthy contemplation on what to do with cinema. What we find as political in Vertov is not only the cinematographic expression he presents through the images, but the political theory of cinema he establishes. For Vertov, cinema is an instrument of cognition and it is political in that sense: It articulates to the political construction of life primarily as a perception machine.

We shouldn't forget the fact that Vertov was filming and editing together with his brother and wife. After Soviet cinema had been consolidated as another form of industrial production, Vertov, Eisenstein, and others were marginalized and excluded from this system. That's why Vertov didn't have any political questions about inner dynamics of film production; what is political was the expression itself (that is to mean the aesthetics of film), with the idea behind that being the articulation between expression as such and the other political processes in life. He recognized that cinema had already started to develop as mass entertainment and such a tendency would render its relation with life that he wanted to establish impossible. However, he thought that this was a problem related to the aesthetic forms in popular circulation. Looking from today, it obviously would be much more proper to relate the historical development of cinema as a form of mass entertainment to the development of industrial production and the distribution models of Fordism.

However, when we arrive to Godard's era, we notice a quite different cinema habitus. The emergence of the New Wave in '59 created a massive aesthetic break; Godard, Tavernier, Resnais, and others did not just turn the formal conventions of mainstream cinema inside out, but what they told in a different way was another story. If mainstream cinema had been just an amalgamation of certain narrative forms and narration techniques, it probably wouldn't have survived New Wave's storm. However, immediately after creating such a sharp break-off, these people actually found themselves surrounded by a gigantic industry, and moreover, they realized how this industry reproduces itself within the social factory, beyond the screen and the movie theatre. At this very moment, Godard took over Vertov's legacy—through the Group Dziga Vertov he founded in mid-70s and through the video and television works he produced together with Anne-Marie Mieville afterwards. What I would like to underline is that Godard's connection to Vertov was not just a formal revival of his heritage; except a few Group Dziga Vertov works, Godard revived the political essence of Vertov's filmmaking and experimented with it towards much richer and more competent forms.

For me, this is very interesting; in order to reach the true form and liberating essence of cinema, Vertov had always tried to purify it from other artistic forms; he tried to achieve the unique expression of cinema through freeing it from theatre, literature, etc. His idea of political cinema was inherently constructed through this purification process. (Because, according to him, as long as cinema could be freed from the burden of these other aesthetic forms, it could relate to life directly; it could register life as it is through the camera-eye and derive an expression out of it through montage). *The Man with a Camera*, as a manifest/film is the most obvious statement of such an effort. Whereas, when he took over Vertov's vision, Godard entirely left out this purification effort. On the contrary, he directly included every instrument and technique of all forms of artistic expression that were available to him: literature, different styles of theatre, poetry, music, even directly philosophical texts, cartoons, and television. Although Godard's materials for political cinema were so extensive and diverging from his stylistic formulas, they were still loyal to Vertov's essential idea: Cinema as a direct relation with life, as an apparatus of thinking, has not been given up in Godard at all. The difference between them lies in the fact that, in Godard's world, life can no longer be considered as separate from these aesthetic segments accumulated on top of it throughout a century of mass media, these aesthetic forms themselves become embedded in everyday life—if Godard would have to reformulate Vertov's motto, he would probably claim, life is no more as it is.

In this sense, Godard redefines political cinema with a reference to practical production conditions of cinema. This is what he means by not to make political films, but to make films politically. That is to say, beyond what film expresses, the important thing is how it is made, what kind of social relations and political mechanisms it reproduces during its production. Not politicized yet are the spheres of the everyday life which we don't recognize as political at the first sight. As Foucault tried to point out by coining the concept of biopolitics, such spheres of life (which are not directly addressed as political) as the school, the family, communications, sexuality, etc. are actually the areas of social reproduction within which social subjectivities are produced. Subjectivation takes place within these areas through power relations and power apparatuses, in an entirely political way. Godard's works after Group Dziga Vertov, especially *Numéro Deux* (1975) and the video/television works he later on produced with Anne-Marie Mieville, such as *Six fois deux: Sur et sous la communication* (1976) and *France/tour/détour/ deux/enfants* (1978–79), focused on these areas. In these works, we cannot find an agitative political discourse in the way of *Le Gai Savoir* (1969), but a more profound and effective political thought on everyday life. For Godard and Mieville, the production process itself in these films and videos is also a political area; oftentimes these films turn around and start to discuss their own political constructs. *Soft and Hard* (1996) is a prime example in this regard. I think this is a very important matter for people who work with video and electronic/digital images, like us. The forms of expression which were developed by the New Wave filmmakers as alternatives to Hollywood language have already became the standard visual rhetoric of MTV and the like now. In a formal sense, Vertov's idea of *The Man with a Camera* and various techniques of cinema vérité are not so distant from what is called embedded journalism today. Then the political substance of the works we make should be considered in relation to their production—how they are made, what kind of subjectivities they produce during their production and circulation, and into which political structures they are incorporated. If we are dealing with art, the political relations it weaves around the production of its object are as important the political expression it creates through its aesthetic layers. Otherwise, it all becomes sterilized; political films like Michael Moore's works can be appreciated by millions, the most radical expressions can receive big praises in the art world, and none of these have any political effect in return.

Can: Photography has developed as a form of art long before cinema. Ulus Baker refers to photography as trace of reality and witness to life. However he also mentions that together with the negative contribution of digital possibilities and the intervention of the press/media, photography is now capable of deceiving, and this situation carries the jeopardy of losing its characteristic of witnessing. On the other hand, he claims, utilizing the digital possibilities, especially of video works, does not carry the same risk for cinema; on the contrary, he thinks that the collage in montage would allow images of cinema to exist in their own reality. Although this seems as a paradox at first sight, when we consider photography as framing, and cinema as a series of montaged images, what Baker explains seems reasonable. How do you consider this analysis?

Aras: In terms of genealogy, photography and cinema are definitely not different from each other—to the degree that Deleuze, Bergson and others assert that cinema became possible at the moment photography was discovered. That is to say, the possibility of mechanically reproducing still images immediately calls for the reproduction of moving images in the same way. Besides, historically, we can see how short the transition of photography to cinema had been; the Lumière Brothers screened the first film almost immediately after Eastman developed the cellulose nitrate film base. Also, Jonathan Crary, Raymond Bellour and others assert that the technological acceleration, which made photography and cinema possible, is the product of an inherent representational logic, a constitutive element of modern subjectivity, which we can trace back to the 18th century and even before. In other words, a preceding collective desire made photography and cinema technologically possible, the transformation of representational regimes themselves necessitated these technologies. In *Film Before Film* (1986), as well as some his other works about the same subject he seems to be obsessed with, Werner Nekes exposes the moving image technologies developed before the birth of cinema and tells us the same thing.

If this is the case, as I tried to explain earlier, the actual expressive power of photography and cinema does not lie in their mimetic capacities (that is, their ability to display reality as it is). But it is hidden in the tension they can create between representation and reality exactly through such capacity. This is what we should understand from the notions of the trace of reality, witness to life: The trace of reality is a trace—not the reality itself; what a witness tells is a story—not the life itself. Traces can mislead you, a story can be a lie, but where we arrive accidentally can be the place we wanted to go to; a lie can make us better understand a larger truth. It is only possible through such relationship of tension for photography and cinema to accommodate affections, and, therefore, to be a form of art.

For sure, what Ulus has recognized as a problem in the age of digital images was not that photographs have now become deceptive; from the very beginning, photography never showed the reality as it is at all. What it did was to establish a new kind of relation to reality. On the contrary, the problem is the tendency for digital images to be realistic and their capacity to surpass this tension. That is to say, computer graphics do not follow the genealogy of photographic images; they do not present a ghostly trace of their objects, they do not witness a moment that is already past. It is not a ghostly shadow of a moment which has already passed as Barthes attributes to photography. Barthes called the camera a clock for seeing. In that sense, computer image is a timeless image—or creates its own time. Therefore, we can consider that this type of image promises different potentials than photographic images. But why is this new type of image, which has the potential to establish an entirely different relationship with reality than the photographic images, simply attempt to achieve some sort of realism (which has never been a primary artistic device for photography and cinema anyways)? This is not simply a question of aesthetics or technology; this is a question related to social conditions, it refers to a social context which should be called medialogical. Ulus has often problematized this context by calling it 'society of opinions': a social condition in which everybody has an opinion that is established through low-cost prefabricated signs about everything, but no one really has the knowledge of anything.

Ulus says, 'No image exists just by itself.' What separates cinema from photography is the time passing between the two frames, the one twenty-fifth of a second long interval that connects every two images. Cinema divides life into fragments, into frames, and shows these frames one after the other by attaching to each other again. It reestablishes blocks of time and space by connecting different ones together, one after another. The time between two frames is a moment of approximation; this interval is actually the duration for two images to connect with each other, not a distance or separation between them. Ulus was asserting cinema's ability to relate two different images to each other as such, as the real power of cinema. This is what Godard did with his famous and's—a blatant cartoonish and connects everything in sight: here and elsewhere...

Video and electronic image did not just simply multiply such moments of approximation and points of connection infinitely, but also liberated them from the linear time, spread them across space in all directions. This is a type of image that is emancipated from the spatial restrictions of the screen and the theatre and the linearity of chronological time. For me this is the fundamental difference of digital images and at the same their promise which is yet to be fulfilled—now images can form entirely different relations with life. Digital and electronic images actualize what cinema has always dreamed of.

Can: Baker defines artistic activity as human resistance. He maintains that as a form of art which has not yet actualized, digital art does not aim to annihilate classic art. On the contrary, he says digital art will create multiple resistance centers and foci. Although video appears as to be the consequence of an effort to expand editing on TV, afterwards, especially in the hands of women like Ulrike Rosenbach, it became the instrument to say 'I see'. He maintains that digital arts, first of all video, will introduce not a postmodern, but a modernist and revolutionary resistance against the perception of image established by Hollywood. According to your own experiences, do you agree with Baker's expectations?

Aras: I would propose to discuss this issue without referring to the terms like postmodernity and modernist resistance. In order to clarify the meaning of these terms, we should follow the debate that started in the end of 80s and the beginning of 90s closely and then look at the positions maintained within this debate. In the last years, everyone started to call anything they don't appreciate postmodern, and modernism simply became some sort of virtue in a world which has lost its dignity. I think the works of Ulrike Rosenbach and the like do not indicate the conservative modernism as advocated by Habermas in those debates, but a new form of avant-garde that Lyotard was pointing to.

Earlier, I mentioned 'a promise which is yet to be fulfilled'. I suppose this promise is related to the inherent potential of digital media for breaking the representational system, and I think Ulus would agree with that.

In the 70s, Ulrike Rosenbach, Valie Export, and others created an image which did not exist before. They created the image of the female body, their own female bodies, by using video. That is how they turned video into the apparatus to say 'I see'—or rather, 'this is how I see my own female body'. This was a serious attack against the hegemonic image regimes in which the female image consisted of only certain clichés, as well as the social institutions and the ideological structures nurturing these regimes. This was a revolt, not resistance... This revolt certainly gained its momentum by the '68 conditions, and it organized its attack by intersecting and overlapping with other similar lines of revolts. Eventually it took 20 years for hegemonic social structures to create resistance apparatuses against such attack, to recover and re-structure themselves. When we look at the art institutions and the cultural production and circulation mechanisms, we can see how they were re-structured and rein-forced to prevent such attacks since the beginning of the 80s. For example, the emergence and functional differentiation of *curatorship* as an institution in the field of contemporary arts should be considered in this context.

Whenever we start speaking about resistance, it means that things are not going so well, and we're actually in deep shit. (Well, that may actually be true at this moment, but that is another issue). The function of avant-garde, its historical mission, is not resistance. We should not forget that this concept, which becomes a key term in the fields of art and politics during modern times, was derived from the military term referring to vanguard forces of an army. The avant-garde sneaks behind the frontlines, hits from behind, and then escapes or quickly moves on; it never organizes its assault in the frontline, it never sets up trenches, foxholes and resistance positions. The artistic and political avant-garde functions in a similar way; it invents the language of a new world by destroying the existing representation systems. It expresses that which cannot be said, and it is always in search of the next expression. As Ulus often reminds by quoting Klee, the avant-garde escapes to the future and waits for the public who are yet to arrive. During the postmodernism debate where he almost accused Habermas of idiocy, Lyotard points that the avant-garde constitutes the substantial core of art. (I think the same is also true for politics. The misery of the left today is due to the loss of its avant-garde quality. It is desperately attempting to set up resistance lines which could hold the large masses behind it; and in Turkey, like in many other places, it finds nationalism as a barricade as such which it could finally position itself into and gather people behind.)

If we attribute a resistance function to avant-garde, we are in trouble. Resistance should be established in the other moments of everyday life, inside the other social institutions. These institutions should be claimed as spaces of liberation and as such, they should be defended, by setting up by fortifying resistance positions. The layers of aesthetics and art, the avant-garde's course of action, of course, intersects and overlaps with these spaces and positions. But resistance positions and lines of flight/escape should not be confused—otherwise we cannot do anything but try resisting until we lose all our positions. We have to gain new positions, while maintaining the ones we already invented.

Today, if you make a random search on the internet, on YouTube, you can find and watch thousands of videos like Rosenbach's works which were called revolutionary then. These videos are not even artworks anymore, they are just ordinary videos whose raison d'être lies in the quality of being videos which anyone could make (This ordinariness itself can be the material of art, but that is another issue). Beyond being an easily available standard raw material, the body of the artist has already become the most banal exhibition object today.

Identity politics discourses of the 80s, and other governmental and economic apparatuses of neoliberalism have already disciplined those immoral bodies Rosenbach and others discovered in 70s. If we want to claim the legacy of the avant-garde, we have to invent new images and new methods like those people did before us, not continue doing what they've already done. For sure, we have to learn what they did, and perhaps apply and repeat the same experiments in the learning process, but that is not the matter.

It is important to know where to look, if we want to find the novelties of digital art; we cannot see the potentials of digital art when we look at digitally generated or altered photographs, because they are limited by the conventions of a representation system established for a previous form of art. Then, where do we search for the aesthetic form of digital technologies itself? Could we find it in the easy, cheap and plentiful production of experimental films like what Hans Richter and Walter Ruttmann did with great efforts in the 20s? Or, could we find it in producing After Effects plug-ins which make it a snap to do genius works like the ones Zbigniew Rybczyński's did by hacking the video technology of the 80s? If what we encounter is a grand-scale technologic transformation which has the potential to transform the production conditions of art and image completely, beyond developing new formal techniques, and these new production conditions do not necessitate the existing public structures and institutions (which have been developed and institutionalized through modern art), then we should look towards different domains and different circulation networks to find the innovative core of digital art. In other words, if what we experience is a new kind of image establishing new relations with life, we cannot find its traces in galleries, museums, biennials, or exhibition halls, in the temples of an already dead cult.

Let's look at the ontological grounds of digital image in a general frame, which I mentioned earlier, and how they transform the practice of art production, and then discuss the political effects within this context, or search for politics in this context.

I can think of two examples for the genuine forms of this new image type. The first one could also help us to theorize what I mean by transforming production relations. There is a group of people in New York, with whom I briefly had the chance to work with in the past years, who work in a format called live video performance. This format is based on live (and mostly improvised) composition and manipulation of video images through computer directly in the presence of an audience. This format should be considered as a novelty by itself since it is made possible through digital technologies. However, when we examine the production relations taking place in this form in depth, we can discern the details which would force us to reconsider fundamental concepts of creative activity and artistic production. For instance, these people don't define the images they produce and present, and the performance itself, as the ultimate product of their creativity, or their artistic production. What they regard as their artistic production are patches, as they call it, the algorithms which they produce to process, manipulate and assemble images and sounds, modules produced for the softwares they use. This is interesting, because this would mean the final product, the artwork, is no more the ultimate object of artistic activity. The artistic product, the object of creativity becomes an ever-lasting, dynamic and transitional material that has the potential to be incorporated into consequent productions endlessly, and produce different products. I noticed a very similar phenomenon while I was in interviewing a breakcore DJ in Berlin for my academic studies. When I asked to see his works, he showed me a number of acetate sample discs, which he considered as his primary work, more important to him than a few music CDs he has published. These beats and sound samples, which never reach the consumer market (at least in the way they are published), are used by other DJs to spin at the clubs or to record their own compositions. He was more proud about the popularity and reputation of his sample discs than his compositions being played on radio, or the circulation of his CDs. He was also using other DJs samples to make his own compositions. The revolution of digital technologies in music is not the possibility of producing weird electronic sounds at a speed of 160 bpm (beats per minute); it is the concept of sample and the new logic of production it brings forward. A finished song is no more a musical work, every sound can be articulated to another, every piece can be re-produced, transform into another infinitely. It is precisely in this context we can talk about images becoming plural within themselves and forming new collectives, beyond the multiple points of contact and multiple resistance centers. What kinds of revolutionary horizons such new forms provide for the urgent political-economy related problems of artistic production under post-Fordist capitalist conditions—that is, how it pushes this mode of capitalist production into a crisis? This can be deduced from the present warfare around the lines of copyright and intellectual property issues, and from the resistance positions fortified by capitalism through legality on this front.

Another interesting example that comes to my mind about digital art/image is the case of Machinima, which are video works produced in a completely virtual environment by using the graphic engines of computer games. I think this is quite a new format, I didn't work on that kind of stuff, but I know, in Turkey, Andreas Treske works on these. This form can allow us to theorize another aspect of the digital image, as I mentioned earlier, that is the virtual character of digital image: It is no more a trace of an object or an event of the outside world, it is a construct by itself, generating its own references.

Certainly, it is possible to find other moments and examples which can be helpful to discover the clues that point to relations transformed by the digital image and digital technologies. However, these examples I mentioned (and others which I suppose could be found) are not produced in the sphere of art institutions and circulated in the hegemonic artistic networks. They are circulated in other spheres of everyday life, within other kinds of social networks. The internet is the primary circulation and sharing platform for people who work on Machinima kind of productions (as well as for many other forms of work produced by digital technology). In other words, these new forms of production bypass the art institutions which became hege-monic in the course of modernism—such as galleries, museums, cinema and exhibition halls, and other cultural temples like art schools. Wasn't such liberation of art (from the hegemonic institutions and the ideological structures these institutions reproduced) already a primary concern for various avant-garde movements developed within modernity as a critique of it?

I don't think that the examples I mentioned above are fully matured yet in terms of their aesthetic forms, and produced the necessary breaks; this is still debatable for me. But this is naturally going to happen, as the potential is already there. Then, the problem is, whether we will venture into collective experiments with these new aesthetic and technologic forms and explore such lines of flight, or will we perpetually wait for the barbarians behind resistance lines fortified by others.

Can: According to Baker, we watch cinema but we see video. You might recall he has an interesting analysis, if a film cannot be told or narrated, then the film is real. He considers video as an instrument for avoiding linguistic virtuality. When you think about his courses in METU-GISAM, how did the students react to such quite new ideas?

Aras: The seminars in METU-GISAM and the videos we made during these seminars become the records of our collective state of mind during those times besides as well as being a quite important product of our work. At that moment, METU-GISAM was redefined for us albeit it was founded a few years earlier, due to strange ironies of life, which I won't go into details here. The center became a place in which we could actualize and develop our collective interests. The technical skills we developed until then, found new intellectual horizons after starting to work with Ulus, and at the same time, he found a new orientation for his intellectual interests and accumulation of knowledge, and directed his intellectual production towards cinema and video. The matters we worked on, read, and discussed about, and the innovations we discovered in the meanwhile, were starting to shape our aesthetic and political orientations. I mean, we already shared similar political tendencies, but together we found new perspectives for our existing desires. Körotonomedya collective was founded in this period. When we look back, I guess, we all find the stuff we did unbelievably exciting and incredibly efficient and productive in those days. For us this was an era of newness, which lasted for a few years. On one hand we were discovering new theoretical perspectives (not only new for us, but new for Turkey as well as the rest of the world), on the other hand we were learning to work with digital technologies, and producing quite experimental works.

Ulus enjoyed what he was teaching, and taught with excitement. He also knew too well how to convey this joy and excitement to us. His style in his seminars was similar to his writings; he explained a concept by weaving around it in detail, he presented an image by associating it with other images. After long lectures, a number of tracks met with each other, ideas find new contexts, some lines appear and certain images begin to take shape in our minds. But the value of Ulus for his students and the people who followed his seminars, was not simply because of the substantial contents of the matters he taught, or how masterfully he conveyed such sophisticated content. I believe that the quality of the socialization in the seminars and courses was quite important as well, and for most of us this socialization was educational and it shaped our orientations in life. These seminars were a communal platform beyond being friendly at the surface level. Ulus never asserted any power through his knowledge and position, he even responded to some very bad questions very seriously, and explained as much as he could. If he had any power stemming from his knowledge, this was a constitutive power he shared with everyone around. People felt rather stronger rather than being intimidated after such difficult and tiring seminars with such sophisticated subject matter.

For video as an important instrument against linguistic virtuality... First of all, we have to clarify what we understand from language and virtuality. Before we started to study with

Ulus, we had been taught to think about cinema through a theoretical framework shaped by structuralist linguistics, semiology, and psychoanalytic approaches. Semiology carried the inherent tendency of structuralism to reduce everything to linguistic processes, although cinema introduced a crisis and deadlock in this regard, and made other approaches necessary. Semiological approaches attempted to construct cinema and visual arts as linguistic processes, and referred to them as signification processes in the same way they treated textuality. The theoretical framework of structuralist semiology, which we can call linguistic, has to exclude virtuality especially at the moments it crosses and overlaps with psychoanalysis. Virtuality, as Deleuze mentions, refers to a potential state; it is not hypothetical or unreal, it indicates a real potential which is yet to be actualized. The flow of time, the corporeal embodiment of the event is the occurrence, the actualization of something that is already virtually present. In this context, for Deleuze, virtuality is the core of reality, not the contrary. The tension between virtual and actual—that's to say, a new potential founded every moment of time when another one is actualized, this provides us with the eternal movement of the world, this is the flow of time itself. It is not a coincidence that while Deleuze constructs such a philosophical gesture, he ultimately circles cinema with virtuality and refines the idea of cinema through virtuality, because his philosophical gesture actually presents a very deep criticism of structuralism. In that case we cannot hold on to linguistic structures and codes to understand events, power relations, and social situations. We can only grasp the events as continuous flows, as the planes upon which such flows take place, and continuous transformations of layers and bodies introduced by these flows. The practice of life is not only a signification process; signification takes place retrospectively, after and about the practice of life. A body is not a subject constructed only through linguistic processes; it is founded by the potential to produce and transmit various affections. Cinema is important for Deleuze beyond a signification process, because it presents a virtual image, a type of image which can directly refer to the virtual. A cinematographic image as such is not the trace of a past reality, following time from behind; it is the intangible and untraceable reality, the event itself. It re-establishes its own time and re-actualizes itself in every time it is shown. The moving image can only be an instrument of cognition if it is related to virtuality in such a way—and cinema had been the only medium capable of such relation until the emergence of the electronic image. Thus, it can show us what has not yet been rendered into any linguistic code yet, what can not be thought, cannot be uttered, cannot be expressed; and then we can derive the idea, the language, the meaning from what we see as such. This was completely peculiar to cinema; that is, to produce the moving image mechanically, being capable of producing the image of the world free form the language and thought that only presented a priori constructions. What Vertov had noticed at the beginning was, (although he didn't define it that way) even in documentary form of cinema, it re-composes the image of the event it witnessed rather than representing it. The power of cinema is not to narrate, or to explain fully. On the contrary, the image it presents will always be somehow lacking certainty, every time it is shown it may lead to different meanings, it will constantly re-construct the event or an event over and over again.

As life itself (and its image) is a priori to its knowledge and signification, cinema (and other technologies of the moving image) allows us to create a relation to life without the mediation of language. Liberating the cinema and images from the domination of representations is only possible with the idea of virtuality. In this regard, Deleuze's theory of cinema is an answer to the question imposed by Walter Benjamin, which haunted our thought through the modern times. (In fact, Deleuze's theoretical approach is not composed as an open answer to Benjamin, since there's only one passing reference to Benjamin in the two volumes of his cinema books. Deleuze mentions Benjamin only once in his discussion of Nazi cinema and Syberberg, yet does not engage with Benjamin's views on cinema in constructing his theoretical framework. But when we look at the origins of their discussions and the formulas they arrive at, it is obvious that Deleuze's theory is quite an answer to Benjamin and his line of thought). Benjamin was asserting that cinema has effectively abolished the distance between the image and the viewer, and this was a problem, because, for Benjamin, contemplation takes place within this critical distance between body and image. For him, cinema is a shock to the brain, and it is capable of presenting these shocks at a speed that does not allow us to think, therefore it makes contemplation impossible. It is possible to consider what he suggests as the distance of language—the critical distance is actually the duration in which the mediation of language is established. Deleuze affirms Benjamin's diagnosis, but he affirms it as the essential power of cinema; cinema doesn't make contemplation impossible, but on the contrary, we can only think after such direct relation, after its shock. We can perceive the world through cinema; cinema is a machine producing perceptions. Contemplation follows such a direct perception, it doesn't precede it.

We should consider electronic and digital images in such context. Besides, as Ulus, Maurizzio Lazzarato, and others indicated, video and electronic images are much more competent than cinema in relating to the virtual for many reasons. So it is more proper to say: Video is an instrument for liberating virtuality from language.

It wasn't difficult for us to adopt these kinds of ideas, especially when we were together with Ulus. As I mentioned earlier, it wasn't only due to Ulus' capacity of sharing his knowledge, there was a fundamental gap we always felt but could not fulfill between our practical works and the theoretical frameworks we learnt until then. And such ideas offered us new perspectives on these matters. We were actually in need of such ideas.

Can: In *What is Opinion?*, while Ulus is telling his philosophical analysis on opinion to a fixed camera, we see him in a long shot sitting on a chair next to a TV monitor screening his close-ups at very same moment. Was it his idea to record it in this way? And how did you manage to make him talk that long without smoking?

Aras: *What is Opinion?* is made as the first part of a series of interview/lecture videos, it was recorded in the METU-GISAM studios. The theme was the central axis of Ulus' PhD thesis. It was my idea to project his close-ups with a second camera onto a monitor next to him, but this wasn't a preplanned detail, I thought of the idea of exposing the video image itself as an aesthetic element, and also make use of the physical space of the studio. I did the same thing in the editing, I tried to expose the visuality of electronic image itself by re-recording the close-ups screened on the monitor, and I used this shots to combine the passages from the interview. It wasn't a problem for me at all to film Ulus, since when he feels comfortable he could talk at length fluently even without the need to repeat or take alternative shots. But, of course, we took many breaks for smoking; it took a few hours to complete the interview. In the end, the interview/lecture you watch is an edited video, not a continuous shot.

Can: He finished his PhD thesis in 7 years, and after the problems he had about the approval of his thesis, he said that he felt a strange sadness rather than joy when it was finished. Can you tell us about those times?

Aras: The writing of the thesis gradually became an emotionally taxing experience for Ulus. There was no problem about the approval of his dissertation, the problem was about him finishing it, and this was not a matter of incompetence of course. In fact, Ulus already had hundreds of pages of written material on his thesis in '98-'99. But he had some issues in his private life during those times, and these affected his work on the dissertation. For people like us, our intellectual and academic activities are not shaped strictly through particular disciplines of these fields, these activities are parts of our general engagement with life, in a general sense, another aspect of our social existence, social relations. So it is not quite possible to make distinctions such as private life, intellectual life, political life, etc. And I believe this is something positive and fruitful. However, in this case, the deeper traumas stemming from elsewhere can affect or destabilize other vital activities. The sadness Ulus mentioned when he finished his dissertation was not about his thesis, he was sad about this whole period of his life. When he expressed this sadness, I made a short film with some material I already had, a 5-minute film I called *Joy*, and sent to him as a present, inviting him to forget resentment. He said he enjoyed my present, but still, he couldn't really recover from that big depression, which consequently turned into a slow suicide.

Can: In his short story, *Ears Not for Hearing*, he tells how he was affected by the mortar shell that fell on their house and did not explode during Turkey's intervention to Cyprus in 1974, when he was 14. Did he tell any other memories about Cyprus? Did he ever think about coming back to Cyprus?

Aras: If what you mean from 'himself' in a general conversation is his 'private' life, his personal past, his desires, dreams, etc., Ulus rarely talked about himself. Ulus' mind did not work with such logic of 'individuality' and 'self'. That's why the stories he told about his past in Cyprus and other places where he grew up were presented as bits and pieces of information, and they have always been told in the context of other issues. He told about these events during our conversations, I didn't know he wrote them as stories until after he died. He didn't tell these to talk about himself; his stories were about something else. I've learned that he wrote these for a periodical publication attempt a few years ago, which was never materialized. What he narrated were bitter and tragic stories. But according to Ulus' story, the reason why the mortar shell which fell on their house didn't explode is because some leftist Greek soldiers, who were forced to fire by their fascist superior officers until the Turkish army seized their position, fired the shells without fuses as result of human consciousness—and it is not hard to guess what had been their reward.

On the other hand, he was closely watching what was happening in Cyprus and he was constantly informing us about Cyprus in our talks and through some pieces he wrote. As we frequently chatted about the political situations in Cyprus, it is impossible not to notice how deeply he was concerned with Cyprus, if we look at another interview I recorded with him in the summer of 2003. I inquired him in detail about the political history of Cyprus for a project I started working on at that time (which was never materialized either). In this interview he explains that he had visited Cyprus in 1986 for the last time and he doesn't plan to go back at all. He points to the political issues gradually going worse and turning into deadlock, as the reason for his reluctance. He simply expresses that he doesn't want to go back to one of the few remaining divided cities that still exist in this world (which nobody wants to be aware of). In other words, what determines Ulus' relation with Cyprus is not his lack of interest, but his disappointment and resentment. We didn't have the chance to finish the project which would include this interview, but I believe what he told there is quite valuable to understand the Cyprus issue.

Can: Although he was such a passionate thinker and intellectual who expressed many ideas about love, I think, he didn't have a long-term relationship. Is this because he never met someone who could help him open up his 'madness', or was he never understood by whom he met, or perhaps, as he always mentioned that love is never something synchronous anyway, is it because of the possibility that one always falls in love when it is already over for the other?

Aras: Ulus was not a lonely person at all. I mean, beyond that place inside where we are always all alone, he had never been just by himself since I got to know him, and I know that he wasn't alone before either. He always had friends around him, there were always people who shared his life. Besides his ever-expanding social circle, even when people moved away for some other reasons, they never ceased their contact with Ulus. For many people, Ulus became the occasion to find each other for long-term friendships. He was beloved for everyone, he never had any hostility against anyone. I know that some of his close friends had been angry with him when he passed away, but when we gathered and poured out our grievances, as they admitted in sadness, it was because Ulus didn't have the power to fulfill some expectations developed in such close relationships. I mean, Ulus never offended anyone knowingly and purposefully in his life, and nobody had any resentment towards him. He never conflicted with anyone, he already innovated plenty of ways to escape from the pressure of conflictual situations. He was at peace with everyone, he had no personal tensions, and he managed to do that without obeying anyone, accepting anyone's domination on his life. He was quite unique in that sense.

We never thought Ulus was mad; on the contrary, he was one of the most sane persons I ever met. I mean, he had problems like everyone, and the reasons for some of these problems were psychological as he was very well aware of; for example, his obsessions about his body, the depressions he avoided reflecting on others, his increasing weakness for alcohol. We were worried about these psychological problems since some time and were concerned about the consequences which eventually lead to his death. However, having such problems is normal, and in that sense Ulus was normal for us. At the very least, there is no doubt that he was more sane than the world he had to live in. If we consider such personal sufferings of somebody who dedicated a large part of his intellectual activities to questions like 'what is intellect capable of?', 'what is thinking?' as insanity, he would remind us the words of French poet Joë Bousquet himself: 'My wounds existed before me, I was born to give them a body…'

He was very sensitive, and he was full of love. He naturally had love affairs, and again, naturally, some of these relations ended sadly, some continued on joyfully. But he was never alone, he never lost his mind. He embraced life with his mind and love, and he shared his mind and love with us. Ulus was someone who showed us how to live in dignity with affection and contemplation, in a world in which disaffection became the norm, and ignorance a virtue.

BIBLIOGRAPHY

Agamben, Giorgio. *Infancy and History: The Destruction of Experience*, New York: Verso, 1993.

_____. *Homo Sacer: Sovereign Power and Bare Life*, trans. Daniel Heller-Roazen, Stanford: Stanford University Press, 1998.

_____. 'Notes on gesture.', *Means without End: Notes on Politics* 20, Minneapolis, MN: University of Minnesota Press, 2000.

Arendt, Hannah. *The Human Condition*, Chicago: University of Chicago Press, 1958.

Aristotle, *Aristotle's Politics*, Oxford: Clarendon Press, 1905.

Aumont, Jacques. *L'oeil interminable: cinéma et peinture*, Paris: Libr. Séguier, 1989.

Austin, John Langshaw. *How to do things with words*, Oxford: Oxford University Press, 1975.

Bachelard, Gaston. *On poetic imagination and reverie*, Washington DC: Spring Publications, 1987.

_____. *Air and dreams: An essay on the imagination of movement*, trans. Edith R. Farrell, Dallas: Dallas Institute Publications, Dallas Institute of Humanities and Culture, 1988 (1943).

Baker, Ulus. *Kanaatlerden Imajlara: Duygular Sosyolojisinde Dogru*, Istanbul: Iletisim Yayın, 2010.

Barthes, Roland. *Camera lucida: Reflections on photography*, London: Macmillan, 1981.

Bazin, André. 'Qu'est-ce que le cinéma', *Ontologie et langages*, Paris: Le Cerf, 1958.

_____. 'The ontology of the photographic image', trans. Hugh Gray, *Film Quarterly* 13.4 (1960): 4-9.

Beauvoir, Simone de. *Must we burn Sade?*, trans. Annette Michelson, Paris: Olympia Press, 2015, (1951-52).

Benjamin, Walter. 'The Work of Art in the Age of Mechanical Reproduction', trans. Harry Zohn, Hannah Arendt (ed.), in Walter Benjamin, *Illuminations*, ed. Hannah Arendt, New York: Schocken, 1969 (1935), pp. 217-52.

_____. *The origin of German tragic drama*, London: NLB, 1977.

Bensmaïa, Réda. 'Le Cinéma comme opérateur d'analyse', *Surfaces* 1, 1991, http://pum12.pum. umontreal.ca/revues/surfaces/vol1/bensmaia.html

Bergson, Henri. *Le rire*, Paris: PUF, 1961.

_____. *Matière et mémoire: Essai sur la relation du corps à l'esprit*, Paris: Presses Universitaires de France, 1964.

_____. *Duration and Simultaneity: With Reference to Einstein's Theory*, Indianapolis: Bobbs-Merrill, (1896) 1965.

_____. *Matter and Memory*, Nancy Margaret Paul and William Scott Palmer (eds.), London: Allen & Unwin, (1896) 1965.

_____. *Les deux sources de la morale et de la religion*, Paris: Oeuvres, PUF, 1970.

Blanchot, Maurice. *L'amitié*. Paris: Gallimard, 1971.

_____. *The Writing of the Disaster*, Nebraska: Univ. of Nebraska Press, 1995.

Bloch, Ernst. 'Erinnerung', *Über Walter Benjamin*, Frankfurt: Suhrkamp (1968): 16-23.

Bonitzer, Pascal. *Le champ aveugle: essais sur le réalisme au cinéma*, Vol. 32, Paris: Cahiers du cinéma, 1999.

Bronner, Stephen Eric. *Of Critical Theory and Its Theorists*, Routledge, 2002.

Burroughs, William S. *Naked lunch: the restored text*, New York: Grove/Atlantic, Inc., 2007.

Cappola, Francis Ford. *Hearts of Darkness: A Filmmaker's Apocalypse* (dirs. Fax Bahr, George Hicken-looper and Eleanor Cappola, 1991).

Carter, Lynn B. *The Quiet Athenian*, Oxford University Press, 1986.

Castoriadis, Cornelius. *Les Carrefours de labrynthe*, Paris: Seuil, 1972.

Cézanne, Paul. *Letters by Paul Cézanne*, John Rewald (ed.), Massachusetts: Da Capo Press, 1995.

Chaplin, Charlie (dir.). *The Tramp*, 1915.

Chion, Michel. *Le promeneur écoutant: essais d'acoulogie*, Paris: Ed. Plume, 1993.

Clastres, Pierre. *La Société contre l'Etat : Recherches d'anthropologie politique*, Paris: Minuit, 1974.

Coser, Lewis A. 'Continuities in the Study of Social Conflict', *Social Forces* 46.4 (June, 1968): 589–590.

_____. 'The significance of Simmel's Work', *Masters of sociological thought: Ideas in historical and social context* (1977): 177-194.

_____. *Masters of Sociological Thought : Ideas in Historical and Social Context*, 2nd ed. Harcourt Brace Jovanovich, 1977.

Daney, Serge. *Cahier critique 1970 - 1982*, Paris: Cahiers du cinema, 1983.

Debord, Guy. *Society of Spectacle*, trans. Fredy Perlmanand Jon Supak, Detroit, MI: Black & Red: 1970 (1967).

_____. *Oeuvres Cinématographiques Complètes*, Paris: Champs Libre, 1978.

Debray, Régis. 'Vie et mort de l'image: une histoire du regard en Occident', *Esprit* (1994): 57-66.

_____. *Media Manifestations: On the Technological Transmission of Cultural Forms*, London and New York: Verso, 1996.

Deleuze, Gilles. *Spinoza et le problem de l'expression*, Paris: Editions de Minuit (1968): 183–196.

_____. 'Postscript on the Societies of Control', *October* 59 (Winter, 1992): 37.

_____. *Negotiations 1972-1990*, New York: Columbia University Press, 1995.

_____. *Cinema 1: The movement image*, trans. Hugh Tomlinson and Robert Galeta, London: Continuum, 2005.

_____. *Cinema 2: The time-image*, trans. Hugh Tomlinson and Robert Galeta, London: Continuum, 2005.

_____. *Pure Immanence. Essays on a Life*, trans. Anne Boyman, New York: Zone Books, 2005.

Deleuze, Gilles and Guattari, Félix. 'L'anti-oedipe', *Capitalisme et schizophrénie 1*, Paris: Les éditions de Minuit, 1972.

_____. *What is Philosophy?*, trans. G. Burchell and H. Tomlinson, London and New York: Verso, 1994 (1991).

_____. 'What is the creative act?', *French Theory in America*, Sylvere Lotringer and Sande Cohen (eds), London: Routledge, 2001.

_____. *A Thousand Plateaus: Capitalism and Schizophrenia*, trans. Brian Massumi, London: Continuum, (1972) 2004.

Delacroix, Ferdinand Victor Eugene. *French Painter*, 1798 – 1863.

Deleuze, Gilles and Parnet, Claire. *Dialogues*, trans. Hugh Tomlinson and Barbara Habberjam, London: Athlone, 1987 (1987).

Derrida, Jacques. *The post card: From Socrates to Freud and beyond*, trans. Alan Bass, Chicago: University of Chicago Press, 1987 (1980).

Descartes, René. 'OEuvres', *Les principes de la philosophie Vol. 2*. Paris: Librairie Albin Michel, 1932.

_____. *Discourse On Method, and Meditations on First Philosophy*, Indianapolis: Hackett Pub. Co., 1993 (1596-1650).

_____. *Discours de la méthode: Part 4*, Paris: Fayard/Mille et une nuits, 2000.

_____. *Selected Correspondences of Descartes*, pp. 207–208, http://www.earlymoderntexts.com/assets/pdfs/descartes1619.pdf.

Detienne, Marcel. *The Creation of Mythology*, Chicago: University of Chicago Press, 1986.

_____. *The Masters of Truth in Archaic Greece*, New York: Zone Books, 1999.

Donzelot, Jacques. *The Policing of Families*, trans. Robert Hurley, New York: Random House Inc., 1979 (1977).

Dufrenne, Mikel. *Phénoménologie de l'expérience esthétique*, Paris: PUF, 1953.

Eagleton, Terry. *The Ideology of the Aesthetic*, Blackwell: Oxford, 1990.

Einstein, Albert. 'What Life Means to Einstein: An Interview by George Sylvester Viereck', *The Saturday Evening Post* 26 (October, 1929): 114.

Eisenstein, Sergei Mikhailovich. *Film Form*, New York: Harcourt, 1949.

_____. *Nondifferent Nature*, trans. Herbert Marshall, Cambridge University Press, 1987.

_____. *Selected Works, Vol 1*, Richard Taylor (ed), Indiana: Indiana University Press, 1992.

Emmelhainz, Irmgard. *Jean-Luc Godard's Political Filmmaking*, London: Palgrave Macmillan, 2019.

Engels, Frederick. 'Feuerbach', trans. Progress Publishers, *Ludwig Feuerbach and the End of Classical German Philosophy,* 1946 (1886), http://www.marxists.org/archive/marx/works/1886/ludwig-feuerbach/ch03.htm.

_____. 'Theses On Feuerbach', trans. W. Lough, *Ludwig Feuerbach and the End of Classical German Philosophy, Ludwig Feuerbach and the End of Classical German Philosophy,* Moscow: Progress Publishers, 1969 (1888), http://www.marxists.org/archive/marx/works/1845/theses/theses.htm.

Faye, Jean-Pierre. *Langages totalitaires: Critique de la raison narrative, critique de l'economie narrative*, Paris: Edité par Hermann, 1972.

Flusser, Vilém. *Towards a Philosophy of Photography*, London: Reaktion Books, 1999.

Foucault, Michel. *Folie et déraison: histoire de la folie à l'âge classique*. 1, Paris: Plon, 1961.

_____. *Les mots et les choses*, Paris: NRF - Idees, 1966.

_____. *The Order of Things*, New York: Pantheon Books 1970.

_____. 'Surveiller et punir', *Paris* 1 (1975): pp. 192-211.

_____. *Discipline and Punish: the Birth of the Prison*, New York: Random House, 1977.

_____. 'About the concept of the *dangerous individual* in 19th-century legal psychiatry, *International journal of law and psychiatry* 1.1 (1978): 1-18.

_____. *This is Not a Pipe*, trans. James Harkness, Berkeley: University of California Press, 1983.

_____. *The Order of Things: An Archaeology of the Human Sciences*, New York: Vintage, 1994.

Frazer, James George. *The Golden Bough; a study in magic and religion*, Abridged (ed), London: Macmillan, 1923.

Freud, Sigmund. 'The psychopathology of everyday life. SE, 6.', in James Strachey (ed) *The Standard Edition of the Complete Psychological Works of Sigmund Freud*, London: The Hogarth Press, 1901.

_____. 'The Uncanny (das unheimliche, 1919).' *The Standard Edition of the Complete Psychological Works of Sigmund Freud* 17 (1919): 1917-1919.

_____. *A General Introduction to Psychoanalysis*, New York: Horace Liveright, 1920, http://www.gutenberg.org/files/38219/38219-h/38219-h.htm.

_____. 'Inhibitions, symptoms and anxiety', *The Psychoanalytic Quarterly* 5.1 (1936): 1-28.

_____. 'Observation of a Severe Case of Hemi-Anaesthesia in a Hysterical Male', *The Standard Edition of the Complete Psychological Works of Sigmund Freud, Volume I (1886-1899): Pre-Psycho-Analytic Publications and Unpublished Drafts*, 1966 (1886), pp. 23-31.

_____. *The Interpretation of Dreams*, New York: Avon 1980.

_____. 'Hystérie', trans. M. BorchJacobsen, P. Koeppel, F. Scherrer, in *Cahiers Confrontation*, 7, 1982 (1888).

_____. *Introductory Lectures on Psychoanalysis*, New York: Liveright, 1989.

Freud, Sigmund & Breuer, Joseph. *Studies in hysteria*, trans. Nicola Luckhurst, London: Penguin, 2004 (1895).

Freud, Sigmund and Cronin, A. J. *The interpretation of dreams*, Vancouver: Read Books Ltd, 2013.

Frisby, David. *Georg Simmel*, London: Routledge, 1984.

_____. *Sociological Impressionism. A Reassessment of Georg Simmel's Social Theory*, London: Routledge, 1991.

Gray, M. A Dictionary of Literary Terms. London: Longman, 1992.

Godard, Jean Luc & Daney, Serge. 'Dialogue entre Jean-Luc Godard et Serge Daney', Paris: *Cahiers du Cinéma* 513, May, 1997 (1988).

Gordimer, Nadine. *Writing and Being*, Nobel Lecture, 7 December 1991.

Hanks, Craig. *Technology and Values: Essential Readings*. Wiley-Blackwell, 2009.

Hegel, Georg Wilhelm Friedrich. *The Phenomenology of Spirit (Cambridge Hegel Translations)*, Terry Pinkard (trans.), Cambridge University Press, 2018.

Heidegger, Martin. 'The question concerning technology', *Technology and values: Essential readings* 99 (1954): 113.

Holz, Hans Heinz. 'Prismatisches Denken', *Über Walter Benjamin*, Frankfurt: Suhrkamp (1968): 62110.

Jameson, Fredric. *Late Marxism: Adorno, or, the persistence of the dialectic*, London: Verso, 1990.

Jünger, Ernst. *The glass bees*, trans. Elizabeth Mayer, New York: New York Review of Books, 2000 (1957),

Kant, Immanuel. *Critique of Pure Reason*, trans. F. Max Müller, New York: The Macmillan Company, 1922 (1781).

Kaplan, Harold I. and Sadock, Benjamin J. *Comprehensive Textbook of Psychiatry V*, 5th edition, Baltimore: Williams and Wilkins, 1989.

Klein, George L. 'Randall's Interpretation of the Philosophies of Descartes, Spinoza, and Leibniz', John Peter Anton (ed.) *Naturalism and Historical Understanding*, New York: SUNY Press, 1967.

Klossowski, Pierre. *The Baphomet,* Colorado: Eridanos Press, Inc., 1988.

[Köronotomedya]. http://www.korotonomedya.net/kor/index.php?index.

Kripke, Saul A. 'Naming and necessity.', in *Semantics of natural language* (1972): 253-355.

Kustorica, Emir (dir.), *Underground*, 1995.

La Mettrie, Julien Jean Offray. *La Mettrie: Machine Man and Other Writings*, Ann Thomson (ed), Cambridge: Cambridge University Press, 1996.

Lacan, Jacques. *Le séminaire de Jacques Lacan. / Livre XI, Les quatre concepts fondamentaux de la psychanalyse*, Paris: Édition du Seuil, DL 1973.

_____. 'The function and field of speech and language in psychoanalysis.', *Écrits: A selection*, trans. Bruce Fink, New York: W. W. Norton, 2002 (1953).

Lanzmann, Claude (dir.). *Shoah*, 1985.

Laplanche, Jean and Pontalis, Jean-Bertrand. *The language of psycho-analysis*, trans. Donald Nicholson-Smith, New York: W. W. Norton., 1973.

Lasswell, Harold D. 'The structure and function of communication in society', *The communication of ideas* 37.1 (1948): 136-139.

Lazzarato, Maurizio. *La Machine de Guerre du Ciné-Oeil*, 2 December 1999, http://nettime.org/Lists-Archives/nettime-fr-9912/msg00010.html.

_____. *Videophilosophy. The Perception of Time in Post-Fordism.* Edited and translated by Jay Hetrick. Columbia University Press, 2019.

Le Brun, Annie. *Soudain d'un bloc d'abime Sade*, Paris: Ed. Pauvert, 1986.

['Le cas Lanzmann'], *Le Nouvel Observateur* (31 janvier, 1991).

Leroi-Gourhan, André. *Le Geste et la parole 1-2*, Paris: Albin Michel, 1964.

_____. *Gesture and speech*, trans. Anna Bostock Berger, Massachusetts: MIT Press, 1993.

Leutrat, Jean-Louis. 'Le Cinéma en perspective: une histoire.' *Nathan Université, Cinéma* 128 (1992).

Lévi-Strauss, Claude. *Les Structures Elementaires de la Parenté*, Paris: Presses Universitaires de France, 1949.

Lynd, Robert and Helen, *Middletown: A Study in Modern American Culture*, New York: Harcourt, Brace, Jovanovich, 1929.

Lynd, Robert and Helen, *Middletown in Transition*, New York: Harcourt, Brace, Jovanovich, 1935.

Maniquis, Robert M. 'Introduction: English Romanticism and the French Revolution', *Studies in Romanticism*, Cambridge: MIT Press, 1989, pp. 343-344.

Marx, Karl. Ben Fowkes, and David Fernbach. *Capital.* London: Penguin Books in association with New Left Review, 1981.

Marx, Karl & Engels, Friedrich. *The German Ideology*, London: Lawrence & Wishart, 1965.

Matheron, Alexandre. 'Remarques sur l'immortalité de l'âme chez Spinoza', Les Études philosophiques 3 (1972): 369-37.

Merton, Robert King. *Social Theory and Social Structure*, New York: Free Press, 1968.

Metz, Christian. *Le significant imaginaire*, Paris: Christian Bourgeois Editeur, 1993.

Miller, Prairie. 'For Ever Mozart: An interview with Jean-Luc Godard', *Cinema=Godard=Cinema*, June 1996, http://cinemagodardcinema.wordpress.com/interviews/for-ever-mozart/.

Mills, Charles Wright. *White collar: The American middle classes*, New York: Oxford University Press, 1951.

_____. *The power elite*, New York: Oxford University Press, 1956.

_____. *The sociological imagination.* New York: Oxford University Press, 1959.

Mulvey, Laura. 'Visual Pleasure and Narrative Cinema', *Visual and Other Pleasures,* London: Palgrave Macmillan, 1989.

Myrdal, Gunnar. 'Conference of the British Sociological Association, 1953. II Opening Address: The Relation between Social Theory and Social Policy', *The British Journal of Sociology* 4.3 (1953): 210-42. Accessed June 27, 2020. doi:10.2307/587539.

Oswald, Ducrot. *Les échelles argumentatives*. Paris: Éd. de Minuit, 1980, http://www.nobelprize.org/prizes/literature/1991/gordimer/lecture/

Ozgun, Aras (prod.). *Ulus Baker, What is Opinion?*, 2001, http://pyromedia.org/redtv/ulus.html.

Pascal, Blaise. *Pensées*, New York: E. P. Dutton & Co., Inc., 1958.

Plato. 'The recompense of life', *Plato's The Republic*, New York: Books, Inc., 1943.

_____. *Meno*, Penguin Books, 1956.

Pollock, Friedrich. 'Empirical research into public opinion', trans. Thomas Hall, in *Critical Sociology: Selected Readings*, ed. Paul Connerton, New York: Penguin, 225-236.

Ruyer, Raymond. *L'Utopie et les Utopies*, Paris: Presses Universitairies de France, 1950.

Sade, Marquis de. *Histoire de Juliette: ou les prosperites du vice*. 1, Alexandria: Library of Alexandria, 1976 (1797–1801).

Sade, Marquis de. *Juliette Birinci Kitap: Erdemsizliğe Övgü*, trans. Mûnire Yilmazer, İstanbul: Chivi Yayınevi, 2003.

Sartre, Jean Paul. *Critique de la Raison dialectique*, Paris: Gallimard, 1960.

Schaff, Philip. *St. Augustine's City of God and Christian Doctrine*, CCEL, 1890, http://www.ccel.org/ccel/schaff/npnf102

Shannon, Claude E. 'A mathematical theory of communication', *The Bell system technical journal* 27.3 (1948): 379-423.

Simmel, Georg. 'Die quantitative Bestimmtheit der Gruppe', *Soziologie. Untersuchungen über die Formen der Vergesellschaftung,* 1908, pp. 68-94.

_____. 'The Metropolis and Mental Life', *The Sociology of Georg Simmel*, New York: Free Press, 1950.

_____. 'On Individuality and Social Forms', in Donald N. Levine (ed.), *Selected Writings*, Chicago: The University of Chicago Press, 1971.

_____. *Bireysellik ve Kültür*, çev. Tuncay Birkan, İstanbul: Metis Yayınlan, 2009 (1950).

Sokurov, Aleksandr (dir.). *Mother and Son*, 1997.

Solanas, Fernando and Getino, Octavio. 'Toward a third cinema', *Cineaste* 4.3 (1970): 1-10.

Spencer, Herbert. 'Social Types and Constitutions', in Herbert Spencer, *The Principles of Sociology, in Three Volumes,* Vol. 1, New York: D. Appleton and Company, 1894, available at: http://oll.libertyfund.org/titles/2642.

_____. 'Social Metamorphoses', in Herbert Spencer, *The Principles of Sociology, in Three Volumes,* Vol. 1, New York: D. Appleton and Company, 1894, available at: http://oll.libertyfund.org/titles/2642.

Spinoza, Benedictus de. *Complete works,* trans. Samuel Shirley and others, Michael L. Morgan (ed.), Cambridge, IN: Hackett Publishing Company, Inc., 2002.

_____. *The Ethics PART IV: Of Human Bondage, or the Strength of the Emotions,* The Project Gutenberg EBook, April 15, 2013 [EBook #971] Release Date: July, 1997 First Posted: July 5, 1997, http://www.gutenberg.org/cache/epub/971/pg971-images.html.

_____. *Tractatus Theologico-Politicus, Part IV,* trans. R. H. M. Elwes, Project Gutenberg Ebook, 2014 (1997), http://www.gutenberg.org/ebooks/992.

Suner, Asuman. 'Specificities: Other Cinemas Speaking the Experience of Political Oppression with a Masculine Voice: Making Feminist Sense of Yilmaz Guney's Yol', *Social Identities 4.2* (March 2, 1998): 283–300.

['Sur les films du groupe'], Paris: *Cahiers du Cinéma* 240, (July, 1972).

Tarde, Gabriel. *L'opinion et la foule,* Paris: Presses Universitaires de France, 1901.

_____.*Psychologie economique, 2 vols*. Paris: Alcan, 1902.

_____. *On Communication and Social Influence: Selected Papers,* Chicago: University of Chicago Press, 1969.

[Tertullian], http://en.wikipedia.org/wiki/Tertullian.

Todorov, Tzvetan. *Face à l'extrême,* Paris: Le Seuil, 2013.

Tylor, Edward Burnett. 'On a method of investigating the development of institutions; applied to laws of marriage and descent.', *The Journal of the Anthropological Institute of Great Britain and Ireland* 18 (1889): pp. 245-272.

_____. *Primitive Culture: Researches into the Development of Mythology, Philosophy, Religion, Art, and Custom,* Cambridge University Press, 2010.

Vernant, Jean-Pierre and Detienne, Marcel. *Cunning Intelligence in Greek Culture and Society,* trans. Janet Lloyd, Chicago: University of Chicago Press, 1991 (1974).

Vernant, Jean-Pierre and Vidal-Naquet, Pierre. *Myth and tragedy in ancient Greece,* trans. Janet Lloyd, New York: Zone Books, 1988.

Vertov, Dziga. *Kino-Eye: The Writings of Dzigo Vertov,* trans. Kevin O'Brien, forw. Annette Michelson, Berkeley and Los Angeles: Univ of California Press, 1984.

Virilio, Paul. *Guerre et cinéma: I. Logistique de la perception,* Paris: Cahiers du cinéma, 1991.

_____. *War and Cinema: the logistics of perception,* Paris: Verso, 2009.

Walter, Benjamin et al. *The origin of German tragic drama,* London: NLB, 1977.

Wittgenstein, Ludwig and Anscombe, G. E. M. *Philosophical investigations,* London: Basic Blackw, 1953.

Woolf, Virginia. 'The waves', *Collected Novels of Virginia Woolf,* London: Palgrave Macmillan 1992, (1932): pp. 335-508.

_____. 'The Cinema, from The Nation and Athenaeum, 1926', *The Essays of Virginia Woolf: Volume 4 1925 - 1928,* Boston: Mariner Books, 2008.

Žižek, Slavoj. *For They Know Not What They Do: Enjoyment As A Political Factor,* London; New York: Verso, 1991.

BIOGRAPHIES

Ulus Baker (1960 - 2007) was a Turkish-Cypriot sociologist, philosopher, and public intellectual. He was born in Ankara, Turkey in 1960, to Sedat Baker, a prominent Cypriot psychiatrist, and Pembe Marmara, a well-known Cypriot poet. He studied Sociology at Middle East Technical University in Ankara, where he taught as a lecturer until 2004. He wrote prolifically in influential Turkish journals such as *Birikim*, *Toplum ve Bilim*, and *Virgul* among others; made some of the first Turkish translations of various works of Gilles Deleuze, Baruch Spinoza, Antonio Negri, and other contemporary political philosophers; actively contributed to körotonomedya collective; and frequently gave public lectures and seminars in alternative scholarly spaces as well as teaching as a lecturer at Middle East Technical University and Istanbul Bilgi University.

Aras Özgün is a media studies scholar and a media artist, who is currently teaching at the Cinema and Digital Media Department at Izmir University of Economics in Izmir, and at the Media Studies Graduate Program of the New School for Public Engagement in New York. He studied Political Sciences (B.Sc.) and Sociology (MS) at Middle East Technical University in Ankara, and Media Studies (MA) and Sociology (Ph.D.) at The New School for Social Research in New York. He writes on media, culture and politics, and produces experimental media, photography and video works.

Andreas Treske is an author, and filmmaker, writing about online video aesthetics and culture. He graduated from the University of Television and Film, Munich, where he also taught film and video post-production. He is the chair of the Department of Communication and Design at I.D. Bilkent University, Ankara, Turkey. In 2015 he published *Video Theory: Online Video Aesthetics or the Afterlife of Video* with Transcript. In 2017, the book was translated to Russian. Since 2008, he is involved in the VideoVortex network.

www.ingramcontent.com/pod-product-compliance
Lightning Source LLC
Chambersburg PA
CBHW062055270326
41931CB00013B/3092